Social Responsibilities of Organized Labor

This book is One of a Series on Ethics and Economic Life
Originated by a Study Committee of the Federal Council
of Churches
Subsequently Merged in the National Council of Churches

Charles P. Taft, Chairman,
Department of the Church and Economic Life

Cameron P. Hall, Executive Director

TOWARD AN UNDERSTANDING OF THE ETHICS AND
ECONOMICS OF SOCIETY

Already Published

GOALS OF ECONOMIC LIFE
Edited by A. Dudley Ward

THE ORGANIZATIONAL REVOLUTION
By Kenneth E. Boulding

SOCIAL RESPONSIBILITIES OF THE BUSINESSMAN
By Howard R. Bowen

AMERICAN INCOME AND ITS USE
By Elizabeth E. Hoyt, Margaret G. Reid, Joseph L. McConnell,
and Janet M. Hooks

CHRISTIAN VALUES AND ECONOMIC LIFE
By Howard R. Bowen, John C. Bennett, William Adams Brown,
Jr., and G. Bromley Oxnam

THE AMERICAN ECONOMY—ATTITUDES AND OPINIONS
By A. Dudley Ward

SOCIAL RESPONSIBILITY IN FARM LEADERSHIP
By Walter W. Wilcox

SOCIAL RESPONSIBILITIES OF ORGANIZED LABOR
By John A. Fitch

Other Volumes in Preparation

Social Responsibilities
of Organized Labor

By John A. Fitch

HARPER & BROTHERS   PUBLISHERS   NEW YORK

SOCIAL RESPONSIBILITIES OF ORGANIZED
LABOR

This volume has been prepared under the direction of a study group authorized by the Federal
Council of Churches in 1949. In 1950 the
Federal Council was merged into the National
Council of Churches. The Federal Council has
retained its corporate entity and continues to
hold the copyright. The National Council of
Churches points out that the volume is not a
statement or pronouncement of the National
Council. The author is solely responsible for its
contents.

Library of Congress catalog card number: 57–6742

Contents

Foreword

by Charles P. Taft

Chairman of the Department of the Church and Economic Life and of Its Study Committee

This volume forms part of a larger study of Christian ethics and economic life which was begun in 1949 by the Department of the Church and Economic Life of the Federal Council of the Churches of Christ in America. At the beginning of 1951 the Federal Council was merged with other interdenominational agencies to form the National Council of the Churches of Christ in the United States of America, made up of thirty Protestant and Orthodox church bodies within the United States.

In recent years religious leaders have recognized that the ethical problems of economic life have become increasingly urgent. The ethics of everyday decisions and practices in economic life, both private and public, are matters of wide concern. We need to go behind individual acts and group pressures for a deeper understanding of the motives underlying what people do in their economic activities, of how the system fits together, of how close our preconceived ideas are to reality.

Change is dominant in our national life and perhaps nowhere so much as in its economic aspects. During the past half-century our ways of life and work have undergone a vast alteration. The change has been accomplished without violence and without great apparent upset, but the tempo of its pace is revolutionary. Certainly if people whose span of life was in the nineteenth century could see what we see in everyday life, they would hardly accept any word but revolution for the process that has brought it about.

This accelerated change demands that all thoughtful people understand its effects upon ethics and human values. How shall we deal with the dynamism in our economic life so as to preserve and extend the dignity of the individual, respect for the rights of minorities, sensitivity to the public welfare, and free discussion and peaceful persuasion? We cannot rely upon business statistics to measure these intangibles. Judgments of even the best qualified individuals about actual or impending changes, affected as opinions are by individual temperament, vested interests, or political partisanship, are also inadequate if considered separately. The fullest use of all our resources for information and discussion is required for sound progress toward solution of our complex problems.

There is no vital threat to our inherited and cherished values either in the *status quo* or in change as such. We cannot separate ethics from practical economic concerns. What is needed is a better understanding both of economic facts and of those ethical convictions and values which have special significance in the meaning and direction they should give to economic activity.

In many parts of the world we find a fanatic cynicism or a false philosophy in opposition to the foundations upon which Western society is based. What earlier generations took for granted, such as the value and integrity of the individual, the character of government as a tool for service of the people, the capacity of human life for essential decency and justice—these are now challenged by conflicting assumptions also claimed to be moral or at least essential for an efficient society.

Here lies the real crisis of the second half of the present century. We must meet this challenge, in so far as it is evil, and clarify in relation to our own institutions the basic ethical affirmations which we support.

The Federal Council of Churches conducted for many years an educational program on the ethical issues involved in economic life. Many denominational bodies have likewise been active in this field. It has become clear, however, that we need a more careful and realistic investigation of economic life and its relation to spiritual and moral values in a Christian frame of reference. We need to make use of the capacities of social scientists and theologians, in close association with other persons drawn from many occupations.

Accordingly, a three-year study was begun in 1949 under a grant from the Rockefeller Foundation, and continued under a further grant from the same source in 1952. The Foundation has not sought to exercise any supervisory control over the study and does not assume responsibility for any of the findings. The results of the study so far are presented in eight volumes: *Goals of Economic Life, The Or-*

ganizational Revolution, Social Responsibilities of the Businessman, American Income and Its Use, The American Economy—Attitudes and Opinions, Christian Values and Economic Life, Social Responsibility in Farm Leadership, and Social Responsibilities of Organized Labor.

Among the other volumes planned are two which continue the social responsibilities theme with respect to mass communication, and to the churches themselves and their agencies in so far as economic policies and practices are concerned. Another volume is being prepared by a group of faculty members at Wesleyan University on formulating public policy in a democratic society in relation to economic growth. The final volume planned will subject to further analysis and interpretation some of the major issues of the study as a whole in their bearing on the work of the churches in social education and action.

Gratitude is due to the several authors for their devotion and creativity in the writing of these volumes. In all the volumes of this series, the authors have been free to write as they wished and to accept or reject suggestions or criticisms; each book is the responsibility of the individual writer.

Others have made valuable contributions to the total study effort of which this volume is an important part. The Reverend Cameron P. Hall, executive director of the department, has given the project his unfailing and effective administrative support. Professor Howard R. Bowen, former economic consultant to the study, made an invaluable contribution in the formulation of the project and aided also in criticism of manuscripts. The Reverend A. Dudley Ward served as director of studies from the beginning until the fall of 1953. He carried out his responsibilities as organizer and coordinator with imagination and efficiency, and also gave help after he had left for other important work. Since September 1953 Dr. F. Ernest Johnson has been in charge of the studies. His long experience in research and education with the Federal Council, and in other connections, has made him exceptionally qualified for this service.

A study committee of the department, including both lay and clerical members and representing a variety of occupations, has reviewed the program of the study at various stages. Mr. Charles H. Seaver, editorial consultant and secretary of the study committee, has

carefully edited the manuscripts and has been available consistently
for counsel.

The National Council of Churches has taken no official position
and assumed no responsibility regarding the content of any of the
volumes. In no sense, therefore, can or should any statement in the
series be regarded as an official declaration of the National Council of
Churches or of any of its units.

Preface

In the fall of 1907 Professor John R. Commons led a group of three University of Wisconsin students to Pittsburgh to study labor conditions in that great center of the steel industry. We arrived in the morning of the first Monday of September, and that being Labor Day we decided to begin our study by attending the picnic that the Pittsburgh Central Trades Council was holding in a park several miles up the Monongahela River. It seemed a good way to make the acquaintance of some steel workers; but we were to know better before we arrived at the park. From the trolley car that carried us toward the picnic grounds we got our first glimpse of the steel mills. We rolled past the famous Homestead Works, which was in full operation. Farther on we could see the Carrie blast furnaces and the Duquesne plant across the river. Then came the borough of Braddock—named for the British general who met disaster there a century and a half earlier—and we were within sight and hearing of the great Edgar Thomson Steel Works, owned, like the plants at Homestead and Duquesne, by the Carnegie Steel Company.

All along our journey smoke was pouring from a hundred stacks. Flashes of fire could be seen here and there. Red-hot ingots, tall as a man, standing in rows on narrow-gauge flat cars, were being hauled to the soaking pits by puffing little locomotives; Bessemer converters, like miniature volcanoes, were spouting flame. There was no picnic that day for the steel men—they were at their jobs.

That was my introduction to the "labor problem" as it existed outside the classroom. That fall the Amalgamated Association of Iron, Steel and Tin Workers reported to the American Federation of Labor a membership of 10,000—less than three per cent of the workers in the industry. Later I learned that there were no unions at that time among the employees of any of the major steel mills of the country; that production workers in the industry generally worked a 12-hour day; that there was no machinery through which a man could appeal for redress of grievances; and that those who joined unions were discharged.

In succeeding years I traveled the country over as industrial editor of the *Survey*. I listened to testimony before the United States Com-

mission on Industrial Relations appointed by President Wilson in
1914 to study the causes of industrial unrest. There I heard some of
the leading industrialists of the country say that they believed in collective bargaining, though none of them dealt with a union in their
own shops. As a reporter I covered strikes for the right to organize in
steel mills, in coal mines, in the textile industry, and elsewhere; and
in all of them I saw the strikers go back to their jobs defeated.

In those early years of my acquaintance with the labor movement I
was deeply impressed and troubled by what I saw of labor's struggle to
organize. I had grown up on a farm in the Middle West. I was struck
with the similarity in some respects between the skilled steel workers
and the farmers whom I knew so well. There were the same shrewd
common sense, the homespun wisdom, the evidences of character
that made me feel comfortable among them as among old friends.
But there was one great difference. The farmers where I had lived
knew hardship, but they were free men and did not hesitate to speak
their minds. It was otherwise with the steel workers. Not only were
they unable to bargain over the conditions of their employment, but
they were not even free to challenge publicly the position of their
employers. They lived under a regime of fear, as did the workers in
other mills and factories where spies reported to management officials
any evidences of independent thought or action.

It seemed strange to me and utterly wrong—a denial of the spirit
of democracy which I had been taught to believe was a fundamental
principle of Americanism.

But with the decade of the 1930s came a turning point in American
labor history. New Deal legislation, the gradual recovery from the
low point of the depression, the demand for labor in World War II—
all these together created a new setting for the labor movement.
Union membership grew at an unprecedented rate. From a weak and
struggling movement slightly more than two decades ago, trade unionism has become not only an accepted movement but a powerful
force—to be reckoned with in the highest circles of industrial management, in state legislatures, and in the headquarters of the federal
government in Washington.

This is a development that calls for a re-appraisal of the significance
of the labor movement in American life. Observers who had some
acquaintance with labor and labor-management relations in the twenty

years preceding the New Deal have some difficulty in adjusting their thinking to the present outlook. There are spokesmen for the National Association of Manufacturers who still invoke the anti-union slogans of 1920. Sympathizers with the labor movement who were not too much inclined to hold the unions to a strict accountability for their acts during the early years when they were struggling for their very existence are still tempted today to think of them, despite their gains, as engaged in a conflict with forces plotting their destruction. On the other hand, those who have become aware of the labor movement only in the last twenty years or so are apt to think of it—in disregard of history—as so powerful, so possessed of resources, as to be impregnable.

The truth can be approximated only by taking both views into account, but both need correction. The unions still need to look out for lurking enemies, but as they have gained in strength and in general recognition, their responsibilities have increased, and it is right that they should meet the test of adherence to the generally accepted moral code.

This book, by one who has lived and observed in both periods of trade-union history—the period of weakness and the period of strength—is in part an attempt to assess the meaning for labor and for society of the revolutionary development that began in the midst of the depression nearly twenty-five years ago.

The first three chapters of the book are in the nature of an introduction. In Chapter 1 I try to show what I mean by social responsibility. Chapters 2 and 3 are intended as essential background for readers who lack knowledge of trade-union history, or have forgotten what they once knew. They may be skipped by the better informed.

In the next five chapters, 4 through 8, some aspects of customary trade-union activity are discussed in the belief that a knowledge of them is a prerequisite to an informed judgment with respect to the trade-union sense of responsibility. In Chapters 9 to 13 the emphasis is on the relation of the unions to the different groups to whom they have obligations. In the following chapters instances of behavior are recorded that are either clearly unacceptable or about which ethical questions may fairly be raised. Attention is directed here also to a strengthened purpose within the labor movement to expose and eliminate malpractice. Finally, I try to sum up the evidence.

In writing this book I have had the help of a group of specially qualified advisers who were appointed by the Study Committee in charge of the series of which this book is a part. They have met with me frequently to discuss the problems involved in the gathering and the presentation of material. Others have read parts or all of the manuscript and have given me the benefit of expert knowledge. None of them is responsible for anything here said. Probably every one of them has reservations about some part of the presentation. All have been encouraging and helpful. I am grateful both for their advice and for the opportunity I had to associate with them.

I owe a special debt to Dr. F. Ernest Johnson for his constant interest and encouragement. As consultant for the series he has given invaluable aid with respect to subject matter, emphasis, and arrangement. He bears no responsibility for any errors that may appear. In fact, there are fewer of them because of his welcome supervision. Many parts of the book have been strengthened because of his wise counsel.

Above all I am grateful to Florence Lee Fitch, my wife. She has read all of the manuscript or has listened while it was read to her. She, like my other advisers, may not agree with all that is set down here, but she has saved me from many a tendency to stray from the announced theme and she has helped me with apt phrases I could not think of myself. Throughout the task of writing I have been encouraged by her wisdom and her patience.

April 27, 1957.   JOHN A. FITCH

Introduction

A major theme of the series of studies of which this volume is one is social responsibility. These words appear in the titles of some of the books and the idea is implicit in the entire inquiry. It is a basic ethical concept, applying to individuals and to groups, signifying a universal obligation to promote the common good.

This ethical imperative is, of course, recognized in other religions than Christianity—a fact of especial importance for our present purpose. For, while this inquiry has been pursued within the framework of Christian assumptions, it is ineffectual to offer judgments or point to principles for the guidance of economic activity in the secular order except as appeal is made to sanctions that are broadly recognized as valid throughout our culture. Otherwise we should be engaged in a sectarian enterprise that would fall short of cogent appeal to the mind of the community as a whole. This is why so little of a specifically doctrinal character can be found in this volume and in those which have preceded it.

On the other hand, these studies, conducted under Christian auspices and by men and women who stand in the Christian tradition, would be less than authentic if the analysis offered and the judgments expressed did not rest on values and convictions that are central to the Christian faith. It is the purpose of this Introduction to point up some of the major issues discussed in the book, by reference to certain values and convictions which Christians hold to be of universal application.

WHY A BOOK ON LABOR UNIONS?

A prior word should be spoken concerning the place of this particular volume in the series. The Federal Council of Churches, which initiated the studies, was from its inception until it was merged in the National Council of Churches deeply concerned with industrial labor and its struggle for status. It was felt that our Protestant churches had been slow in developing a sympathetic attitude toward the aspirations of workingmen and in discerning the significance of the labor movement. The *Social Ideals of the Churches*—often called the "Social Creed"—which for several decades served as an expression of Protestant social concern, focused attention sharply on the needs of the workers and on their right to organize for the purpose of collective bargaining.

Indeed, it may be argued that preoccupation with this "right" and its social significance—which was due to widespread interference with its exercise—today gives a one-sided character to the official Protestant "witness" with respect to industrial issues. For organized labor has now acquired a large measure of power, and this correspondingly increases its responsibility. Although there are regions in the United States where labor is still battling for the most elementary rights— too often with scant support from the churches—it is nevertheless patent that the strength of organized labor in many key industries has now reached approximate equality with management in terms of bargaining power. A distinguishing mark of this book is the fact that the author has set the "labor problem" in a context that makes possible a fair appraisal of the labor movement. He has traced for us the historical development which is a necessary background for an understanding of the present situation.

One who would appraise a movement or an organization must first interpret it. And a valid interpretation must place the subject in the context of experiences and events in which it came to be what it is. Historical perspective is essential. It is a grave error to take the contemporary at face value, disregarding the process by which it came to be. It is well to heed the admonition of the eminent divine of an earlier generation who said: "Beware the sin of contemporaneity." Scant attention to history is a cultural defect that is nowhere more lamentable than in the field of social ethics.

As the reader will discover, Mr. Fitch is convinced of the validity and functional importance of the labor movement. His testimony on this score is the more persuasive because of his intimate contacts over many years with the developments he records. On the other hand, he is able to deal frankly and severely with what he deems organizational faults and individual derelictions.

There are many church people who still have need of a sympathetic interpretation of the labor movement. Yet some liberal churchmen who, before labor's coming of age, learned to defend it consistently as the "underdog" may profit by the realism reflected in these pages. A labor union is, in its very nature, an instrument of power, and the tendency of power to corrupt is thrown into sharp relief in the Christian view of man. This is a fact which the more insightful among labor leaders know well, and their gratification over the great increase in labor's strength is tempered by apprehensiveness concerning the possible abuse of newly acquired power.

This change in the industrial balance of power has inevitably made "labor problems" a focus of great public concern. Labor-management relations have become a major tension area in the power structure of American society. The primary aims of labor unions are to increase wages and lighten working conditions, and to promote "job security" —all this in the face of counterclaims of employers and of consumers. The labor movement should therefore welcome an appraisal by the conscience of the community in accord with the requirements of social justice. And it is a function of the church to assist in the process of making the conscience of the community articulate.

In our culture, influenced as it has been so largely by the biblical tradition, there are two basic values by reference to which such an appraisal must be made: the inestimable worth of persons and the well-being of the community as a whole.

THE WORTH OF PERSONS

The starting-point then for an inventory of ethical values is the worth of individual persons as ends in themselves. In this primary affirmation is grounded all Christian concern for safeguarding and promoting human welfare. Much of what has been said about it, however, has an aspect of unreality because the reference is usually to the worth of *other* persons. A conviction of one's own worth as a child of God is basic in Christian ethics. Reverence for all life presupposes reverence for one's own. Responsible action, in the full sense of the term, is possible only to a person who considers his life a sacred trust.

In a sense, therefore, self-regard is an ethical principle. At the lowest level it is a drive toward self-preservation. At a higher level it supports a discipline of living that sustains health and conserves physical and mental resources. In its finest form it impels a person to supreme self-dedication to a cause that includes but transcends the self.

Basically and in the first instance, the labor union is an instrument for improving the material well-being of its members. Again, basically and in the first instance, this is a holy purpose, grounded in the worth of persons. To the extent that material goods are a means to cultural and spiritual enrichment, "materialism" is not antithetic to Christian values.

In his book *Christian Materialism*, the late Bishop Francis J. McConnell decried the tendency among idealists to discredit everything that may be characterized as "material" or "materialistic." Taking money as an example he said: "Money means food and clothing, books and works of art, chances to help one's fellows—in a word, life! If we could actually trace the history of a coin from the day it leaves the mint, with its image and superscription clear and sharp, to the day when it returns to the melting-pot, we should find that the coin has been closer to human life than any other material agency, that the pressure of human hands upon it has known an indescribable tensity, that the coming of the coin has been looked to with more anxiety and its departure often with more sorrow than those of any other forms of the material."

The labor union as an instrument for improving the workers' status has an ample ethical foundation. Yet here a paradox appears—one of the great ethical paradoxes that life presents. For, since persons live in society and attain development in a social context, the drive for self-realization and fulfilment creates innumerable involvements and conflicts of interest, among the most serious of which are those related to competitive economic effort. Psychologists and theologians alike are aware that our most grievous conflicts develop around our most authentic values and our most elemental concerns. Self-respect easily becomes pride; self-defense readily becomes aggression; and love almost imperceptibly degenerates into possessiveness and jealousy.

Naked evil is quickly recognized and readily condemned; it is the potential evils—pride, avarice, and love of power, which lurk in the urge to self-expression and achievement—that give rise to the most grievous ethical dilemmas. Keeping this in mind may help to preserve perspective on the problems weighed in this book. Mr. Fitch documents by historical narrative and descriptive analysis the capacity of human nature to find fulfillment in pursuit of high purposes—along with the ever-present tendency of high motive to degenerate into prideful self-seeking, and even exploitation of one's associates or of the community itself. Paradoxically, the most subtle moral dangers assail men in their "moralistic" moods; that is, when they are preoccupied with their own praiseworthy ends. "Let him that thinketh he standeth take heed lest he fall."

This account of the labor movement, with its high aims and its temptations, has theological significance in that it throws light on the nature of man. It shows the spiritual possibilities and the moral hazards that inhere in collective human effort.

THE CLAIMS OF COMMUNITY

The discipline of the individual self, which the Christian faith holds to be morally necessary, is effected through a consciously ethical relating of the self to a community of persons, a fellowship that binds them together. The church is such a fellowship—the "beloved community" which has provided the main strand of Christian history in its institutional phase. It is related to the "covenant" concept that runs through the Old Testament: a covenant between God and the people whose ultimate aim is to build a "kingdom of righteousness."

But the experience of community is relevant also to secular life. Indeed, in biblical thought there is no division between sacred and secular. And one of the major present concerns of Christian leaders is to infuse all secular expressions of community—trade and professional associations, labor unions, and the like—with a spiritual purpose and intention. This is the meaning of Christian "vocation," which is now being given renewed emphasis in our church programs. In that context, responsible leadership in all socially useful group activity is an expression of religious vocation.

The labor union is one manifestation of community of interest and intention. In sociological terms the union is one example of a "functional organization of society" whose purpose is to develop the capacities and resources of distinct groups of workers and to pool them in the pursuit of commonly approved ends. It is often assumed that corporate, or collective, action is necessarily on a lower moral plane than individual, private, action. This is a questionable assumption. The business corporation and the trade union are alike "collective" entities, but neither is necessarily "soulless." They are neither immoral nor amoral, per se. As this book shows, labor unions have, at times, been characterized by something akin to missionary motive. It is implicit in the concept of social responsibility that this motive should be nutured and deepened.

But it is equally questionable to assume that an organization which comes into existence for the benefit of its members and the furtherance of their common interests can ever fully express the needs or serve the ends of the community as a whole. It is simple ethical realism to recognize the primary role of self-interest in determining the policy of any economic group. To insist that "the interests of employer and worker are identical" and therefore should never be in opposition is not only fanciful; it is to deny the very principle that brings workers' and employers' organizations into being. Every organization of the group-interest type, if conscious at all of social responsibility, is continually confronted with the problem of reconciling its interests and aims with those of other groups that are pursuing their legitimate ends.

A Christian view of labor unions is, then, both appreciative of their social role and critical of any tendency to obscure basic economic and political realities by means of a halo of humanitarian concern.

COLLECTIVE BARGAINING

It follows from these considerations that the common good requires the cooperation of groups which have not identical but reciprocal interests—interests that are often difficult to reconcile. This is why it has become so important to develop a workable ethics for group behavior to supplement the traditional "personal" ethics which, while indispensable, throws little light on group responsibility. And this, in turn, requires some instrument and some established procedures whereby reciprocal claims based on real or assumed equities can be brought into confrontation with intent to reconcile them.

Such an instrument is the institution of collective bargaining, which is designed to adjust conflicting claims. Its ethical foundation necessarily comprises the "right to organize," the corresponding obligation to "bargain in good faith," and the further obligation to carry out any "contract" that may result. This right and the obligations it implies are grounded in "first principles." Moreover, the viability of the contract depends not only on the degree to which it embodies genuine group interests, but also on the degree to which its terms are felt to be both ethically sound and operationally feasible. An eminent American labor leader, when asked how much the issue of a labor conflict depended on the "right and wrong of it"—as contrasted with sheer power—made a revealing answer. "It is," he said, "when men know they are right that they can fight to win." The distinction between acting merely in pursuit of interest on the one hand, and pursuing interest as supported by an over-all principle of justice on the other hand—this distinction is the essence of ethics in the economic sphere.

It is when we move from the statement of principles to their implementation that the major difficulties in defining social responsibility are encountered. The issues discussed in these chapters have come to be issues largely because the opposing contentions put forward with respect to them have an undeniable element of validity and hence are pressed with much conviction and tenacity. The crucial fact is that while all normally endowed persons are capable of making such a moral distinction they are likewise prone to allow it to become blurred by the glare of self-interest. Ethical analysis must be directed toward penetration of the complex of group interests so as to disclose overarching concerns that have the character of moral imperatives.

At present, both labor and management are especially obligated to take serious account of the impact on the community as a whole of wage increases which they tacitly assume will be compensated by price advances. Disinterested economists, as Mr. Fitch has shown, are much concerned over the "wage-price spiral." An increase in the wage rate that, by necessity or by choice, is absorbed in the price that is to be charged for the product or the service involved is, of course, paid by the consumer, who is not a party to the negotiation. The increase may be warranted in whole or in part, but it may be on the other hand not only a burdensome tax on the consumer but an inflationary threat to the entire community. This is a pressing issue. It rests heavily on both parties at the bargaining table—more heavily than is commonly recognized by either.

A glance at some of the sharply debated issues may clarify what has just been said.

"Union Security"

It was perhaps inevitable that sharp controversy should arise over measures taken by labor unions to maintain a strong bargaining status through pressure on workers to join and to maintain their dues-paying membership. The "union shop," which is permitted under federal law except as state legislatures may forbid it, makes the employer who signs a work contract a partner of the union in maintaining its strength, since membership becomes a condition of continued employment.[1] Is this a simple denial to a nonunion worker of an elementary right to work for any employer who is ready to hire him? Many people so believe. Or is it, rather, a situation in which individual responsibility and prerogative are in part superseded through collective contractual agreement, as the unions maintain? If so, what ethical conditions and requirements are involved when a union thus takes over responsibilities that formerly belonged exclusively to individuals?

There is also the matter of conscientious objection to union membership, which results from the discipline of some of the smaller religious sects. The churches are bound to be sympathetic with this appeal to the principle of religious liberty. A suggested compromise is the payment of an amount equivalent to the union dues into the organization treasury, with exemption from the responsibilities of "membership." Whether this is a compromise in the good or in the bad sense of that term is a matter calling for discriminating thought.

These questions illustrate the complexity of group ethics in the economic sphere. The advent of unionism has raised issues quite as difficult as those raised by the advent of the corporation with respect to individual rights and responsibilities in a business society. The serious reader of this book is challenged to wrestle with them.

"The Right to Strike"

The labor strike is a special aspect of industrial relations in that, although labor regards it as a necessary potential weapon, it is seldom deliberately resorted to as an instrument of policy. The vast majority of labor disputes are settled without recourse to the strike. The importance of this statistical fact may be overestimated, however, since

[1] The "check-off" of union dues (deducting them from regular pay) is a milder form of pressure.

the few major strikes that do occur constitute an undeniable threat to the public welfare. The mere fact that a stoppage of indefinite duration may occur in transportation or steel or coal in spite of all existing mechanisms for negotiation and arbitration constitutes a continual hazard of which we are all fully aware, no matter how little time we may give to discussing it. Also, many a "peaceable" settlement may reflect a prudential reaction to an implicit strike threat. Here the strike is a potential weapon—a weapon, so to say, of "cold" warfare.

The ethical problem thus presented is complicated and stubborn. Such common values and ends as social order and the supply of essential goods and services must be balanced against the claims of economic groups to freedom from coercion by government in order to engage in voluntary, responsible action in the pursuit of legitimate objectives. To put it another way, the community is continually required to choose between values that are equally real and important. And the choice may involve the deliberate acceptance of an evil that is judged to be the "lesser of two." Such choices are as truly moral as the simpler ones where the issue is a matter of "black and white."

Ethical solutions in the area here explored are not arrived at by applying rigid principles and making absolute judgments. Rather, they are reached by devising compromises that carry the largest freightage of human values and embody the highest degree of common justice attainable in a given situation.

When a stalemate is reached in a crucial contract negotiation, government intervention may become a practical necessity. With such a temporary shift of responsibility new ethical issues emerge. How shall the government, as a political body, discriminate between the public good and the public's immediate convenience as reflected in the press and in the demands of citizens whose votes are coveted? How far is governmental coercion justified in implementing a decision that hundreds of thousands of workers are disposed to defy? And if as a matter of public policy government denies to public employees the right to strike, is it obligated to compensate them with a quid pro quo in respect to wages or working conditions?

In the present state of national policy we have, generally speaking, no set limits to the extent of disturbance and privation the public can be expected to take before cracking down on either labor or management, or both. Even the stern measures provided for in the Taft-Hartley Act stop short of ultimate curtailment of the right to strike. In the years just ahead the safeguarding of the community as a whole from the consequences of economic paralysis due to industrial disputes may well become the most crucial domestic problem of democratic government. This book offers no final solution of that problem, but it presents factual and ethical considerations necessary to any possible solution.

LABOR IN POLITICS

Another current issue—a hotly debated one—is the propriety of labor's participation in politics through contributions to political campaigns and through propaganda paid for out of labor's often ample funds. It is contended by some that the restrictions placed on corporations with respect to direct campaign contributions should apply equally to labor unions. This is plausible on its face, and there seems to be a trend in that direction. On the other hand the members of a labor union are much more likely than the stockholders of a corporation to feel a common interest in a particular campaign. The union membership is apparently less diverse in political outlook than the stockholders of a big corporation, who include not only the wealthy but large numbers of wage workers. Moreover, union leaders see a grievous inequity in prohibiting a pooling of workers' financial resources designed to match the political influence which men of wealth exercise through individual giving.

Even so, what of the minority, however small, of union members who may feel that the dues they have paid are being used for a political cause to which they do not wish to be committed? To many, such objection is ethically overriding. To others the issue seems no different in principle from that raised when a contributor to a church budget strenuously objects on religious grounds to some item in the budget which he must support, at least indirectly, if he contributes at all.

The increased concern on the part of organized labor with "ethical practices" is impressive and promising. It indicates an awareness on the part of the AFL-CIO of the ethical dilemmas and the individual and corporate delinquencies to which Mr. Fitch gives so much attention. There is always a danger that "codes" may serve merely to verbalize ideals and obligations which are not only far beyond existing practices but beyond any present readiness for implementation. Nevertheless the existence of a concern and the devotion of vigorous leadership to the realization of higher ethical practices warrant confidence and public support. Such a mood seems appropriate as one approaches Mr. Fitch's informing and stimulating analysis.

F. ERNEST JOHNSON

Social Responsibilities of Organized Labor

1

The Concept of Social Responsibility

Social responsibility, whether of an individual or a group, recognizes the existence of obligations to others in an ever-widening area—obligations to individuals, to groups, and to society. We are concerned in this book with the responsibilities of labor organizations, but the unions are not alone in facing the questions that arise. Some of these questions have universal application, and require consideration by all thoughtful men and women.

A dictionary definition of the word "responsibility" declares it to be "the state of being accountable or answerable," and, by way of amplification, "as for a trust or office, or for a debt." This definition assumes the existence of an obligation to another, based upon an understanding or a contract. However, beyond the area of such obligations created by agreement, there exists an underlying imperative which arises from ethical convictions that are imbedded in the prevailing culture. The parable of the good Samaritan is a case in point, as is the tradition of the sea which sends one vessel to the aid of another in distress, regardless of nationality. It is this same sense of urgent necessity that leads one to offer assistance to a stranger who has suffered an accident, or causes neighbors to rally to the aid of the victims of a fire or hurricane. It extends into a broad area of humanitarian considerations, which includes the brute creation as well as mankind. Even on the Sabbath Day an ox or an ass fallen into a pit will be rescued.

The ethical concepts at the root of this underlying imperative are the outgrowth of human experience. Through the ages men have searched for principles and action suited to their needs. The search is unending, but it results at any given time in the existence of an unwritten (and sometimes written) code of behavior whose general acceptance is essential to the existence of the prevailing culture. The elements of the code vary with the experience and outlook of the particular society in which it is developed. Hence in one part of the

1

world primitive tribes may be practicing cannibalism while elsewhere, at the same time the doctrine of the infinite worth of human personality is diligently taught. These elements also tend to be altered in time, for better or for worse. As the generations pass, polygamy gives way to monogamy, slavery to freedom, capital punishment for minor offenses to more enlightened practice; or the trend for a time may be in the reverse direction, as the circumstances out of which World War II emerged so clearly show.

So this code consisting of many canons of behavior comes into being slowly and painfully over the centuries. It represents what man, in his continuing search for an acceptable way of life, has found practicable or useful or excellent. It is the basis for man's moral conduct.

In the Western world the development of the code has been influenced by innumerable forces, but primarily by a Judeo-Christian philosophy. Basic in that philosophy is an upward look toward God, and an outward look toward fellow man. The admonitions of Moses to the children of Israel contain these two elements:

Thou shalt love the Lord thy God with all thine heart, and with all thy soul, and with all thy might. (Deuteronomy 6:5)

Thou shalt love thy neighbor as thyself. (Leviticus 19:18)

"On these two commandments," said Jesus, "hang all the law and the prophets." (Matthew 22:40)

The Scriptures are rich in variations on the theme:

The stranger that dwelleth with you shall be unto you as one born among you, and thou shalt love him as thyself. (Leviticus 19:34)

What does the Lord require of thee but to do justly, and to love mercy, and to walk humbly with thy God? (Micah 6:8) [1]

And beyond these are the magnificently extended horizons of the Sermon on the Mount, in the words of Jesus:

Ye have heard that it hath been said, thou shalt love thy neighbor and hate thine enemy. But I say unto you, love your enemies, bless them that curse you, do good to them that hate you, and pray for them that despitefully use you, and persecute you. (Matthew 5:43, 44)

[1] The scriptural references are to the King James Version.

DEVELOPMENT OF STANDARDS

These approved canons of behavior are not always spelled out. What is meant in specific terms by the admonition to love God or one's fellow men? Many of the terms in common use to denote types of responsibility—terms such as "fairness," "justice," "mercy"—are incapable of exact definition. Nevertheless organized society attempts in two ways to define the areas of acceptable behavior.

The first is an evolutionary process, described by William Graham Sumner and his followers, who traced the progress of ethical concepts through custom, folkways, mores and morals, to statute law. The last stage is reached when certain types of behavior have come to be thought of as so essential to the existence of an approved society as to require punishment for deviations from them. Thus we arrive at specific definitions in such areas as sex morality, parental responsibility, property rights, public and personal safety. At the center of the area covered by statute we have reasonably exact indications of what is required: "Thou shalts" and "thou shalt nots" are not only spelled out but may be vigorously enforced. On the fringes uncertainty exists. Some legal enactments still on the statute books are enforced laxly, or not at all, because general public opinion no longer supports the assumptions on which the laws are based. Examples are the so-called "blue laws" of an earlier day, which are not yet entirely obsolete but tend in that direction. On the other hand there are social convictions now being written into law that represent a widespread consciousness of need, or sense of right, that has not yet received universal approval. Examples include such matters as public health, child labor, and social legislation generally.

The second way of defining and enforcing ethical standards both precedes and supplements legal enactment. Public opinion develops the conventions that are written into law, supports and thus makes enforceable the laws that it approves, and gives sanction to a host of ideas and convictions that lie outside the area of legislation. This is a force that is more extensive than law and, in some of its aspects, more powerful. Its milder means of enforcement consist of expressions of opinions from the pulpit, the lecture platform, or the editorial desk, and even personal exchange of views. Its severer forms involve coercion through discrimination, boycott, and social ostracism.

The direct application of ethical concepts as molded by public opinion occurs when administrative agencies attempt to give body to general principles as set forth in statute law. An example is the work of the National Labor Relations Board in its rulings under the Wagner and Taft-Hartley Acts. While the Board continues to function in a highly controversial area, many of its decisions, protested at first, are now accepted and represent a general consensus.

Social responsibility, then, is a response to the generally accepted code of behavior that includes respectful consideration for all of it, and a sense of obligation to adhere to its major and most firmly established principles. The obligation is primarily to society itself, but its practical manifestations generally involve relationships with individuals and groups.

THE PURPOSE OF THIS BOOK

The discussion above relates to social responsibility as it impinges upon the whole of society. In this book we are directly concerned with the response of organized labor to the obligations implied in the term. The main purpose is to attempt to give some insight into the nature of that response through an examination of significant acts and pronouncements of organized labor in the current scene. In order to do this we must take a brief look at the past. The labor movement today, like other social and economic movements, is the result of forces that have molded attitudes and practices over the years. We shall see how profoundly the labor movement has been affected by social and governmental forces, and especially by the new direction of those forces in the last few decades.

We shall see also that labor organizations, like employers' associations, civic bodies, and churches, have responsibilities in more than one direction. The union that has a broad view of its functions recognizes the existence of obligations to its members, to other workers, to employers, and to the community. In all of these relationships the obligations are reciprocal. While we are concerned here with the responsibilities of unions it must not be overlooked that unions do not stand alone as inheritors of obligations. They, like all other groups, will be able to discharge their responsibilities to the fullest extent only in an atmosphere in which the element of mutuality in such relationships is recognized.

We shall here be giving attention both to rights and to obligations. No formal presentation will be made in which those concepts are enumerated or defined, but they will underlie the whole presentation. The history of the labor movement reveals its emergence from a period of individualism and limited organizational rights into a period in which the individual worker has achieved significant advantages through collective action. Among these are the right to organize and to bargain collectively; to resort to economic pressure through strikes and enlist support through the medium of peaceful picketing; and to use the collective power of organization to increase the political importance of the individual.

With the development of these rights the several types of responsibility referred to above become apparent. The collectivity known as the union derives its power from the willingness of individual members to give up some of their independence and to accept the rule of the majority, or of authorized leaders. An obligation is thus imposed upon the union to assure to the individual member a democratic right to a voice in the determination of policy, and a right to protection against malfeasance on the part of elected representatives.

The right to bargain collectively engenders an obligation to bargain in good faith, to recognize the rights and obligations of management and of ownership, and to exercise such self-restraint at the bargaining table as will promote the ends of justice. Similarly, the expanded economic and political power due to organization creates an obligation to act with regard for the welfare of society.

Before turning to these matters, however, we must consider more specifically what we mean by "trade unionism."

2

The Essential Nature of Trade Unionism

For some purposes we might theoretically equate unionism with the 17 million individuals who constitute the membership of the various unions. Unfortunately the difficulties involved in doing this are insuperable. Each of these individuals, besides being a union member, has his own personal objectives and ideas. No union and no agency can speak for even one of them in his totality as a human being. Moreover these union members are distributed unevenly among some two hundred international unions [1] which differ from one another in structure and method and to some extent in underlying philosophy and objectives.

When we turn from the individual to the institution, we find that unions, like corporations, are not conscious and self-activating entities. They are shaped by circumstances and by the composite personalities of their members. Yet a union tends to have an individuality of its own. When it has become well established it develops group characteristics that differ from the individual characteristics of its members. It may have at any given time certain objectives that transcend those of its members,[2] the most significant one being institutional survival. The union is more than the instrument of those who happen at any particular moment to belong to it. Ideally it is a continuing body dedicated to the task of improving conditions of life and labor, not just for a single generation but for generations after.

---

[1] Most American unions of some significance are nationwide in scope. A considerable majority of these have members in Canada as well as in the United States and are known as "internationals." Because of this, and for reasons of convenience as well, the major unions discussed in this book will be referred to as internationals, whether or not their membership extends across an international frontier.

[2] "As long as one looks at this or that man, the personal objectives may take precedence. But when one looks at the actions of a group of men, he is confronted with something more than the sum of the objectives of the group's members. There are institutional objectives which may at any time be just as important as the goals of the individuals. . . ." Harbison and Coleman, *Goals and Strategy in Collective Bargaining* (New York: Harper & Brothers, 1951), p. 7.

The union, as an institution, is influenced by a host of abstract concepts, contributed to by history, tradition, and experience. This is especially true of the older bodies; but the newer organizations also are profoundly affected by the history and experience of other unions, and by their own variously derived concepts of a labor movement—of which trade unionism is the modern expression—stretching back into an unmeasured past (See Chapter 3).

Because of this it is difficult to put one's finger with certainty on a particular body of opinion, philosophy, and method and say "this is unionism." For this reason, and in view of the specific purposes of this book, we shall be concerned neither with individual members nor, generally, with unions as corporate entities, but rather with the effect of the behavior of members and officers who, acting together in the name of the union, outline policy, make decisions, initiate action, and determine methods. The total of the policies and decisions so arrived at constitutes trade unionism as understood in this book.

The union in the United States in the twentieth century exists or comes into being primarily as an agency for determining the rights and status of employees vis-à-vis the employer. It brings to an end the stage of bargaining by individuals about wages and working conditions, and inaugurates an era of representative or collective bargaining in behalf of the employees.

On the management side, collective bargaining may be said to have come into being with the development of the corporation. Management officials spoke for the owners—stockholders—in arranging terms of employment first with individuals and later at the bargaining table with spokesmen for the employees. But long before the corporation became the major factor in business activity, the individual employer became the more powerful bargainer whenever his accumulated resources became greater than those of any of his employees, thus enabling him to outlast them in an economic contest.

Labor's collective bargaining has been practiced within narrow limits for a hundred years, and in greater magnitude over wide areas since the mid-1930s. Thus it has come to play a role similar to that of management when management acts as bargainer for owners of the facilities of business enterprise.

AREAS OF UNION ACTIVITY

Although the primary purpose of the union is to deal with the employer as agent for the employees—and that is perhaps the only purpose at the outset—other purposes emerge as the union grows in membership and experience. It is apparent that as time goes on the union encompasses three major areas of activity: dealing with the employer, providing nonbargained services for its members, and acting in various ways on the stage of public affairs. These areas may be outlined in brief.

Bargaining Aims

The union bargains with the employer for the economic advancement of the employees. More important than anything else at the outset is the wage bargain: the union seeks higher wages, or opposes a reduction.

Following closely on the heels of the wage issue is concern about working conditions. In earlier trade-union history the length of the working day was a matter that loomed nearly as large as the question of wages. In the early 1800s the standard working day was from dawn to dark. In this period there were frequent strikes to obtain the 10-hour day. It was not until the middle 1880s that this objective was generally won in unionized industries, and the struggle for the 8-hour day began. By the end of World War I the 8-hour day had become universal for skilled craftsmen in building, printing, and other mechanized trades, and was coming to prevail to a considerable extent in manufacturing. The unions then turned their attention to securing the 48-hour week. The next twenty years saw a reduction in the length of the work-week to 44, and then to 40 hours. In 1938 Congress passed the Fair Labor Standards Act, which required employers engaged in interstate commerce to pay overtime for hours worked beyond 40 in a week.[3] And this is unlikely to be the end of the story. A 36-hour or even a 30-hour week may be in store.[4]

[3] This progressive reduction in working hours did not proceed evenly over the whole of industry. The continuous industries were conspicuous laggards.

[4] The U.S. Bureau of Labor Statistics reports that a 37½-hour week now prevails in a number of industries and 97 per cent of the workers in the ladies' garment industry now have a 35-hour week. *Monthly Labor Review*, November 1956, pp. 1263 ff.

Other "working conditions" which the unions have improved through bargaining with the employer include the extent of the work load and protection against bodily hazards.

The third bargaining area involves security—job security and union security. The unions attempt to protect their members against arbitrary lay-offs, whether due to technological developments within the industry, a decline in business, union activity, or misconduct. Discharge for any of these reasons is regarded as beyond the unilateral decision of the employer.

Organized labor attempts to obtain "union security" by making arrangements with the employer that are designed to bring about as nearly as possible 100 per cent union membership. This means that an agreement is reached under which membership in the union is, to greater or lesser degree, made a condition of employment. The degree of compulsion involved ranges from the closed shop, which requires a worker to be a union member before he can be considered for a job, to the maintenance-of-membership plan, which does no more than require a worker who has voluntarily joined the union to stay in it for the period of the contract. This arrangement makes provision also for an "escape period" during which members may withdraw. The different forms of union security will be further considered, and pro and con attitudes toward them discussed, in a later chapter.

Unbargained Benefits [5]

Once the job is made relatively secure, and the fear that the union may be ousted is allayed, the union is free to turn to other matters. It discovers membership needs that lie outside the original area of union-management bargaining. These needs include education, health services, recreation, and cultural development. Not all unions provide services for their members in all these fields, and some provide none. But the great health clinics maintained by several unions of garment workers—jointly with their employers—are notable contributions to group medicine. The United Mine Workers maintains a hospital service which, under successive agreements over a dozen years, is financed by the companies through payments based on tonnage of coal mined. Most of the other health and hospital services are financed jointly by unions and employers.

[5] See Chap. 8.

Even more widespread among the unions are provisions for the educational needs of members. These range from courses in economics, English, parliamentary law, industrial relations, and trade-union history, all of which are open to all members, to instruction of union officers and stewards in the performance of their duties.

Public Affairs [6]

The third area of union activity referred to earlier is that of public affairs. Although the American Federation of Labor under the Gompers leadership was extremely skeptical of the value of legislation dealing with any area that was a proper subject for collective bargaining, it was keenly aware of the danger of anti-labor legislation. The slogan "Reward our friends and defeat our enemies" was adopted early in the present century to induce trade-union voters to go to the polls and vote for or against legislators according to their record with respect to labor laws.

In more recent times, and particularly since the emergence of the New Deal in the 1930s, organized labor has moved far from the Gompers attitude and has espoused an extensive legislative program. Both AFL and CIO had committees which engaged the year around in lobbying for desired legislation and in promoting the election of persons friendly to labor aims to legislative positions and to high posts in government administration. Under the merger of December 1955 these bodies were combined in the Committee on Political Education.

The area of labor interest in legislation is by no means limited to proposals affecting the worker as a worker, but has come to include matters involving the interests of the consumers and the welfare of the community as a whole. Beyond this broader concern for domestic affairs, organized labor has developed intense interest and activity in international problems.

THE INFLUENCE OF UNIONS

It remains to consider briefly in this chapter the relation of union activity to employee welfare.

The extent to which trade-union action has contributed to the financial well-being of the wage earners is a question about which

[6] See Chap. 13.

economists differ. These differences have to do more with labor's total "share" in the national income than with the effect of union pressure for higher wages in particular industries.[7] Moreover, the influence sometimes exerted by union agreements in part of an industry over the level of wages in nonunion plants in the same industry is not to be overlooked. In the period during the 1930s when company unions were being rapidly installed by managements as a barrier against self-organization, it was not unusual to insert a clause in the basic understanding between management and company-union representatives to the effect that wages should be at least equal to those provided for in union agreements in that economic field. Today there are occasional large, independent, nonunion plants in industries partly organized which maintain a wage level slightly above the union scale.[8]

The influence of the unions in reducing daily and weekly hours of labor is perhaps clearer. The progressive shortening of the working day and week followed consistently on the heels of the development of a stronger labor movement.

A strong influence toward improved relations between employer and employee has been the inclusion of "grievance machinery" in union contracts. Practically all of the 125,000 negotiated agreements now in existence [9] provide the machinery for settling grievances at the lowest level of authority, where most of them are in fact settled. For those grievances not satisfactorily disposed of at that level a system of appeals provides a step-by-step procedure up to a final conference between high-ranking officers representing management and

[7] See reference to Red Caps and Pullman porters, Chap. 9, pp. 86–87.

[8] A treatise dealing with wages and employment sums up a chapter entitled "Union and Nonunion Wages" as follows: "The preceding discussion provides no answer to the question whether or to what extent unionism has improved, or can improve, the real wage position of workers *as a class.*" (Emphasis supplied.) But "Unionism is a dynamic factor in the determination of labor conditions. Its influence is not confined to union members. . . . A wage increase granted by a nonunion firm may have been greatly influenced by wage increases secured in other firms by union action. Nonunion firms on occasion raise wages in anticipation of the outcome of collective bargaining negotiations involving other firms or to frustrate union organizing efforts. At least in part for this latter purpose, some nonunion firms adopt a policy of maintaining wages above levels in the industry and area." Woytinsky and Associates, *Employment and Wages in the United States* (New York: The Twentieth Century Fund, 1953), p. 501.

[9] *Monthly Labor Review* (U.S. Bureau of Labor Statistics), July 1956, p. 805.

union, and finally, if necessary, a referral of the problem to an outside arbitrator whose decision is by agreement final and binding.

The new rights thus obtained give to the worker a sense of status. They tend to restore an essential which is said to have been lost by the changes arising from the industrial revolution. "When the tool was taken from [the worker's] hand," a competent team of writers assert, ". . . the satisfaction which comes from the individual creation of a product was largely gone. [He] had lost something which wages alone could not replace . . . , a certain dignity as a human being." It was in part to recover this lost status that unions were organized "through which many could work together as a group . . . and regain to a certain degree their earlier independence and importance as human beings." Trade unions were "an inevitable result of the industrial revolution." [10]

[10] Faulkner and Starr, *Labor in America* (New York: Harper & Bros., 1944), p. 29.

3

Historical Background

The labor movement has its roots deep in human history. As a movement for individual rights its impetus comes in part from the political evolution of the Anglo-Saxon peoples, which has progressed by a series of historic achievements: the signing of Magna Carta, the rise of a parliamentary system, the enunciation of a bill of rights, male suffrage, and universal suffrage; and for Americans in addition the Declaration of Independence and the Emancipation Proclamation. Thus the rights of the individual as a citizen emerged.

The struggle of the workers for status has led through slave revolts, peasant wars, revolutions, rent riots, strikes, and parliamentary action to an industrial citizenship corresponding in many respects to political citizenship. The two types of struggle are intermingled, and each is essential to the other. From these struggles modern concepts of democracy have emerged. In both areas of advance there seems to be something inevitable.

Basically, the *labor movement* was in being when the Israelites, in bondage in Egypt, revolted against making bricks without straw. The *union movement* is its modern phase. But only in recent decades have the unions achieved anything like full recognition. After labor organizations began to emerge in this country, legal obstacles hampered their progress for more than a century.

In 1806 a Philadelphia court found striking shoe workers "guilty of a combination to raise their wages," and fined them eight dollars apiece with costs.[1] Knowledge of this famous case and of much that followed it is essential to a full understanding of modern American trade unions. For, with the exception of the last three decades, during the century and a half of the existence of a union movement in this country, the energies of the promoters of unionism have been largely devoted to a struggle for survival.

[1] John R. Commons, *Documentary History of American Industrial Society* (Cleveland, Ohio: Arthur H. Clark Co., 1910), Philadelphia Cordwainers Case, Vol. III, pp. 59–248.

Unions and Individualism

The hurdles that had to be taken before the road lay open for trade unionism were sociological and economic as well as legal. First, the rural, largely agricultural society of the America of 150 years ago made an individualistic philosophy almost inevitable. An apparently unlimited supply of free land beyond the slowly receding western frontier made escape from wage bondage both possible and attractive. Under such conditions it was easy to believe that the individual could fend for himself. Groups of workers who combined to improve their lot incurred popular disapproval and this disapproval was often shared by the workers themselves, who looked forward to climbing the economic ladder without the help of either unions or government. In the early 1840s a society of workingmen in New York declared that the future of labor—its salvation—lay in access to the land. They urged the government to open up the vast public domain to actual settlers without cost, thus anticipating the Homestead laws of the early days of the Lincoln Administration.[2]

The judges shared the current philosophy. Some judges were so confident that the wage earner of that day would become the "master" of the future that stopping along the way to organize and press for his rights seemed to them a waste of time. Moreover such action, they felt, tended to hinder the activities of employers upon whom the welfare of the community depended. So, following English common law, combinations of workers were held to be illegal conspiracies. When that doctrine was on the wane, the combinations were permitted to exist but their customary defensive acts—strikes, picketing, refusal to work with others who accepted less than the union scale— were declared illegal. Not until 1842 did a major court hold otherwise. In that year the Massachusetts Supreme Court upheld the right of workers to organize, and even to strike for the closed shop.[3]

While that decision had a considerable influence in modifying the conspiracy doctrine as applied to the organization and activities of unions, judicial hostility continued to be manifest. Sixty-six years after the Massachusetts decision, in 1908, the Supreme Court of the United States held that a law forbidding a railroad company to dis-

[2] 12 U. S. Statutes 392, May 20, 1862.
[3] Commonwealth v. Hunt: 4 Metcalf (Massachusetts), p. 111.

charge an employee because of membership in a union was unconstitutional.[4] And in 1915 the same court ruled against a state law which forbade an employer to require a worker to sign a "yellow dog"[5] contract. In this latter case the court said that the law was designed solely to benefit the unions and that it was "unable to conceive" of any justification for such a purpose.[6] Somewhat later a New York court, in an opinion setting forth its reasons for issuing an injunction against picketing, declared that it was the duty of the court to "stand at all times as the representative of capital, of captains of industry."[7]

EFFECT OF IMMIGRATION

Another obstacle to the growth of unionism, particularly in the latter part of the nineteenth century, was the presence of a heterogeneous population due to practically unrestricted immigration. An influx of migrants from all the countries of Europe increased after the Civil War until the annual average number of arrivals was nearly 900,000 by the first decade of the present century; in some of these years the number was over a million. This created particularly in the large industrial centers a situation whereby the bulk of the workers, especially the unskilled, were not only alien to the native population but divided into groups that were alien to each other because of both differences in language and inherited nationalistic or racial hostilities.

Under such circumstances there was no such thing as labor solidarity. The native American worker despised the new immigrant because he accepted any wages he could get, and because he was not averse on occasion to taking the place of a striker. The foreigners, moreover, distrusted each other and "scabbed" on each other. Employers took advantage of this situation. Professor John R. Commons found that a leading packing house in Chicago in 1904 hired Slovaks one week and Swedes the next. On asking the "employment agent" for an explanation, he was told: "We change about among different

[4] Adair v. U.S. 208 US 161.

[5] A term that refers to an individual contract, the acceptance of which is made a condition of employment, and by which a worker agrees not to join a union during his term of employment.

[6] Coppage v. Kansas 236 US 1.

[7] Schwartz and Jaffe v. Hillman, 115 Miscellaneous Reports (N. Y.) 61.

nationalities and languages. It prevents them from getting to-gether." [8]

The study of the steel strike of 1919 by the Interchurch World Movement revealed that the same tactics were employed in that industry.[9]

Some of the craft unions had developed considerable strength at this time, notably the printers and the building trades unions, but these were unions of native Americans. Under the circumstances organization of the new workers was in many cases virtually impossible. The language difficulty alone was almost insurmountable, let alone the hostilities between national groups. The labor organizations could not carry their message to these workers through the medium of the English language. To cover the ground in a typical industrial area they needed organizers capable of speaking a dozen different tongues.

As time went on these two socio-economic obstacles tended to become less serious. Free land with its stimulus to individualism had practically disappeared by the end of the nineteenth century. With its passing industrialism and urbanization began to change the outlook of the people.

Somewhat later the immigration problem reached a new phase. World War I had the effect of reducing the influx of foreigners to a trickle, and after the war restrictive laws made a return to the excessive figure of the prewar period impossible. The effect was to alter drastically the nationality and language barriers of the first two decades of the present century. Linguistically at least, the population has since become relatively homogeneous. We have now a new

[8] John R. Commons and Associates, *History of Labour in the United States* (New York: The Macmillan Co., 1918), Vol. III, *Working Conditions*, by Don D. Lescohier, p. XXV.

[9] The resulting lack of facilities for communication between employer and workers sometimes made this policy an obvious disadvantage to the employer. Sometime in the late 1920s the writer attended a meeting called by the mayor of a town where a factory employing only non-English speaking workers was strike-bound. The mayor had been asked by the employer to convey his offer to the strikers. To facilitate this objective the mayor brought to the meeting two interpreters of the same nationality as the strikers. Each attemped to convey the message to the strikers and then each accused the other of misinterpreting it. Neither mayor nor employer had any means of knowing which interpreter was right!

generation of job-seekers, thousands of whom bear the names of immigrant parents or grandparents to whom English was an alien tongue. But these new workers do not stand apart, nor do they or their fellows find communication difficult. They come from the same schools; they share a common language.

Nowhere is the change more apparent than in the great industrial centers. In the period 1907 to 1910 I spent a considerable amount of time in the steel towns around Pittsburgh. I came away with two major impressions: the existence of a general, all-pervading state of fear that made it difficult for a stranger to penetrate to the real thinking of the steel workers, particularly with respect to their attitude toward unions, and the presence of a vast unskilled labor force composed almost entirely of immigrants who could not, or would not, speak the English language. Any conversational approach to one of them was almost certain to be frustrated by the constantly repeated sentence "Me no fustay!"

In 1919 when the AFL was making its ill-fated attempt to organize steel, a group of steel workers standing on a street corner in one of the mill towns denied that they had any knowledge of the existence of such a movement or the whereabouts of the union office. This was during a time when the mill was closed down by a strike. Later I found the union office about a block from where I had made my first inquiry.

In 1935 when, under the influence of the Recovery Act, a new movement to organize the steel workers was under way, I found a different situation. It was all summed up for me when I stopped a steel worker on a street in Homestead, Pennsylvania, to repeat my question of sixteen years before. Where was the union office? The man, it turned out, was a skilled worker and a son of immigrant parents. With a voice that could have been heard a block away, and in pure American, he said, "Why, buddy, you go to the left one block and then to the right, and there's the union office." A new day had dawned!

Two of the obstacles to unionism had been removed. But, in speaking of an agrarian economy and of a heterogeneous society as obstacles, we have disregarded the force that through all the years down to the 1930s exercised the greatest influence in retarding the development of unions. That was the opposition of the employers.

EMPLOYERS' OPPOSITION

From the beginning, anti-union employers have been active on two fronts, legal and economic. The early cases in which strikers were indicted and tried for conspiracy were initiated by employers. Later the employers appealed to the courts to issue injunctions against union activities. The types of behavior that were forbidden at different times by court injunction not only included strikes for the closed shop, peaceful picketing, and other aspects of employer-labor struggle, but in various ways the very right to organize was hampered or altogether nullified by court action. In West Virginia in the 1920s the United Mine Workers, in a series of cases in different courts, were enjoined from attempting to organize coal miners. The national organization was forbidden to send money into the state to be used in organizing campaigns, and employers already dealing with the union were enjoined from "checking off" union dues.[10]

The most effective and far-reaching legal restraint on organizing activities during this period of judicial attack was the result of a decision by the United States Supreme Court. This case involved the use of a "yellow-dog" contract. The court upheld an injunction by a lower court which had forbidden the union to attempt to recruit as members persons who had signed such a contract.[11] This decision considerably stimulated the use of such contracts by employers. The effect was to make organizing campaigns illegal in numerous industrial communities.

The point of view of organized labor with respect to these legal obstacles to union activity was expressed in a report made to the American Federation of Labor in 1922, when the trend of court action in this field was at its height. "What confronts the workers of America," said the report, "is not one or several casual court decisions favoring the interests of property as against the human rights of labor, but a series of adjudications of the highest tribunal of the land, successively destroying a basic right or cherished acquisition of organized

---

[10] Most of these injunctions were modified or set aside on appeal, but were in full effect between issuance by the lower court and decision in the Appeals Court. See Fitch, *The Cause of Industrial Unrest*, New York: Harper & Brothers, 1924, pp. 325 ff.

[11] Hitchman Coal & Coke v. Mitchell 245 US 229 (1917).

labor, each forming a link in a fateful chain consciously designed to enslave the workers of America." [12]

Employers' opposition to the growth of unions, however, did not await the action of courts. Through various tactics on what was referred to above as the "industrial front," anti-union employers took other steps to oppose union organization. Employers often "made an example" of workers trying to start a labor organization, by discharging and blacklisting them. Thus the movement was nipped in the bud, and notice was served on the rank and file that joining a union was a dangerous thing to do.

At the root of this sort of aggressive action was a method that came for a time to be characteristic of a large section of American industry—the use of spies. Not infrequently employers maintained an organized secret service, including a staff of undercover men who worked in the various plants and made reports. How this worked, and the intimidation resulting from it, has been described in various articles and reports.[13]

Supplementing the work of the industrial spy was the cooperative activity of police officers. Arrests of pickets, physical assaults on organizers, sometimes deportation [14] of strikers from the areas affected, all resulted in an atmosphere of fear that militated against successful organizing. In remote areas, or company towns, guards employed by the companies were deputized by county sheriffs and thus were enabled to carry arms. In the coal industry this practice sometimes led to something approaching local civil war, as in southern Colorado in 1914. The methods used and their effect on the life of a community were vividly set forth in a report of the National Labor Relations Board [15] on one of the first cases to come before it, that of the Jones & Laughlin Steel Corporation and the Amalgamated Association

[12] AFL Convention Proceedings, 1922, pp. 371–373.

[13] Sidney Howard, The Labor Spy (New York: Republic Publishing Co., 1924); Violations of Free Speech and Rights of Labor: Hearings and Reports of Subcommittee of the Committee on Education and Labor, U. S. Senate (La Follette Committee) pursuant to Senate Resolution 266. 74th Congress; John A. Fitch, The Causes of Industrial Unrest (New York: Harper & Brothers, 1924), pp. 171–185.

[14] See Report on Labor Disturbances in Colorado, by Carroll D. Wright, Commissioner of Labor, Government Printing Office, 1905.

[15] The agency set up by the Wagner Act and continued under Taft-Hartley to administer its provisions.

of Iron, Steel, and Tin Workers, on April 9, 1936.[16] This case involved an attempt to organize a plant at Aliquippa, Pennsylvania. The following is an excerpt from the Board's report.

Aliquippa is a city of about 30,000 inhabitants, 10,000 of whom are employed by respondent. . . . The union sought . . . to organize the men in the Aliquippa works. Their efforts were countered by systematic terror. Officers of the union and organizers who came into Aliquippa were followed about by the private police of the respondent. . . . The house of Gerstner, the financial secretary, at which an organization meeting had been held, was surrounded day and night by the J & L [Jones & Laughlin] police, and the employment agent of the respondent sat near Gerstner's doorway noting down the names of those who entered the house. Persons coming out of the house were questioned. Some were mysteriously beaten and hit on the head while walking in the streets.

Earlier a union organizer who came to Aliquippa and distributed union pamphlets, as he went along the street was set upon by two persons who beat him severely. He was then taken before a Justice of Police, fined $5, and refused a transcript of record for purposes of appeal.

The officers of the unions were unable to obtain a hall in which to hold meetings and were "refused the use of open lots." Therefore they held their meetings across the Ohio River in an open lot in the town of Ambridge.[17]

The Board reported the circumstances of the dismissal of ten employees,[18] decided that the dismissals were because of their union activities and therefore in violation of the Wagner Act, and ordered their reinstatement with pay for lost time. This was one of several cases appealed to the United States Supreme Court, which upheld the constitutionality of the Wagner Act.[19]

In this brief description of judicial and industrial activities against

[16] From Decisions and Orders of the National Labor Relations Board, Volume 1, pp. 503–509.

[17] Ibid., p. 509.

[18] The original complaint which was presented to the Board included twelve cases of discharge, one of which was dismissed by the Board for lack of evidence. The twelfth man asked to have the complaint as to himself withdrawn. He wrote a letter to the Board stating that he feared the use of his name would do him harm. Ibid., p. 503.

[19] NLRB v. Jones and Laughlin Steel Corporation, 301 U.S. 1 (1937).

unions, the past tense has been used because the labor-management scene has in the main undergone great change. The use of injunctions has been curbed by federal law and by similar statutes in several states. While the labor injunction is still employed it no longer constitutes the basic threat to union organization that it did a quarter-century ago.[20] Moreover the Wagner Act of 1935 gave legal protection to the unions, a protection that basically is maintained under the Taft-Hartley Act of 1947, and the present legal status of the unions is fully recognized by most large employers. Largely as a result of these developments trade-union membership has quadrupled since 1933.

The purpose of this glimpse at the past is to indicate the nature of the struggle that went on for a hundred years before the basic right to organize was firmly established. Organized labor today seems to be facing an entirely different situation, but its outlook and some of its methods are deeply influenced by its past.

Also, the new era is not yet in full effect in every corner of the country. In certain areas, particularly in the South, most if not all of the anti-union devices referred to above are still in everyday use. Indeed, some new devices have been discovered. Moreover, in the greater area where unions are accepted, efforts are constantly being made, and with some success, to obtain legislation to restrict union activity.

But the present status of unionism, legally and industrially, is in general so strong that there seems little likelihood of a reversion to the earlier stage of struggle for existence.

[20] A union lawyer writes me as follows: "The labor injunction is now not a basic threat or an important factor in national disputes between major unions and employers. However, injunctions issued by state courts are still a major factor in negotiation by the smaller unions and are a major barrier to organizing unorganized plants. They are particularly effective in the 17 states with 'right-to-work' laws."

4

Union Objectives

Trade unions attempt to obtain for their members some of what they, and all other persons, believe are the major essentials of living. As a matter of course food, clothing, and shelter come first. An investigator going through a factory asked a woman, "Why do you work?" "What else are you going to do?" was her response. "You have to eat." [1] After these essentials other wants emerge.

The worker, whether manager or sweeper, architect or ditch-digger, desires the respect and esteem of his fellows—recognition, status.

He dislikes anything that challenges his standing, such as disrespect, injustice, an affront to his dignity.

He desires an opportunity to satisfy his spiritual and emotional needs. [2]

These are the basic and minimum essentials that all men recognize who seek a full and satisfactory life. It follows, by an obvious syllogism, that these are the things that workingmen and women desire.

What the unions attempt to get for their members in detail depends upon the particular situation surrounding each group and each individual. Doubtless sculptors and public accountants differ from each other with respect to particular requirements. Similarly the needs of machinists are not identical with those of hod carriers. Nevertheless wage earners, by virtue of the similarity of their relationship to the prevailing economy, have much in common with each other, not only in a particular shop or industry or geographical unit but throughout the world.

George Meany said in his presidential address at the opening of

[1] A. Dudley Ward, *The American Economy—Attitudes and Opinions* (New York: Harper & Brothers, 1955), p. 165.

[2] Mr. Ward reported that the more economically secure persons interviewed in the search for "attitudes and opinions" mentioned as "tending toward satisfaction" not only income and working conditions "but also a sense of job security, good human relations on the job, constructive features, and a certain status that steady employment conferred."

the 1953 convention of the AFL: "We recognize the community of interests of every worker on the face of the earth. The things that bother us as workers, the things to which we aspire as workers, are the same things to which the workers of Burma, the workers of Japan, the workers of Italy, and the workers of Germany aspire."

With this as background, we may proceed with our inquiry about "what unions want."

HIGHER LIVING STANDARDS

Speaking for the American Federation of Labor, Samuel Gompers said in 1914: "The general object of the Federation is to better the condition of the workers in all fields of human activity. Economic betterment in all directions comes first." [3] In 1955 George Meany wrote: "We . . . seek an ever-rising standard of living—by which we mean not only more money but more leisure and a richer cultural life." [4]

The union's first interest, therefore, is in jobs and wages. Statistical records of industrial disputes in every country that has compiled them make it clear that the wage question precipitates more strikes than any other issue—strikes in prosperous times for an increase; strikes in periods of recession to prevent a reduction. Everyone who reads the papers knows that contract negotiations, especially since the end of the last world war, have dealt primarily with wage questions or related issues.

JOB SECURITY

Having settled the wage issue for the time being, the union concerns itself with tenure. The problem is not alone how to make the job remuneratively satisfactory but how to hang onto it. So the union attempts to set up barriers to arbitrary discharge. At first glance many union contracts seem to recognize the right of the employer to discharge at will. For example, such clauses as these often appear in collectively negotiated contracts: [5]

[3] The American Labor Movement (AFL pamphlet, 1954), p. 13. Reprint of testimony before the U. S. Commission on Industrial Relations, May 1914.
[4] Fortune, March 1955.
[5] These and other excerpts from contracts are taken from Union Contract Clauses (Chicago: Commerce Clearing House, Inc., 1954).

"The employers reserve the right to exercise their discretion in the laying off and discharge of their employees."

"The company has the exclusive right to discharge any employee for just cause."

The limitation of "just cause" raises questions which open the way to negotiation with the union. Even the first clause quoted above would not necessarily—and probably does not—prevent the union from taking up a particular discharge as a grievance, if in its judgment an injustice has been done. Frequently, however, the contract lists certain offenses justifying discharge as a penalty, and presumably excluding others, though some contracts precede such a list with the words "including, but not being limited to, the following."

Sometimes a contract contains such a clause as this: "All new rules and regulations for the breach of which an employee may be discharged shall be discussed with the union before adoption." Or the contract may provide for negotiation concerning the propriety of discharges, as in the following: "The union shall have the right to challenge the propriety of any discharge and may present the matter as a grievance to be settled under the grievance and arbitration procedures in this agreement."

A clause in another contract provides that an employee who has been discharged "by way of discipline" shall be given a hearing by the employer if he requests it, to review "both the justice of [the] disciplinary action and the appropriateness of the penalty," and that a union officer may be present to represent the employee. This contract provides further that the decision reached after review shall itself be "subject to further review as provided in the grievance procedure."

In general the view held by most unions is that a man has a right to keep his job unless the evidence to the contrary is strong and convincing. This leads in some cases to protests and sometimes to strikes when management acts to curtail operating activity. The farming-out by a company of a part of its operations to a contractor almost invariably leads to strenuous opposition, particularly if there is an evident purpose to have the work done by nonunion workers, or by employees willing to accept a lower wage. The Hatters Union staged a prolonged strike at Norwalk, Connecticut, in 1955 when the Hat Corporation of America announced its intention to move a part of its work to another state. The strike was settled by an agreement that protected the jobs of the Norwalk employees, whereupon the union, which had been using newspaper ads to enlist public support, published a final statement entitled "The Hatters Are No Longer Mad."

SENIORITY RIGHTS

The job-security objectives discussed above involve equal protection of all workers regardless of length of service from arbitrary discharge. Another type of protection now found in most union contracts apportions the degree of job protection according to seniority. These rules favor the oldest employee in terms of tenure with respect to promotions and layoffs. Seniority clauses in most union contracts recognize ability as well as term of service as a basis for preference. This often leads to controversy, since the union tries to protect the older employee and the employer desires to promote efficiency.[6]

THE THREAT OF TECHNOLOGY

Seniority rules and contractual barriers to arbitrary discharge have done much to promote job security, but technological changes in industry that tend to substitute machinery for men are more difficult to deal with. This type of threat has been a problem since the dawn of the Industrial Revolution. Fear of loss of jobs because of such developments resulted in labor action ranging from destruction of the new machines, as in the case of the power-driven looms in England in the eighteenth century, to strikes against their use in the nineteenth.

---

[6] The degree of protection afforded through seniority rules varies with the area within which rights may be exercised. Plant-wide or company-wide seniority gives the senior employee greater protection than can be obtained under departmental seniority. Where the protection is on the broader basis the right to "bump" obtains. This means that an employee who has been laid off in one department, in deference to the right of a longer-service employee to be retained, may go into another department and demand the job of another employee whose term of service is less than his. The practice of "bumping" is thus set forth in a union contract: "Employees having attained seniority with the company who are laid off on account of curtailment of work may claim seniority in other departments over employees who have less than six months' departmental seniority, provided they have more company seniority than the employee whom they seek to displace, and the ability and qualifications to perform the work performed by the employee whom they seek to displace."

Nowadays American unions generally accept technological change but bargain with the employer for protection against loss of jobs. Contracts sometimes guarantee the employer's right to install labor-saving devices, but either provide for notification of the contemplated action, or make provision for affected employees through transfer or retraining or require severance pay in the case of actual loss of jobs.

With the existence of such arrangements for meeting the short-run effects of technological advance and with convincing evidence that the long-run effects tend in one way or another toward increased employment, the fear of technological unemployment has to a considerable extent been allayed. But now something new in the field of technology is arousing old fears.

The name given to this phenomenon is "automation," a term that has been said to have evolved "in less than two years . . . from a fairly simple designation of certain kinds of industrial processes to a symbol of a complicated, almost awesome way of industrial life." [7] It is for engineers to offer definitions in this field. Walter S. Buckingham, Jr., has said: "Automation means a continuous and integrated operation of a production system using electronic equipment to perform routine functions and regulate and coordinate the flow and quality of production. . . . The immediate effects in the plant are to substitute machinery for labor, set a continuous pace at which the plant must be operated, greatly increase production, and provide a more comprehensive and efficient system for information gathering and handling.[8]

The nontechnical observer might say that automation is something introduced by the new forces comprehended under the term electronics, and that not only does it make possible the incredible performance of computing machines in handling complicated mathematical formulae in a few moments that formerly required hours of laborious mental effort, but it enables a few individuals or even one man to direct a continuous flow of productive energy formerly requiring the combined efforts of many. Walter Reuther told the 1954 CIO convention: "We have places in the automobile industry . . . where an

[7] Monthly Labor Review, May 1955, p. 519.
[8] Monthly Labor Review, May 1955, pp. 521–522.

automatic electrical brain has replaced five hundred clerical workers, where automation makes an engine block in less than fifteen minutes without a single human hand touching that engine block."

Carl J. Demrick, Vice-President of the Chrysler Corporation, describes an aspect of automation in the Plymouth Engine Plant that at once illustrates its weirdness and its astonishing effectiveness:

The new engines, loaded onto pallets, roll onto this [hot test] line looking for a place to stop and be tested. When an engine finds an empty test stand it automatically stops and rolls onto the stand. It is automatically hooked up to water, gas, oil, and electric power lines. Then the new engine is automatically started by an air motor. The complete test cycle takes twenty minutes.[9]

This new development has been called by some commentators the second industrial revolution. As to its possible impact on the work force the experts have both warning and reassuring words. Mr. Buckingham refers to the "fear" that automation will produce technological unemployment. "As an economy-wide problem," he says, the argument supporting this fear "may be overdrawn." Automation "will probably be limited to industries which employ at the most 25 per cent of the labor force . . . ," new jobs will be created, and the extensive training that will be required "will to some extent counteract unemployment by delaying entry into the labor market." While "there is a real danger that imperfections in the labor market will seriously delay absorption of the displaced workers," he reaches the optimistic conclusion that "automation, together with atomic energy, *if properly understood, applied, developed and controlled,* may provide the means of eliminating poverty for the first time in the history of the world." [10]

[9] *Advanced Management*, May 1956, p. 6.

[10] Walter S. Buckingham, Jr., *op. cit.* Emphasis added. An industrial relations expert writes me as follows:

"Automation changes the character of the work force. It greatly enhances the demand for highly skilled mechanics and for engineers. The demand for laborers and relatively unskilled workers is greatly decreased since the automatic processes, formerly performed by a punch press operator, for instance, are now performed automatically by machine.

"This has resulted in some drastic changes in educational programs. A prominent engineering college has developed a two-year course to train employees for work in automated factories and other places where high skills are required. These semi-engineers are trained to understand and perform engineering work of a

Edgar Weinberg of the United States Bureau of Labor Statistics, referring to the probable intensification of "the shifting of productive resources of workers, management, and capital among various activities of the economy," writes that "some individuals inevitably suffer losses as a result of displacement; others are benefited as a result of upgrading." Employees may lose their jobs in "firms that do not adopt advanced techniques of production," and employment may be expanded where firms adopting cost-cutting equipment "may gain a significant competitive advantage." [11]

Caution and hope are combined in the comment of labor leaders. Speaking further at the 1954 CIO convention, Walter Reuther predicted that automation "will create deep-seated economic and social problems." Depending on the degree of social and moral purpose that accompanies its adoption, it can "solve the problems of poverty and hunger and ignorance . . . or [it] can dig our economic graves." If it is used for "moral human purposes," he said, "automation ought to be welcomed" since, after it has met our basic economic needs, there will be more time that can be devoted to "facilitating man's growth as a spiritual and cultural and social human being." [12]

---

routine nature, which tends to waste the time of an engineer who is a graduate of a four-year college course in engineering. Their skills and training are considerably higher than those of skilled workers, but less than those possessed by a fully trained engineer."

[11] A Review of Automatic Technology," *Monthly Labor Review*, June 1955, p. 637 ff.

[12] Writing in a symposium on automation in *Advanced Management* (published by the Society for the Advancement of Management), May 1956, Nathaniel Goldfinger, AFL-CIO economist, mentioned the possibility that automation "may result in the displacement of many thousands of workers." Automation, he said, "promises, in the long run," to provide lasting benefits, but "in the shorter run" it will raise "countless problems of adjustment."

In the same symposium Edward Falkowski, UAW shop steward, made similar references to the "long" and the "short" run. He had found "disquieting" the "complacency among so many top-level thinkers." "We are assured," he wrote, that "automation is no new thing," but merely an extension of previously known techniques. "Yet there is a point at which a rainfall becomes a flood, a wind, a tornado."

Other participants in the symposium registered a moderate degree of optimism about short-run effects. Mr. Demrick reported an increase in employment at the Plymouth plant since the adoption of the new methods, but he wanted to be the "first to say" that the importance of such comparisons "should not be exaggerated." Edgar Weinberg noted that many monotonous tasks are becoming "relatively less important," while "jobs requiring the exercise of judgment are

The 1954 CIO convention adopted a resolution calling on Congress to investigate the effect of technological developments on employment, discover what plans industry may have for further advance, and "based on their findings to make recommendations to ensure full production and full employment in peace time."

The AFL-CIO convention of 1955 gave consideration to automation only as it affected federal employees, for whom it recommended reduction of weekly hours of work to 35. In private industry, apprehension about the effects of automation seems to have influenced the emphases of union bargaining, particularly in relation to security of income.

INCOME SECURITY

It has been suggested that the economic interests of the union are centered first in wages and then in job security. Basically, of course, pressures for these objectives are pressures for income security, but the history of organized labor's economic struggles indicates so much absorption in these immediate objectives as to preclude consideration of their ultimate significance until a comparatively short time ago. In other words, organized labor has tended to emphasize the hourly or weekly wage more or less to the exclusion of consideration of the hazards that threaten its very existence.

It was not until the end of the first decade of the present century that the unions, at first reluctantly, began to advocate legislation to insure compensation for accidents incurred in the course of employment.[13] Unemployment insurance, after a period in which organized labor strenuously opposed it, became an orthodox objective for the American Federation of Labor in 1932. In 1935 leaders of organized

---

becoming relatively more numerous." Displacement of workers "so far" has been "relatively low," but legislation and collective bargaining will have to be concerned with action "to cushion the impact of technical changes on workers." Arthur N. Turner of Yale spoke with tempered optimism of the "short run" effects, but spoke of the "very dangerous" possibilities of "overconfidence in the long run," which makes the need for research "very urgent."

[13] Before this, the unions had endeavored to secure modifications of the common law of employers' liability in the interest of a modicum of justice in its application; but they were at first fearful of the workmen's compensation laws, which while they substituted a certain amount of assurance of compensation for the almost complete lack of such assurance under employers' liability, took away for the most part the right of the injured worker to sue for damages.

labor actively supported social security legislation and thus came to favor economic protection for the aged. Shortly afterward, they became for the first time advocates of health insurance.

Since the mid-1930s labor has come to think of various forms of insurance against economic hazards as proper subjects not only for legislation but also for collective bargaining. Hence, pensions, health and hospitalization measures, compensation for nonoccupational accidents, and other welfare plans are well-established provisions in collectively negotiated contracts.

"SUB"

A further step in the direction of income security resulted from agreements which were first negotiated on a large scale in 1955. What had long been sought by several unions under the slogan "guaranteed annual wage" emerged in the automobile industry in a form better suited to the descriptive term "supplementary unemployment benefits" now generally used. The agreements fell far short of the popular supposition that the guaranteed annual wage would mean full wages for an entire year, regardless of employment possibilities. One is reminded of the comment of an engineer who pointed out that automation would not bring about the "seven-day week-end." Neither has the guaranteed 52-week pay envelope arrived. To be sure, union officials have, at times, spoken as if their objective were the same as the popular notion regarding it, but when serious negotiations were begun with the Ford company the union did not ask for 100 per cent security, and when the agreements were signed they provided for considerably less than the original union demands.[14]

[14] Speaking before the 1954 CIO convention Walter Reuther said: "We are asked many times by people who make up the general public, 'do the CIO unions want workers to be paid for not working . . . ?' and we answer without hesitation and the answer is no. We do not want to be paid for not working, but we do not want our people to be penalized when they haven't got a job through no fault of their own. . . . We are going to give the employers a most powerful incentive. We are going to shift the cost of unemployment from the backs of the workers onto the backs of the management, where it belongs, and they will have an incentive to plan for full employment."

Later the convention adopted a statement on guaranteed annual wage which said that their plans are "geared to the specific conditions of the industries in which they operate. They take account of the problems confronting business, and in many cases state clearly that the employer's liability shall be limited to a certain per cent of his current payroll. Such a limited liability approach is the answer of

In brief, what Ford, General Motors, Chrysler, and some other companies agreed to in 1955 is as follows:

The guarantee is for 26 weeks instead of 52. During the first four weeks of unemployment an eligible employee will be entitled to receive 65 per cent of his basic rate of pay, after taxes. If unemployment continues beyond the fourth week, he will receive 60 per cent of wages for any part of the remaining 22 weeks during which he may be unemployed. Moreover, the liability of the companies for payment of the supplemental benefit will be limited to the difference between the amount the worker may have received under the unemployment compensation laws and the amount of the guarantee. A further limitation fixes the maximum weekly benefit for which the company can be held liable in any case, at $25.

Subject to these limitations, an employee whose take-home pay was $70 a week would be entitled—benefit plus supplementation—to $45.50 a week during the first four weeks of unemployment, and $42 a week during the remaining weeks, respectively 65 and 60 per cent of his net earnings after taxes. If the state law entitled him to $20 a week as unemployment compensation, the amount that the company would be obligated to pay would be the maximum of $25 in the four-week period and $22 after that. This would bring the company's payment down approximately to 36 and 31 per cent of the worker's former take-home pay for the two periods.

When the plans were inaugurated in 1955 the unemployment compensation laws of most of the states provided that an unemployed person could not receive benefits under the law if he were at the same time receiving any payments from his employer. The agreements stipulated that they would take effect only when, in states where at least two-thirds of the employees lived, these laws were so amended or interpreted as to authorize supplementary payments. By June 1, 1956, the date on which supplementary payments were to begin, this goal had been reached, mostly through administrative interpretations.[15]

---

the major CIO unions to the argument that guaranteed wage plans would result in an impossible burden."

[15] However, because of limitations in the agreement, the plans did not go into full effect on June 1, 1956. These limitations included the following: 1. Full payments are possible only when the funds set aside by the companies have approached an agreed-upon minimum. In none of the companies had the funds been built up to that point. 2. Eligibility depends on seniority and accumulation

The second industry-wide "SUB" plan was instituted in August, 1956, by agreement between the major steel companies and the United Steel Workers. This plan covers a maximum of 52 weeks of unemployment and in its financial provisions represents an advance over the plan in the automobile industry. It is described more fully in the Supplementary Notes.

This chapter has been devoted mainly to the economic objectives of the workers—the basic concern for wages, job security, and income security. As stated at the outset, there are other objectives, non-economic in character, related to status and to intellectual and moral advance. The desire for the right to participate in the making of decisions concerning matters of direct interest to the employee is among other things an aspect of the quest for status. Collective bargaining, which is both a means for achieving economic objectives and a practice that enhances the standing of the individual, is the subject of the next chapter. Nonbargained or self-obtained advantages in the fields of education, recreation and cultural advance are discussed in Chapter 8.

In considering the nature of union objectives, emphasis has been on the union as an instrument for attaining ends desired by its members. However, the union as such has also certain organizational objectives, some of which concern the union as an entity. The objective of integrity—in the sense of wholeness and growth—or, perhaps a better term, the objective of survival is an end that concerns the union as a corporate body. The means by which the union seeks to attain this end are discussed in Chapter 7, "Union Security."

---

of "credit units." The latter are evidences of previous employment. A worker with a ten-year service record is entitled to one half credit unit for each week of working time. If he works 52 weeks prior to being laid off, he will have 26 credits which will entitle him to supplementation for the full 26 weeks. A worker with less than 10 years' service receives a quarter credit unit for each week worked and would have, after 52 weeks, 13 credits, which would entitle him to 13 weeks of supplementation. These major factors—size of fund, seniority, and credit unit restrictions—had the effect of limiting claims upon the fund when the plans took effect on June 1, 1956. After June 1, 1957, all workers will be entitled to half credit for each week worked.

For the text of state rulings on supplementation of unemployment benefits, with an extended discussion, see *Supplementary Unemployment Benefits* Industrial Union Department AFL-CIO, December, 1956.

5

Collective Bargaining

The impact of collective bargaining on American life is impressive. A bulletin of the United States Bureau of Labor Statistics states that it constitutes "the main reason for the existence of unions. . . . [It] is the central fact, the focal procedure, of labor-management relations."[1] According to a leading American economist, "the influence of the American trade-union movement upon the American economy . . . that stands out most conspicuously is the unique importance of collective bargaining."[2]

To John R. Commons collective bargaining was a method of transcending importance. In his *The Economics of Collective Action*, published in 1950, he wrote: "I contend that the preservation of the American economic system against a totalitarian world, and against its own internal disruption, consists mainly in the collective bargaining between organized capital and organized labor . . ." (p. 262).

In similar vein, a member of the National Labor Relations Board said to a convention of employers: "It may well be that free collective bargaining is the final stand of economic freedom as we know it. For in every nation where this process has failed, the dignity of man and the institutions of free men have failed with it. This prospect places a sobering burden on the shoulders of all those who lead unions of men and enterprises of commerce. It is my sincere hope that both, within reason and law, will preserve and strengthen the processes of free collective bargaining in this country."[3]

The term "collective bargaining" is accurately descriptive of one of the most common procedures in industrial relations—the procedure that involves a meeting between representatives respectively of workers and management for the purpose of discussing, and if possible

[1] *Witt Bowden, American Labor and the American Spirit*, Bulletin No. 1145, 1954.

[2] Sumner Slichter, *Connecticut Federationist*, 1953.

[3] From address by Philip Ray Rogers, member of the NLRB, before the Associated General Contractors of America at New Orleans March 15, 1955.

reaching an agreement on, the terms and conditions of employment to prevail over a fixed period. Neither the term nor the practice, however, was characteristic of American trade unionism at its beginning a century and a half ago. "The early trade unions started out with individual bargaining. . . . Not even conferences were held between the individual employers and the representatives of the men. They merely determined a scale of prices and pledged one another, as in the case of the shoemakers, 'not to work for any employer who did not give the wages, nor beside any journeyman who did not get the wages.' " [4]

While there were occasional instances of a modified form of collective bargaining in the earlier period, general recognition on the part of the unions of the importance of joint negotiations seems to have been lacking until after the Civil War, and then its exercise was postponed by the unwillingness of employers to recognize the unions. Such agreements as were reached between employers and unions, often after strikes, were not products of the bargaining process as it is now understood.

The term itself seems to have been generally unknown until toward the end of the nineteenth century. The English labor historians Sidney and Beatrice Webb, writing in 1914, were "not aware of any use" of the term prior to its use by Beatrice Potter (Mrs. Webb) in her treatise on the cooperative movement published in 1891.[5] Professor Richard T. Ely published in 1886 the first book [6] by an American economist to be devoted in its entirety to unionism and other aspects of the labor movement. Nowhere in its pages does the term "collective bargaining" appear, nor is it to be found in any of the earlier reports of the American Federation of Labor. Not until 1920 did the words "collective bargaining" appear in the index of any of the annual proceedings of the AFL.

The comparatively late emergence of collective bargaining as a general practice was not due to failure on the part of the unions in

[4] John R. Commons and Associates, *History of Labour in the United States* (New York: The Macmillan Co., 1918), Vol. I, p. 121.

[5] Sidney and Beatrice Webb, *Industrial Democracy* (New York: Longmans, Green and Co., 1914), p. 173.

[6] Richard T. Ely, *The Labor Movement in America* (New York: Thomas Y. Crowell and Co., 1886).

the later years to regard it as an essential. Despite the long history of resort to other methods, there is abundant evidence of a keen desire on their part, during the fifty years preceding the inauguration of the New Deal, for negotiated agreements. During this period strikes to obtain "recognition" of the union were numerous, and refusals on the part of management to confer with union committees were common. The Pullman strike of 1894, the anthracite strike of 1902, strikes at the Bethlehem Steel Company in 1910, of textile workers at Lawrence, Massachusetts, in 1912 and 1919, in the Colorado coal fields in 1914, and in the steel industry in 1919—all these followed either refusals on the part of management to confer, or the discharge of employees who had served on committees attempting to bring about a conference.

Nevertheless the practice of collective bargaining had become well established among unions of skilled craftsmen before the legislation of the 1930s opened the way for its general acceptance. The National Industrial Recovery Act of 1933 and the Wagner Act of 1935 offered legal protection of the right to organize, and the latter made it an "unfair labor practice" for an employer to refuse to bargain collectively.

Good Faith in Bargaining

As union membership grew under the protection of these laws, collective bargaining entered upon a new phase, not only because of the increased membership but also because of the impact of the laws on the nature and practice of bargaining. The question of "good faith" in bargaining was posed in 1933 by the National Industrial Recovery Act, which required the "codes of fair competition" to include protection of the right to organize and bargain collectively. The "first" National Labor Relations Board, set up to administer that provision, declared in a notable case that "the employer is required by the statute to negotiate in good faith with his employees' representatives; to match their proposals, if unacceptable, with counter-proposals; and to make every reasonable effort to reach an agreement." [7] The Wagner Act of 1935 did not attempt to spell out what is involved in collective bargaining, but the National Labor Relations

[7] Houde Engineering Corporation v. U.A.W. Local 18839, Aug. 30, 1934.

Board created by that act continued to interpret the law as requiring good faith. "Collective bargaining," the Board said in a leading case, "means more than the discussion of individual problems and grievances with employees or groups of employees. It means that the employer is obligated to negotiate, in good faith, with his employees as a group, through their representatives, on matters of wages, hours, and basic working conditions, and to endeavor to reach an agreement for a fixed period of time." [8]

The Taft-Hartley Act of 1947 defines collective bargaining as the "performance of the mutual obligation of the employer and the representative of the employees to meet at reasonable times and confer in good faith with respect to wages, hours, and other terms and conditions of employment, or the negotiation of an agreement . . . and the execution of a written contract incorporating any agreement reached if requested by either party. . . ." [9] Before passage of the Taft-Hartley Act the National Labor Relations Board had held that the requirement of a signed agreement as evidence of good faith was implied in the Wagner Act, and the Supreme Court had upheld the ruling.[10]

Subject Matter of Bargaining

The subject matter of bargaining also has been affected by the Wagner and Taft-Hartley Acts. Matters that had previously been thought to be within the unilateral discretion of management have

[8] In the matter of Atlantic Refining Co. and International Association of Oil Field, Gas Well, and Refinery Workers, 1 NLRB 359.

[9] Section 8-d.

[10] Heinz v. NLRB. 316 U.S. 514, January 6, 1941, "It is true," the court said, "that the National Labor Relations Act, while requiring the employer to bargain collectively, does not compel him to enter into an agreement. But it does not follow . . . that having reached an agreement, he can refuse to sign it, because he has never agreed to sign one. . . ." The absence of a signed contract "as experience has shown, tends to frustrate the end sought by the requirement for collective bargaining. A businessman who entered into negotiations with another for an agreement having numerous provisions, with the reservation that he would not reduce it to writing or sign it, could hardly be thought to have bargained in good faith. This is even more so in the case of an employer who, by his refusal to honor with his signature the agreement he has made with a labor organization, discredits the organization, impairs the bargaining process, and tends to frustrate the aim of the statute. . . ."

become subject to negotiation between management and union. An order issued by the National Labor Relations Board in 1948, requiring the Inland Steel Company to bargain with the United Steel Workers over the details of a pension plan, was upheld by the courts. More recently (October 1954), the Board ruled [11] that a unilaterally established stock-purchase plan for employees, to which the employer contributed, is subject to the bargaining requirements of the statute. Both rulings depend for their validity on the inclusion in the statute of "wages . . . and other terms and conditions of employment" as subjects for collective bargaining. Other matters with respect to which the employer is required to bargain, under various rulings, include "bonuses, hospitalization insurance (and other forms of insurance), merit increases, incentive pay plans, vacation and holiday pay, . . . work standards and loads. . . ." [12]

Employers are placed under a further obligation as the result of NLRB interpretations of the bargaining provisions of the Taft-Hartley Act. They must, under certain circumstances, provide the bargaining union with data in their possession and not otherwise available which may be essential to an effective presentation of the union case. This ruling has its most striking application where the employer resists a wage demand on grounds of inability to pay. In such a case decided in 1954 [13] the Board said, ". . . it is settled law that when an employer seeks to justify the refusal of a wage increase *upon an economic basis* [emphasis as in original] . . . good-faith bargaining under the . . . Act requires that upon request the employer attempt to substantiate its economic position by reasonable proof." [14] Similar rulings requiring the furnishing of financial data under varying circumstances,

---

[11] Richfield Oil Corporation, 110 NLRB 356. A note in *Labor Law Journal*, March, 1955, p. 152, refers to this decision as "in principle" a "landmark case of novel impression." The Board's ruling was upheld by a Federal Court of Appeals, January 1956. Richfield v. NLRB 231 F. 2nd 717.

[12] Max J. Miller, *Labor Law Journal*, March, 1955, p. 152.

[13] This decision of the Board was upheld by the Supreme Court (six to three) in May 1956. The Court said "If such an argument [i.e. inability to pay an increase] is important enough to present in the give and take of bargaining, it is important enough to require some sort of proof of its accuracy. . . . Such has been the holding of the Labor Board since shortly after the passage of the Wagner Act." NLRB v. Truitt Manufacturing Company, 351 U.S. 149, May 7, 1956.

[14] Truitt Manufacturing Co. and Shopmen's Local No. 729, AFL Iron Workers Union. 110 NLRB 856.

many of which have been upheld by the courts, go back at least as
far as 1948.

UNIONS AND COLLECTIVE BARGAINING

In the foregoing discussion of the effect of the legislation of the
past quarter century on the practice of collective bargaining, we have
been considering primarily the obligations of the employer. The
Wagner Act required the employer to bargain collectively, but no
corresponding duty was placed upon the workers or the unions; the
employer was required to bargain, and the union was not. This seem-
ing discrimination was due to the historic fact that it had been the
unions that were asking for collective bargaining and the employers
who had been opposing it. Moreover, at the time of the passage of the
Wagner Act the unions were relatively weak. Vast areas of industry
were wholly devoid of union organization. In 1935 the unions were in
the main petitioners for the right to extend their organizations and
to bargain collectively.

What was true of the unions in 1935 is still true, so far as their
attitude toward collective bargaining is concerned. Today, as Witt
Bowden wrote for the Bureau of Labor Statistics in 1954, and as
quoted at the beginning of this chapter, "collective bargaining is the
main reason for the existence of unions." Yet Congress in 1947 included in the Taft-Hartley Act a clause *requiring* unions to bargain
collectively.

This Act dealt with a great variety of subjects, involving problems
that were, as Senator Taft put it on the floor of the Senate, "infinitely
complicated." And these problems had been accentuated by the fact
that between the passage of the Wagner Act in 1935 and the Taft-
Hartley Act in 1947 the membership of unions had grown from less
than $4\frac{1}{2}$ million to approximately $13\frac{1}{2}$ million, an increase of 200
per cent.

The Taft-Hartley Act reflected a fear that the unions had become
too strong and a belief that they could, and sometimes did, misuse
their strength. As to collective bargaining, it was believed that a few
of the more powerful unions had on occasion manifested something
less than a bargaining mood. A former chairman of the National
Labor Relations Board, writing in 1950, said: "of course instances
occur in which a union adopts the policy of 'take this proposed con-

tract or else,' " though adding, "an outstanding fact has been that unions have desired collective bargaining 'in good faith.' " [15]

Discussion on the floor of Congress of the bills which finally emerged as the Taft-Hartley Act revealed little evidence of abuses of collective bargaining by unions. The annual reports of the National Labor Relations Board since the passage of the Taft-Hartley Act do not provide much evidence of refusal to bargain on the part of unions. Most of the charges of such refusal brought to the attention of the Board seemed to relate to collateral issues affecting bargaining, rather than to outright refusal to negotiate.

In its 1951 report the Board said:

Because labor organizations are formed primarily when employees desire to negotiate with their employer, the cases in which unions are charged with unlawful refusal to bargain rarely involve any allegation of an outright refusal by the union to meet or negotiate with the employer. Ordinarily, cases in which a union is alleged to have refused to bargain involve the legality of some proposal insisted on by the union, or upon a technical point of bargaining such as the question of the legality of a union dealing individually with an employer who has been represented in bargaining by an association. This pattern prevailed in cases decided by the Board during 1951 fiscal year as during past years.[16]

On the other hand, a powerful union may be in a position at times to impose terms on a small or weak employer without being guilty of a technical "refusal to bargain." An experienced public official writes me as follows:

Where a contract is negotiated on an industrial or association basis, many employers who are not members of the association or who did not participate in industry-wide bargaining are required to sign a contract with practically no bargaining at all. . . . What actually takes place . . . is that the leaders of the association sit down with the union and negotiate a contract. The association is, of course, dominated by the larger concerns. After the contract has been negotiated, it is mailed to all of the smaller concerns, many of whom may not be members of the association. If an individual employer appeals to the union to make some change in

---

[15] H. A. Millis, in Millis and Brown, *From the Wagner Act to Taft-Hartley* (Chicago: University of Chicago Press, 1950), p. 449.

[16] 15th Annual Report, NLRB, for fiscal year ended June 30, 1951, pp. 220, 221.

the contract so that it will fit his particular needs, there is practically no chance that the union will even discuss his problem with him, much less make any change in the standard contract. Consequently, what actually happens is that the contracts are mailed out to the small employers who sign them and return them to the union. They must then carry out the provisions of the contract without regard to the effect of those provisions on the operation of their businesses.

This problem presents many difficult and complicated issues. It can be argued that the standard working conditions created by the association contract result in the greater good to the greater number so far as both employees and employers are concerned, even though some employers may find it extremely difficult to implement the provisions of the contract. Also, if the union were to make one exception in an industry such as the trucking industry with thousands of employers, hundreds of other exceptions would be demanded, and a chaotic situation might result.

THE PRACTICE OF COLLECTIVE BARGAINING

The definition of collective bargaining as a meeting between representatives, respectively, of workers and of management for the purpose of discussing and if possible reaching an agreement on terms and conditions of employment implies an over-simplification of the process. First, before collective bargaining can take place there must be an organization of the employees. Second, there must be recognition on the part of management that the employees, or a considerable number of them, are members of the organization. Third, management must be willing to negotiate with the representatives chosen by the employees to bargain in their behalf. The greater part of the history of the development of trade unionism in the United States has been devoted to a struggle to bring about these three steps precedent to collective bargaining.

These essential conditions having been established, however, the door is open for the various forms of collective bargaining which have been developed to suit the requirements of different industries and different types of unions. At the outset local unions delegated certain of their members, regularly working in the shop or work place, to meet with managment and confer over wages and working conditions. This is still the practice in a limited number of cases where unaffiliated locals exist. Because these representatives played a dual role as bargainers with and at the same times as employees of the management representatives, they were not always effective bargainers. They were dependent for their jobs on the very men from whom they were attempting to obtain concessions. At the same time they were inexperienced bargainers, and by reason of the necessity of working at their regular employment throughout each working day, they were often limited in their ability to acquaint themselves with the economics of the industry, competitive conditions, and other factors involving the employers' ability to pay.

It is in part because of the limitation of worker-bargaining that locals have joined with other locals to form regional and nationwide organizations. Extension of organization has as one of its major purposes the development of labor unity and, through the power of numbers, the strengthening of the whole body in dealing with employers. But perhaps the most important aspect of union growth as a factor in bargaining is the development of techniques it made possible. The union bargainers are no longer exclusively employees of management; the leaders in the bargaining process are employees of the union. Thus they are freed from economic dependence on management. At the same time they are enabled to give full time to the task of gaining the knowledge essential to informed bargaining, and to developing the skills to make it effective.

Collective bargaining, therefore, as practiced by organized labor, is in the hands of experts who are salaried officers of the unions. Supporting them are statisticians, economists, and other professional research people who are in the larger unions permanently-employed staff members.[17] In consequence, it is sometimes said that the unions approach the bargaining table with better knowledge of the underlying conditions affecting the ultimate agreement than do the management representatives, when the latter are concerned with other problems in addition to those directly involving labor-management relations. This, of course, is not the situation where the employer has taken steps to provide equal bargaining skill on the management side of the table. Most large employers now recognize that planning and adjustments to meet employers' responsibility in industrial rela-

[17] The number of unions employing such experts is growing. "In 1943 there were research directors in 51 unions and the total now is double, at 96." *Business Week*, October 6, 1956.

tions constitute an area requiring specialized equipment and knowledge. Consequently "directors of personnel," "vice-presidents in charge of industrial relations" or specialists bearing similar titles, with their staffs, devote themselves exclusively to the field of labor-management relations, meet problems as they arise, and bring expert knowledge to the bargaining table.

In practice, method in collective bargaining varies considerably from industry to industry, and sometimes from plant to plant in the same industry. In industries such as steel, operating in a national market, a basic agreement is negotiated between the national union as such and the leading manufacturers, after which district or local agreements are reached with smaller companies and with fabricating concerns. These agreements embody the applicable elements of the basic agreement and additional items relating to the particular plant or company involved.

In the automobile industry bargaining takes place separately with each of the three largest companies. The union is represented by a separate committee for each company, headed by a director. The whole process is coordinated by the leadership of the national executives of the union.

THE SCOPE OF BARGAINING

The leading example of nationwide bargaining is found in the railroad industry. Here the operating unions—commonly referred to as the "Brotherhoods"—sometimes bargain as a group with all the principal railroad companies on matters of wages and rules; sometimes the bargaining is conducted by two unions working in concert; sometimes one of the Brotherhoods decides to go it alone. In every case, however, the bargaining is on a national basis and any agreement reached is signed by the spokesmen for all of the Class I railroads.

The nonoperating unions (shopmen, car builders, electrical workers, machinists, telegraphers, signalmen, maintenance-of-way men, etc.—about fifteen unions in all) have been negotiating as a unit with the railroads for many years. The negotiating committee for the unions consists generally of the presidents of the fifteen unions headed by the president of the Railway Employees Department of the AFL. The management committee is made up of representatives of each of the three main area divisions of the railroads of the country—the Eastern, the Southern, and the Western division, respectively.

The resulting national agreements cover wages and operating rules; other questions, which vary in character from one railroad to another, are bargained over between individual railroads or railway systems and system federations of unions. Matters of concern only to a particular craft may be dealt with by the craft union involved.

In marked contrast is the bargaining that takes place in industries operating in a local or limited area market, such as the building industry. Here bargaining is conducted by the craft locals with the specialty contractors organized generally in local associations.

As suggested above, responsibility for conducting negotiations in behalf of the unions is coming to be concentrated largely in the executive officers of the national organizations. In local bargaining the negotiating committee generally includes officers of the local union and sometimes rank-and-file members. But the committee is under the direction of a national or district officer, who is chief spokesman. Rank-and-file opinion is made fully manifest, however, when—as is sometimes the case—the chairman encourages each committee member to express himself as he sees fit. This procedure sometimes results in the introduction of subjects irrelevant to the immediate purpose of negotiating a contract, but it enables individuals to put before their employers complaints and "beefs" that they would hesitate to bring up under less protected circumstances. Some union officials believe the results of such a procedure are salutary, giving the committee member a sense of participation, and at the same time enabling him to get something important "off his chest."

Collective Bargaining and the Employee

The first effect of successful collective bargaining from the standpoint of the worker, as well as its only purpose in its early development, is improved economic conditions. This is apt to be the net result of good-faith bargaining.

Despite the doubts of some economists that the unions have been effective in raising general wage levels, there is much evidence to support the thesis that great impetus has been given by collective bargaining to wage increases in specific areas.[18] Moreover, the wiping out of geographical wage differentials in certain industries through collective bargaining agreements has resulted in raising the lower wage levels without causing a decline in the higher levels. The development in recent years of negotiated agreements providing for "fringe" benefits, such as noncontributory pensions, sickness and hospitalization benefits, and paid vacations, has manifestly improved the economic condition of the workers. And the reduction of daily and weekly hours of labor which has proceded slowly for a century and then rapidly in the last two or three decades has been largely a result of collective bargaining.

Also, the economic advantages cited here are not necessarily limited to those in whose behalf the bargaining is conducted. Such agreements benefit all within the bargaining unit whether or not they are members of the union conducting the negotiations. Nor is the effect always limited to the bargaining unit. In a plant where bargaining takes place in one department and not in all, a favorable financial settlement in the one department usually results in its application to other departments as well. Moreover, wage agreements in unionized plants are apt to have repercussions in other plants in the same industry even if they are unorganized.[19]

Another effect of collective bargaining on the worker is a sense of improved status. The bargain is made in his behalf by his designated representatives. He no longer has to look at a notice on a bulletin board to discover what conditions of employment are to prevail. Collective bargaining makes him a citizen of industry, with a vote. Said Lester Granger, executive director of the National Urban League, "The rise and strengthening of collective bargaining is social progress, not because it exalts the place of the labor unions in our social structure, but because it dignifies the individual worker in his job and citizenship status." [20]

COLLECTIVE BARGAINING AND THE EMPLOYER

For the employer, collective bargaining presents aspects that both

[18] Chap. 2, pp. 10–11; Chap. 9, pp. 86–87; and Chap. 15, p. 188 ff.
[19] See p. 11, footnote.
[20] Social Work Journal, January 1955, pp. 5–6.

attract and repel. An advantage to the employer is the opportunity presented to know better what is in the mind of his employees. The late Joseph Shaffner, of Hart, Shaffner and Marx, told the United States Commission on Industrial Relations in 1915 that the only criticism he had to make of the 1910 strike in his plant was that it should have happened sooner than it did. He confessed that he had been ignorant of the impact of company policy on the workers. He had thought that they were satisfied until the strike convinced him of his error and at the same time provided him with facts of which he had been unaware.[21]

Where good-faith bargaining takes place between experienced bargainers, the result is likely to promote stability in industrial relations. Stability is promoted also when collective bargaining is conducted on a broad enough scale to include the principal competitors in a particular market. The tendency then is to equalize the terms of the wage bill and thus to protect each producer from undercutting by his neighbor.

On the other hand, there are aspects of collective bargaining that create apprehensions in the mind of the average employer. Whatever later experience may prove, the employer is bound to be influenced by them when contemplating the initial request for union recognition. As a team of writers in the management field put it, "the union possibly represents the unknown, the outside factor bent on disturbing what management considers a happy and intimate relationship and formalizing what has been the friendly first-name kinship of people working together to do a job." When the workers organize, the employer "frequently regards it as an act of betrayal by persons whom he has trusted, or as a vote of no confidence in him or his policies." [22]

MANAGEMENT PREROGATIVES

Of all the aspects of collective bargaining that trouble the employer, however, the one that concerns him most is loss of "management

---

[21] U.S. Commission on Industrial Relations, Final Report and Testimony, Vol. I, p. 519.
[22] Black and Piccoli, Successful Labor Relationships for Small Business (New York: McGraw-Hill Book Company, Inc., 1953), Chap. 7, "Comes the Union."

prerogatives." The very thing that enhances workers' status seems to lessen that of management. Before the workers are organized the employer is in a large sense master in his own house. His power is far from absolute, it is true. What he may do with respect to matters that concern the workers is limited by his resources, by conditions of the market, and by what his employees individually are willing to accept. But there is a difference between a thousand individual decisions as to what is acceptable and the united voice of the same individuals expressed through an organization. Where formerly the employer was free to make all minor decisions and most of the larger ones, he now must bargain over all of the large matters and an impressively increasing number of those that had seemed to him to be of lesser significance. Moreover, matters that had been thought to fall without question into the realm of management discretion tend now with increasing frequency to emerge as questions to be bargained over. Said A. J. Hayes, president of the Machinists Union: "Unions came into being specifically for the purpose of interfering with management's right to make unilateral decisions affecting the welfare of its employees." [23]

The management representatives at President Truman's industrial conference in 1945 tried in vain to induce the labor delegates to agree on an area within which management decisions could not be questioned. The labor men did not deny the existence of such an area, but they were unwilling to set limits to it. This is a subject over which differences of opinion will continue to exist for perhaps an indefinite period.

Rulings of the National Labor Relations Board requiring the employer to furnish information to a union in order to enable it to bargain intelligently fall within the area referred to here. Speaking of these rulings, the general counsel of the Board said in a public address: ". . . the job of fixing wages and conditions of employment, which Congress has made a joint undertaking through negotiations, and the job of managing the business, which belongs to the employer, are not necessarily mutually exclusive undertakings. The same considerations may affect both. Ultimately then the problem is one of balancing the interests of the parties, of providing a union with suffi-

[23] *Machinists' Journal*, February, 1955.

cient access to information to enable it to bargain intelligently without unduly invading management's prerogatives which are recognized under the Act." [24]

Despite these unsettled problems, unions and management have come a long way from the time when, as the Commons history reports, employers felt that "meeting committees of their own workmen on a basis of business equality was 'beneath the dignity' of employers" [25] and when unions "bargained" merely by announcing the wages they were willing to accept. Modern collective bargaining is a businesslike way of reaching agreement on matters of mutual concern. Powerful employers have not lost their dignity thereby, and workers have gained in status and self-respect. For the most part the practice has led to better relations based on more complete understanding.

[24] Address by Theophil C. Kamholz, General Counsel, National Labor Relations Board, before the Labor Law Section of the Texas State Bar Association, July 1, 1955.
[25] Commons and Associates, op. cit., Vol. II, p. 33.

6

Strikes

Most collective-bargaining negotiations in the United States lead to peaceful settlements; only a minority end with resort to strike and picket line. Yet the possibility of a strike is present in the consciousness of every negotiator and influences every bargaining conference.

To be sure, as management and labor grow in their experience with and understanding of the value of collective bargaining and as, through manifestations of honesty and fair dealing, each develops greater confidence in the other's integrity, reason and logic will play an increasingly important role in contract negotiations. Nevertheless, even where these conditions exist, each side is well aware of the fact that if negotiations fail, a resort to the economic pressure of the strike is possible. Each side may have to consider how far it can go without incurring the danger of a walkout, which means loss of wages to the worker and loss of profits to the employer. Under the best of conditions, therefore, the potential resort to a strike continues to be the union's ultimate weapon. On the other hand, in the words of a management spokesman, "the ability and willingness of a company to take a strike is the company's ultimate weapon." [1]

How Strikes Are Called

There are spontaneous strikes which erupt apparently without previous consideration, and "wildcat" strikes which are called by local groups or their leaders in disregard of what appears in the rule book.

[1] J. Ward Keenan (Vice-President of B. F. Goodrich Co.), *Management Record*, February 1954, p. 51. C. M. White, President of the Republic Steel Corporation, told a Presidential fact-finding board in 1949 that "there are worse things than a strike. Everybody gets a lot of things off their chests. . . . I think that labor has got to be as big as industry in seeing that the right results are reached. If labor is not big enough, then we have got to fight this thing out. That is the way I look at bargaining. If they think we are wrong, they strike us. That is the way this thing should work."
The New York Times, August 20, 1949.

Most strikes, however, emerge only after careful consideration and in accordance with principles laid down in union constitutions. In an introduction to a report on these constitutional provisions made for the National Industrial Conference Board, the investigators quoted labor leaders as saying that "strikes, once started, are a union's most expensive single activity. . . . Therefore, in writing their unions' constitutions, they deliberately establish procedures that make it hard, rather than easy, to call a strike." [2]

Studies of strike provisions in union constitutions were made in 1954 both by this management research agency and by the United States Bureau of Labor Statistics.[3] Both studies included most of the labor organizations of the United States, with a total of more than 15 million members. Both revealed a high degree of members' participation in decision-making with respect to calling strikes on both the local and the national level.

The Bureau study showed that a high proportion of the union constitutions required a vote of the membership affected before a strike could be called; many of them specified that the vote was to be taken by secret ballot or by referendum. The size of the vote required to sanction a strike ranged from a simple majority to three-fourths of those voting.[4]

But the membership is not the sole judge of the wisdom of a strike. The Bureau study revealed that 97 of the 133 unions studied, representing 13⅓ million members, required approval of the strike by international officers, either the president or the executive board or both. Thirty of these unions gave sole authority over strikes to the national officers and sixty-seven required a vote of the membership as well as that of the union leaders.

[2] James J. Bambrick, Jr., and George Haas, "Strike Authorization Procedure," *Management Record*, November 1954, p. 429; see also *Handbook of Union Government Structure and Procedures* (National Industrial Conference Board, 1955), p. 42.

[3] *Monthly Labor Review*, May 1954, p. 497.

[4] In detail, the study showed that 59 per cent of the union constitutions studied, covering 9¼ million members, required a vote of the membership before calling a strike. In unions with 5½ million members the vote was by secret ballot, and other unions with three-quarters of a million members voted by referendum. Of the unions whose constitutions specified the size of the majority required to sanction a strike, a simple majority was sufficient in nineteen unions, a two-thirds vote was required by thirty-three, and a three-fourths vote in eleven.

The National Industrial Conference Board study,[5] obviously covering almost the identical ground as the Bureau study (the latter covered one hundred and thirty-three unions with 15,066,000 members, and the former one hundred and thirty-six unions with 15,270,000 members), corroborates the Bureau findings in almost every respect. There is a minor difference in that the Board study reports that none of the constitutions "made any provision whereby nonmembers could vote" on the question of striking, while the Bureau states that three unions made such provision. Otherwise the two reports are in substantial agreement.

The Conference Board, however, adds some interesting notes on union practices not mentioned by the Government report. It states that the local union generally votes overwhelmingly for a strike at about the same time that it is formulating its demands, and therefore before the attitude of the employer is known. This is to be accounted for, the report states, on the ground that "in effect, the union members are voting on whether they want a raise. If they don't vote to authorize a strike, they figure they will never get anything in the subsequent bargaining."

The usual procedure where a single local is involved, according to the Conference Board, begins with a secret ballot by the local which then attempts to negotiate with the employer. If it fails to reach a settlement, the second step is to call in a representative of the parent union who attempts to settle the matter. If he fails, he makes recommendations to the national office, after which the executive board of the union votes approval or disapproval of a strike.

In most cases, then, both the membership and the national executives must register approval before a strike can be called. In exceptional cases the initiative may be taken by the national office without waiting for action by the members. For example, a clause in the constitution of the United Automobile Workers provides as follows: "In case of great emergency, when the existence of the international union is involved, the president and the international executive board may *declare* a general strike" by a two-thirds vote of the execu-

[5] See *Management Record*, May and November 1954.

tive board, but "under no circumstances shall it *call* such a strike until approved by a referendum vote of the membership." [6]

That the whole story of union procedure in authorizing strikes is not told in the constitutions is indicated by some off-the-record information obtained by the Conference Board. For example, the constitution of the International Union of Electrical Workers (IUE) makes no reference to a vote by the members. It provides merely that "no strike shall be called by any local without the president or his representatives having made an effort to adjust the dispute"; and that the president of the local must "notify the president [of the union] immediately if a strike is proposed or pending." But a representative of this union told the Conference Board investigators that "a majority of the local union constitutions contain provisions requiring a secret ballot membership vote by a two-thirds majority before a strike can be called."

The constitution of the International Brotherhood of Electrical Workers (IBEW) provides simply that a local union must get the approval of the union president before calling a strike. Further light on the whole matter of strikes by that union was contained in a letter to the Conference Board from a union representative:

The problem of strikes in the electrical contracting industry has been largely eliminated by a procedure in contracts for a final and binding decision of labor disputes by the 34-year-old council on industrial relations which is composed of an equal number of representatives from management and labor. Many of our agreements with public utilities and other industries provide for final and binding arbitration of changes in agreements.

An examination of about eighty international union constitutions by the writer produced further justification for hesitancy about assuming that final conclusions can be drawn from what appears in union constitutions. For example, several large unions make no reference in their constitutions to procedure in calling strikes. Yet their strikes are matters of record and must somehow have been "called." Some constitutions that are completely silent on pre-strike procedure casually mention steps to be taken when a "legally authorized" strike

[6] Emphasis added. The distinction between "declaring" and "calling" a strike is not made clear.

takes place, or "in the event of a strike," or when a strike is "sanctioned." These vague references clearly indicate prior strike approval, probably by a high authority in the union.[7]

On the other hand, it is probable that the membership is consulted even where a constitution seems to place all authority in the hands of the president. In the constitution of the United Steel Workers, there is a single reference to strikes: "No strike shall be called without the approval of the International President." But current practice involves action by the union's executive board and a "wage policy committee" consisting of delegates elected by the locals.

The constitution of the Transport Service Employees (Red Caps) makes the simple statement that the president "shall have the power to authorize strikes." Presidential power is defined explicitly in the constitution of the Textile Workers Union of America:

Neither the International Union nor any of its local unions . . . shall have the power or authority to induce, call . . . or engage in any strike . . . except as expressly authorized or ratified in writing by the General President. Such power and authority resides exclusively in the General President and he exclusively may withdraw such authorization or ratification, once given, and he exclusively may declare any strike . . . terminated at any time.

Despite these grants of sweeping powers to union presidents, the political aspect of high elective office in unions is such as to justify doubt that any strike of considerable proportions would be called without in some manner sounding out membership opinion. However, a "doubt" is a weak reed to lean upon. Where such powers are granted the supposition that they are to be used is also justified.

DEFENSE FUNDS

One of the oldest methods made use of to keep a strike going is the payment of strike benefits. Most of the union constitutions examined make reference, either explicitly or implicitly, to the payment of weekly sums to strikers from union funds. The payments range from sums as low as three or four dollars a week to substantial

[7] The lack of references to procedure in constitutions of internationals does not preclude their being in by-laws of the locals.

amounts. Most unions maintain a strike "defense" fund from which payments are made.

At the convention of the United Automobile Workers held in March 1955 (with wage negotiations pending), the delegates "by an overwhelming majority" voted to increase monthly dues from $2.50 to $7.50 in order to create a strike fund of $25 million. This increase was to remain in effect until the anticipated fund was obtained, when dues were to revert to $2.50. If the fund should later fall below $20 million, monthly dues should be increased again to $3.50 and remain at that point until the amount in the fund again reached $25 million. A vice-president of the union was quoted as saying that the building up of this strike fund was "the most important action our convention has ever taken with respect to collective bargaining." [8]

The defense funds of most unions are usually inadequate to meet the demands of a prolonged strike and they are often supplemented by contributions from other (nonstriking) unions. The financial reports of unions quite commonly include among expense items contributions to other unions. Sometimes these are substantial, as in the rather famous gift of $100,000 by the Amalgamated Clothing Workers to assist the AFL in its effort to organize the steel industry in 1920. Since then such contributions in time of emergency have become less unusual.

The importance to the striker of even a small weekly payment during strikes is obvious. Most union constitutions provide as a penalty for wildcat strikes the withholding of benefits.

The AFL-CIO Community Services Committee, which is engaged in a great variety of welfare services throughout the country (see Chapter 13), makes assistance to strikers its first obligation.

[8] *Monthly Labor Review*, U. S. Bureau of Labor Statistics, May 1955, p. 529. With a membership of over one million, it is obvious that this large sum could be accumulated in less than five months. Its effectiveness should be measured against any possible claim that might be made upon it. It was pointed out in the debate on the resolution that if all the employees of General Motors, said to be 325,000, were to go on strike, and if they were paid strike benefits of $20 a week, the fund would be exhausted in less than four weeks. The strike fund of the Automobile Workers is cited merely by way of illustration. Most unions accumulate such funds in greater or lesser amounts as protection against possible emergency.

PICKETING

The first step in most strikes is the organization of a picket line. Picketing may involve the presence of one or two strikers at the entrance to the place of employment, or it may include large numbers—even the whole body of strikers—who march up and down before the mill gates.

Picketing may be said to have two major purposes: first, to prevent access of workers to the plant; second, to interfere with management activities. Frequently all that is necessary to tie up the plant is to make known the fact that a strike is in progress. The single emissary at the plant gate—"missionaries," Chief Justice William H. Taft once called pickets of this type—may have nothing more to do than to carry a banner stating that a strike is in progress, or to convey that information by word of mouth. On the first day of the walkout some employees may come to work who had not heard of the strike and who need only to receive that information to impel them immediately to join it. Job seekers from out of town often learn of it only on arrival at the plant entrance. If they are union members or in sympathy with the purposes of unionism, they will decide to seek employment elsewhere.

This type of picketing, involving no more than conveying information, has been approved by the courts, both because of its peaceful nature and as an aspect of free speech that is protected by the First Amendment to the Constitution.[9]

If, however, the mere announcement that a strike is in progress is insufficient to deter persons who desire to work from entering the plant, picketing takes a new form. Strike leaders call for larger numbers to patrol the area. The tactics of obstruction are now added to the tactics of information and persuasion. What follows then is the phenomenon known as "mass" picketing. Strikers appear in great numbers before the plant entrances and march in close ranks so that

---

[9] Thornhill v. Alabama. 310 U.S. 88, April 22, 1940. The Supreme Court said: "The freedom of speech and of the press guaranteed by the Constitution embraces at least the liberty to discuss publicly and truthfully all matters of public concern without previous restraint or fear of subsequent punishment. . . . In the circumstances of our times the dissemination of information concerning the facts of a labor dispute must be regarded as within that area of free discussion that is guaranteed by the Constitution."

one wishing to enter would have to shoulder his way through, since the marchers do not open the way for a free passage. If the marchers were run-of-the-mill citizens on their way to a ball game, or attracted by some exciting event such as a fire, they would be indifferent to the purposes of other persons desiring to pass through their line of march. But in mass picketing the marchers are not indifferent to the purposes of the others. Their presence is an effective deterrent to those who want to go to work. The would-be worker is powerfully affected by the single-minded mass will of the pickets. However peaceable their conduct, the nonstriker hesitates to incur their displeasure—to be the object of mass disapproval—or he may withdraw for fear of injury. If, however, he is exceptionally determined and attempts to force his way through, his act stimulates resentment, which can lead to physical resistance and then to acts of retaliation.[10]

The ultimate purpose of mass picketing is to prevent anyone, regular employee or strike breaker, from going to work, by peaceful means if possible but if that is unavailing, by force. How far the average man on the picket line is willing to go in the use of force is uncertain. As a rule he is no more likely to commit acts of aggression, or assault persons on the highways, than are the general run of members of any normal community. But the psychological atmosphere of the picket line is such as quickly to generate heat. The resort to violence in dealing with a determined strike breaker may be the result of an unforeseen impulse.[11]

[10] When the strike reaches this acute stage union discipline asserts itself. A clause in the constitution of the United Rubber Workers reads: "If during a strike or lockout a member does not obey the instructions and orders of his local union or those of the international representatives entrusted with the strike, he shall not be eligible for the assistance [strike benefits] provided for in . . . this Section."

[11] "Violence on the picket line is rarely a premeditated union plan of action," writes Jack Barbash, but it is "likely to occur" when the employer tries to "break the strike by operating the plant and getting the employees to go through the picket line." Illustrating the latter situation, he quotes from an account given by a union business agent of picket line tactics. A group of pickets met workers as they got off a street car "and asked them, 'Are you with us or against us?' and there wasn't anything in between—it was either yes or no, and if the answer was no and they were against us, Wham! There was fighting then and there and a lot of people were hurt." Jack Barbash, *The Practice of Unionism* (New York: Harper & Brothers, 1956), pp. 227–229. See also article on "Intimidation," *Encyclopedia of the Social Sciences* (New York: The Macmillan Company, 1932), Vol. 8, pp. 239 ff.

IS THERE A RIGHT TO A JOB?

Behind this attitude are two powerful contributing factors, one of which is peculiar to the strike situation; the other arises out of the economic status of the wage earner.

In the first place, there is no article in the trade unionist's creed more universally accepted and adhered to in practice than that no one has a right to take a striker's job. This leads to an attitude regarding the rights of strikers that is in some respects unique. Picketing for the purpose of informing and persuading, and without the show or threat of force, is conceded to be a reasonable procedure. Use of force, intimidation, or violence to prevent workers from seeking employment or to prevent employers from having access to such persons appears to be asserting a right for the strikers in derogation of rights undoubtedly possessed by others. It seems basic to a democratic society that seeking work should be a legal right, regardless of how much anyone may deprecate the ethical standards of the seekers. Nevertheless, the belief is widespread among union leaders that whether or not strike breakers have a legal right to take the jobs vacated by strikers, the latter have a right, perhaps a "natural" right, to prevent them from doing so.[12]

The other factor, which accounts in part for the striker's belief that he has a right to prevent access to the plant, has to do with the wage earner's assumption that the job is his. It should be remembered that for the typical wage earner there is no such thing as a legal right to a job. That is one reason for the bitter criticism in the labor movement for the use of the title "right-to-work" to describe laws whose purpose is not to establish any such right but rather to deny to unions and employers the right to make a contract providing for "union security."

To be sure, a right to hold a job sometimes exists as a result of a

[12] In a case before the U. S. Supreme Court involving the constitutionality of right-to-work laws, counsel for the appealing union declared "that the right of a nonunionist to work is in no way equivalent to or the parallel of the right to work as a union member; that there exists no constitutional right to work as a nonunionist on the one hand while the right to maintain employment free from discrimination because of union membership is constitutionally protected." Commenting on this argument, the Supreme Court said: "We deem it unnecessary to elaborate the numerous reasons for our rejection of [the union's] contention. . . ." Lincoln Federal Union v. Northwestern Iron and Metal Co., 335 U.S. 525, 1949.

contract, as in a case when a plant manager or an orchestra leader is engaged for a term of years; but wage earners are practically never hired on such a basis. Labor contracts are almost invariably "at will," which means that the worker may quit when he sees fit and that he may be fired at the employer's discretion, subject to the limitation of the National Labor Management Relations Act (Taft-Hartley) that he may not be discharged for union activity, and to the clauses in union contracts providing for seniority or requiring that dismissals must be for "cause."

These are important rights, but they do not protect the jobs of strikers.[13] Altogether, then, despite the fact that laws and collective bargaining have brought us some distance from the time when an employer could discharge at will, "for any reason or for no reason," the legal right to a job as a property right has not yet come into being.

Even if this were not the case, the fact would remain that the striker has not been discharged: he has quit voluntarily. How then can it be supposed that he has the right either to claim the job as his own or to prevent others from taking it if it is offered? Here we need to try to understand the union point of view. Over thirty years ago I offered a statement and an explanation of that point of view which I see no reason to modify now. I wrote:

The striker . . . has quit his job, not because he is through with it but because he wants to make it a better job. He has no thought of abandoning the industry or the employer. He has withdrawn temporarily in the hope that his withdrawal and the consequent inconvenience to his employer will have an effect on the job. He hopes that changes will be made as a result of which the job will be a more satisfactory one when he goes back to it. He thinks of it, therefore, as his job. He is undergoing hardship and loss in behalf of that job. He has an eye on the future and on the opportunities that it will hold for his children, as well as for himself. Now, along comes a rank outsider and walks into the plant and takes the job that belongs to another man, and for which he has sacrificed nothing. Despite the fact that he has had the same opportunity that the striker had to get a job of his own, he has deliberately chosen to reach out and take what belongs to another. He is worse than a thief, in the striker's

[13] Subject to the provision in the Taft-Hartley Act that if the strike is against a violation of contract by the employer, or to end an "unfair labor practice" forbidden to the employer by the Act, the strikers are entitled to be reinstated in their jobs.

opinion, for the ordinary thief only takes money or goods, the results of past effort. The strike-breaker steals the future; he takes hope and opportunity and the worthwhileness of living from a man who has done him no wrong.[14]

It must be apparent, then, why the striker tries to protect and hold what he believes to be his own. Even if it is true that he is mistaken in his belief that the job is his personal property, it is possible to understand how he comes by such a belief. His ability to do useful work and his skill, which he has built up and increased by application over the years, are among his most valuable possessions—valuable in the economic sense as well as in other respects. But their economic value has no existence unless he can make use of them in the production of goods. Therefore he has come to think of holding a job and the attempt through a strike to make it a better one as a right not entirely dissimilar from the right to own property and to improve it.[15]

There can be no doubt that the freedom once possessed by the employer to hire and fire at will, and to answer to nobody for his action, has in one way or another come to be somewhat circumscribed. But to recognize that as a fact is far from suggesting that a legal right to prevent ingress to and egress from a struck plant has now been conferred upon the strikers. What is needed further before we can find a way through the maze of industrial conflict is recognition that the psychological and emotional atmosphere engendered by strikes has its origin in attitudes and points of view that are capable

[14] John A. Fitch, op. cit., pp. 221–222.

[15] In this belief he is doubtless fortified by the provisions in the Wagner and Taft-Hartley Acts forbidding discharge for union activity, as well as by the job-security clauses that have been written into collective bargaining contracts. It is possible, however, that the nearest approach to recognition of a property right in a job is to be found elsewhere. Unemployment insurance laws were not written to establish such a right. On the contrary, they recognize loss of employment as an expected hazard, but they require payment to be made to a worker who has lost his job "through no fault of his own" in much the same way that a property owner is indemnified for an injury caused by another. And in most of the American states it is the employer alone who is required by law to provide this indemnity. Whether or not the possession of a job is ever to be held to be a legal right, it is hard to avoid the inference that the law requiring compensation for the loss of it through the act of the employer is something of a recognition that the thing that was lost and is now to be compensated for had some of the elements of the assets that are accounted for in a balance sheet.

of being understood. It is such understanding that is the prerequisite of enlightened action.

FREQUENCY OF STRIKES

It was stated earlier that most collective bargaining negotiations result in harmonious settlements. This fact may well receive further emphasis, since the belief is widespread that American trade union- ism is constantly embroiled in strikes. During the preparation of this study I have frequently asked persons of high intelligence, but who were not students of labor relations, to tell me what proportion of total working time in their opinion is lost each year because of strikes. The answers have ranged from 3 to 25 per cent. Yet the statistics of strikes compiled by the United States Bureau of Labor Statistics show that, in the period of thirty years during which information on that point has been made available, only once has the figure been above 1 per cent. It was 1.43 per cent in 1946. The annual average for the whole period is a trifle over .3 per cent. In 1956, the "pre- liminary" figure was about .3 per cent.[16]

In this chapter an attempt has been made to deal with the strike as an aspect of collective bargaining, to examine the nature of the controls set up by the unions to insure a degree of deliberation with respect to use of the strike weapon, and to consider the picket line as the traditional and most powerful device for making strikes ef- fective.

From the standpoint of moral principle there would seem to be no question about the reality of the right to strike. A particular strike may seem to the onlooker unnecessary or unreasonable, or the calling of it a mistake, but that in itself does not raise questions of moral right. Such questions may, and often do, arise in connection with the conduct of strikes. Picket-line behavior is a difficult and complicated issue, not easily dealt with simply by reference to concepts of right and wrong. But just as what is right on the picket line is at times obvious and at other times hard to define, the same is true of what is wrong. An area in which labor leaders sometimes appear to be lax in the discharge of their responsibilities is in dealing with the obvious wrongs and in finding clear definitions for what is right. This matter is discussed in more detail in Chapters 13 and 15.

[16] For information on the compiling of strike data, see Supplementary Notes.

7

The Demand for Union Security

In the controversial matter of union security, labor and management confront one of their more difficult problems. The unions generally consider contractual safeguards so important that they affect their very existence. To many spokesmen for organized business, on the other hand, the desired safeguards appear to be not only unnecessary but so unjustifiable both economically and morally that they ought to be forbidden by law. The respective positions are so far apart that they call for examination.

When an employer agrees to deal with a union committee acting as spokesman for his employees, he is said to have "recognized" the union. If, in the ensuing negotiations, an agreement is reached and a contract signed, the union seems well established. Its position is even stronger if the union has been accepted by the employees in a secret ballot, and as a result has been "certified" by the National Labor Relations Board as representative of all the employees in the bargaining unit.

When all this has taken place something has been achieved that might be considered as contributing to what is called union security. Undoubtedly it is so considered by the union; but the labor spokesmen mean something more when they use that term. They desire additional safeguards.

The principal forms of union security sought by the unions are three. Stated in descending order, according to the degree of security provided, these are the closed shop, the union shop, and maintenance of membership.

Briefly stated, the closed-shop plan requires an employer to hire union members only. In other words, under such an agreement a worker must be a union member in good standing before he can be hired.

In a union shop the employer is free to hire whom he will, unionists or nonunionists. After being hired, however, the worker must join the union within a short period. Thus the employer has greater freedom under the union shop since he may select his employees as he sees fit; but after the waiting period, with all employees in the union, the arrangement bears a close resemblance to the closed shop. Under either type of shop, the employer formerly was bound by the agreement to discharge any employee who for any reason lost his good standing in the union. This was true until the enactment of the Taft-Hartley Act. That law made the closed shop illegal [1] and modified the effect of the union shop by limiting the obligation of the employer to discharge a nonmember to cases where the employee had lost his membership for failing to pay his union dues.

Maintenance of membership, the third form of union security, leaves the employer free to hire whom he will and no one is required to join the union. The arrangement provides for an "escape" period of about fifteen days immediately after the signing of the agreement. During this period persons who are already members of the union may withdraw, if they wish to do so, without losing their jobs. Nonmembers may join or not as they see fit. At the end of the escape period, all who are then members and all who join later must remain in good standing throughout the period of the agreement, subject to the same requirement to pay union dues as in the case of the union shop.

These three types of union security involve compulsion in varying degrees. Under either the closed shop or the union shop the worker is under pressure to belong to the union if he wants to keep a job. Under maintenance of membership he must stay in the union once he has joined it, for the period of the agreement. All three forms reflect a fear that without some form of compulsion the worker will either refuse to join, or, having joined, will withdraw or lapse in the payment of dues.[2] This fear stems not alone from possible worker

---

[1] The closed shop still exists, though to what extent is difficult to ascertain. The Taft-Hartley Act applies to employer-employee relations in interstate commerce. Wholly intra-state activities are unaffected by it. However, the closed shop and other forms of union security are illegal by legislative enactment, in eighteen states. In the other thirty states there are doubtless closed-shop agreements relating to intra-state activities only. In addition, by mutual and more or less tacit agreement between management and unions in certain instances, the closed shop still prevails in areas to which the Taft-Hartley Act applies, in disregard of that law.

[2] The dues matter is frequently handled by the "check-off," which is in itself a

indifference. It is historically an outgrowth of employer coercion *not* to join unions. "Union security arrangements are not new," says an AFL pamphlet. "They developed from necessity, as the bitter opposition of employers to union organization forced unions to seek agreements under which the union's status would be secure from anti-union attacks" sponsored, openly or secretly, by the employers.

THE CASE FOR COMPULSORY UNIONISM

Prior to the passage of the Recovery Act in 1933, and the more effective Wagner Act in 1935, employers were legally free to discharge employees who joined unions. Because anti-union employers made full use of this freedom, unions that were strong enough to enforce such a demand saw to it that closed-shop clauses were written into their contracts with the employers. Some of the methods used by employers in the earlier period to prevent union growth are referred to in Chapters 3 and 12. Although unions are now stronger and more firmly established, their leaders still believe that protection against employer's efforts to dislodge them is required. The belief is widespread among present-day union leaders that most employers would destroy the unions if they could.[3] This belief is bolstered both by the fact of active employer opposition in some sections of the country and by the campaign of employing interests to secure the passage by state legislatures of so-called "right-to-work" laws, which have as their purpose the outlawing of union security agreements of the types described.

---

fourth form of union security. By agreement with the union the employer holds out on pay day, or "checks off" the union dues and pays them over to the union. Thus each member is automatically "paid up."

[3] A prominent interpreter of union objectives and attitudes says: "The history of workers' attempts to extend union organization and secure employers' recognition and acceptance has been characterized by resistance and conflict. . . .

"The great railroad strikes of the 1870's and 1880's" and the major industrial conflicts of the first two decades of the present century, "marked the period of conflict." A by-product of this period, he states, was "the creation of workers' fear of the vast power and influence of corporations and industry. This heritage of fear has become a part of the folklore of the labor movement which has been bequeathed to the present generation of union members."

Clinton S. Golden, Executive Director, Trade Union Program, Harvard University, in his Introduction to *Causes of Industrial Peace Under Collective Bargaining* (New York: Harper & Brothers, 1953), p. 3.

The union desire for contracts that require all the workers to join a union or to continue their membership arises also in part from evidences of indifference among the workers themselves. The period of almost religious fervor in union organization drives—the period when workers were pouring into the unions as in a crusade, smarting with a sense of unrequited wrongs—has largely come to an end. In the major areas of industrial activity collective bargaining has become a commonplace; and at the same time younger workers have been recruited by the hundreds of thousands who have had no experience with the difficult days of union building, and no recollection of unemployment or starvation wages. Some of these, having joined unions, wonder why they should continue to pay dues. Others have no wish to join, being satisfied with the existing conditions.

Union leaders admit that workers who join the union under the compulsion of a union-shop contract may do so with reluctance and in some cases with resentment. They assert, however, that such recruits soon recognize the advantages of unionism and become willing members.[4] Moreover, experience under the Taft-Hartley Act indicates rather clearly the existence of a large body of rank-and-file labor opinion that is favorable to the union shop.

The Taft-Hartley Act as passed by Congress in 1947 permitted the union shop, but made sure that it could not be imposed on rank-and-file workers without their consent. Before the leaders could negotiate with management for a union-shop agreement, the workers affected had to have an opportunity to express their opinions pro or con in a secret ballot supervised by the National Labor Relations Board. It required the approval of a majority of the workers in the bargaining unit—not merely of those voting—to authorize negotiations for a union shop.

This provision of the law was in effect for a period of four years and two months. During this period over 46,000 union-shop elections were held, in which about 6½ million workers were eligible to vote, of whom 5½ million (84.6 per cent) did vote. In all, 97 per cent of the elections and 91 per cent of those voting approved the union shop. This 91 per cent majority may be compared with the approxi-

---

[4] Some unions assist their new recruits in understanding the advantages of union membership through classes, published material, and movies.

mately 57 per cent majority in the "landslide" Presidential election of 1956.

The requirement of a vote on the union shop was repealed in 1951 with Senator Taft's approval. Under the circumstances the holding of elections was considered an unnecessary expense.[5]

The convinced trade unionist believes that compulsion to join a union, as under the union shop, is justified on several grounds. The union, he states, must have some means for "policing" the contract. Under the Taft-Hartley Act, and as emphasized by the Supreme Court, a union that has been certified by the National Labor Relations Board as representing a majority of the workers in the bargaining unit must protect the rights of all workers in the unit, including nonmembers. The law also provides penalties for nonobservance of the contract. The unions hold that since they are charged with such responsibilities they must have "adequate authority to deal with workers" who violate the contract.

A CIO statement points out that negotiating agreements covering wage and other advantages for "all the workers in the unit," processing grievances for all, and paying the costs of arbitration if the grievance goes that far, all constitute a heavy burden on the union treasury. It asks why the nonmember beneficiary should be relieved of the necessity of helping to meet these costs. "The individual," the statement adds, "not only has rights, he has obligations."

This is the "free-rider" argument, a term the unions apply to workers who accept benefits obtained by the union but do not help

[5] The National Association of Manufacturers in a published statement discounts the significance of these elections. They were, it states, "hand picked" in that they were held only in highly organized plants where the unions "felt sure of winning decisively." The more significant fact, the statement continues, is that only "approximately five million" trade unionists out of 17 million in the country, and out of "60 million employed persons," voted for the union shop. Thus "less than a third" of union members and "less than 10 per cent of all employees voted for compulsory unionism."

It should be noted that the "60 million employed persons" is derived from the census enumeration of the "labor force" in the country. This term is used by the Census Bureau with reference to persons engaged in any form of economic activity, and so included employers, executives, professional persons, etc., as well as wage earners. The large majorities in the areas in which elections were held do not support the inference that other union members not participating in the elections were opposed to the union shop.

pay for them. As an AFL pamphlet put it, "All workers receive the benefits of unionism, but only the union members through their dues carry the cost of supporting the union. . . . In order that all workers receive equal consideration, unions must be allowed to negotiate an arrangement under which all the workers would help support their collective bargaining representative."

The unions call attention also to the union security agreements negotiated over the years. A study by the United States Bureau of Labor Statistics, of 1,716 collective bargaining agreements in effect in 1954 covering 7.4 million workers, showed that 65 per cent of the agreements contained a union-shop clause, and 14 per cent provided for maintenance of membership. In the remaining 21 per cent the union was recognized as the sole bargaining agent.[6]

These facts, the unions contend, indicate that coercion is a limited factor in union-security arrangements, and that these arrangements are willingly accepted by many employers.

EMPLOYER ATTITUDES

Employers are not unanimous in their approach to union security. Some employers state that they prefer a closed shop because it eliminates bickering between union members and nonmembers, relieves the union leaders of fear that the union may be undermined, and creates a comfortable atmosphere in the shop. Some employers believe that a majority of the skilled workers are in the unions anyway and that a closed shop goes far toward insuring a competent force. Moreover, under a closed shop the union is under a moral obligation to assist the employer in obtaining workers in accordance with his needs.

These employers are undoubtedly a minority. Opposition to the union shop and other forms of union security appears to be the more typical employer attitude. This seems to be indicated by employers' support of the campaign in favor of so-called "right-to-work" laws.

The statutes under that designation now in effect in eighteen states differ in phraseology but are alike in purpose. The Virginia law was described by the Supreme Court of that state as follows: "It provides in substance that neither membership nor nonmembership in

[6] *Monthly Labor Review*, June 1955, pp. 649–658.

a labor union shall be made a condition of employment; that a contract limiting employment to union members is against public policy; and that a person denied employment because he is either a member of a union or not a member of a union shall have a right of action for damages."

The movement for this type of legislation appears to have been launched about twenty years ago by an organization called the Christian American Association, which was incorporated in Texas in 1936. At one time this organization advocated an amendment to the Constitution of the United States to forbid discrimination in employment on account of membership or nonmembership in unions, but later it turned to advocacy of action by the states. In 1944 two states, Arkansas and Florida, wrote into their constitutions amendments barring union-security agreements. Two years later Arizona, Nebraska, and South Dakota took the same action. All of these except Florida have since enacted legislation to implement the constitutional amendments. Other states have followed suit, the latest statute being that of Indiana in 1957. A national Right-to-Work Committee led by former Congressman Fred A. Hartley, Jr., co-author of the Taft-Hartley Act, was formed in 1955 to support the movement.[7]

Statements issued by the National Association of Manufacturers and the Chamber of Commerce of the United States set forth the views of those organizations on union security. Of the right-to-work laws, the Manufacturers Association said "these laws clearly are designed to protect the freedom of individuals to make their own choice in regard to joining or not joining a labor organization, without restraint or coercion by employers, union officials, or other persons. . . . The principle behind these laws is neither anti-union nor pro-union; it is one of the simple morals of freedom."

The Chamber of Commerce takes the position that "employees should be free to join or not to join a labor organization. . . . A labor union should recruit and hold its members on its merits, not by making membership a condition of employment." It sees in the union shop danger of a "nation-wide labor monopoly," and it assails the

[7] Bills embodying the restriction appearing in these laws have been introduced in several other state legislatures. One that was passed by the Kansas legislature in 1955 was vetoed by the governor. In a few states such laws, once enacted, have been repealed. The Louisiana law was repealed in 1956.

union contention that the union shop is a democratic arrangement, growing out of the principle of majority rule.

"Most right-thinking citizens," says the Chamber, "would ignore as ridiculous any suggestion that because a majority in a state voted Republican, all Democrats and members of all other political parties in the state had to join the Republican party and pay dues to it, or leave the state." [8]

The employers' associations are quick to compare the unions' condemnation of the "yellow-dog" contract with their attitude toward the closed or union shop. Under the former the worker was compelled, as a condition of employment, to stay out of the union, and the unions denounced and fought it. Under the latter the worker is compelled to join the union, and the compulsion is a plank in the union platform. To be sure, the two forms of compulsion are not strictly comparable. The "yellow-dog" contract was held by the United States Supreme Court to be entitled to the protection of the government.[9] Incitement to violation of the contract was made subject to injunction, with attendant penalties of fine or imprisonment. The union shop, on the other hand, is a matter of voluntary agreement between employer and union, and enforceable by the private action of the strike. But both are examples of coercion of the individual.

In insisting upon the union shop the unions may be over-influenced by the "heritage of fear" that Clinton Golden says has become "a part of the folklore of the labor movement." The unions were weak when the "yellow-dog" contract was in its heyday. They are now strong enough in the major industrial sectors of the country to protect themselves against open-shop campaigns.

There is, to be sure, nothing new in the union demand for security.

[8] On the whole, there seems to be an element of irony in the emergence of the National Association of Manufacturers and the U.S. Chamber of Commerce as champions of the right of the individual worker to be free of coercion with respect to joining a union. Coercion to prevent a worker from joining a union has never seemed to them equally obnoxious. However, the claim of organized labor that if laws forbidding union-security contracts become general the unions will be destroyed seems not only exaggerated but manifestly erroneous. Nevertheless, experience and history seem to justify their belief that the purpose of the promoters of such legislation is to weaken the unions rather than to liberate the individual.

[9] Hitchman Coal & Coke Co. v. Mitchell, 245 U.S. 229, 1917.

More than a hundred years ago John Stuart Mill made reference to it as a potential economic factor in the England of his time. After expressing his belief that trade unions are essential as the "necessary instrumentality" of a free market, he wrote: "It is, however, an indispensable condition of tolerating combinations that they should be voluntary. No severity necessary to the purpose is too great to be employed against attempts to compel workmen to join a union, or take part in a strike, by threats of violence." [10] It is to be noted that it was specifically compulsion by "threats of violence" which he said should be opposed with unlimited severity. It may be observed in this connection that violence has seldom if ever been resorted to by English unions to enforce the closed shop. Indeed the English trade unions generally deny that they favor the closed shop. Their practice differs from that of American unions in that they do not ordinarily ask the employer to sign a contract limiting employment to members of the union; they merely refuse to work with nonunionists! [11]

In this country the British practice obtained at the very beginning of significant trade-union action. One of the counts against the union in the famous Cordwainers Case in 1806 was that its members refused to work with nonmembers. Later the closed shop as now understood came into the picture and was alternately condemned or approved by the courts.

SOME PERTINENT QUESTIONS

The fact that the demand for union security is at least a hundred years old does not dispose of all the questions. An aspect of the closed-shop policy that has received wide criticism is the combination of closed shop and closed union. When a union refuses to accept new members, or accepts only certain privileged persons such as relatives of members, a closed-shop agreement gives it a degree of power in the industry that may be antisocial in character. Such arrangements have been condemned by the courts in various jurisdictions. The Cali-

[10] *Principles of Political Economy*, Revised Edition (London and New York: The Colonial Press, 1900), Vol. 2, p. 439.

[11] Cf. Jean T. McKelvey, "The 'Closed Shop' Controversy in Postwar Britain," *Industrial and Labor Relations Review*, July 1954.

fornia Supreme Court upheld an injunction against a union that was closed in effect against Negroes.

Unions organized on an industrial basis are seldom, if ever, "closed." The CIO textbook on right-to-work laws declared: "The CIO is against the 'closed' union which discriminates against the admission of workers on account of race, color, or creed and has expressed itself many times in support of legislation that would prohibit such discrimination. . . . Nor is the CIO in favor of a closed union in any case." In the same treatise Walter Reuther is quoted to this effect: "I personally think it is wrong for a union to have a closed membership in which they attempt to build a labor monopoly, in order to exploit the advantages of a monopoly. I think it is morally wrong; I think it is economically wrong." [12]

Curiously, the statements by employers' agencies condemning union security do not mention the closed union, perhaps because in their opinion the union shop itself, without the closed union, represents an equally unhealthy degree of power. The union shop, the Chamber of Commerce states, is "an instrument of tremendous power." It controls members by the threat of expulsion from the union; it can compel employees to strike even when they think the strike is "unnecessary or wrong" and "it is obvious, too, that in a union shop employees may feel compelled to support union officials they believe to be corrupt or with whose views they strongly disagree."

These sweeping generalizations not only are presented without supporting data but overlook the clauses of the Taft-Hartley Act which curb the freedom of the union under a union-shop agreement. Yet it is true that in many unions devices or practices exist which give the officers extraordinary power. Some of these, together with more democratic practices, are dealt with in Chapter 9. It must be recognized, however, that where rule or practice, or seizure of power confers on leadership any of the functions of dictatorship, such a dictatorship is easier to maintain under a union shop than without it.

Another aspect of compulsory membership of any sort calls for thought. This is its effect upon members of religious groups who believe membership in unions to be a sin. Granted that such religious

---

[12] *The Case against Right-to-Work Laws*, pp. 87, 88.

bodies have a limited membership, as in general appears to be the case, and that not all their members are wage earners, the application to them of the compulsory principle seems to violate what are generally recognized as essential individual rights. Everyone would probably agree that a union rule compelling a member who was of the Orthodox Jewish faith, or a Seventh-Day Adventist, to work on Saturday or lose his union standing would be an invasion of his religious liberty. It seems to me to be equally so to compel a worker to join a union when to do that would do violence to his conscience, or to offer him a choice between such violation and expulsion from the union and his means of livelihood.

The Seventh-Day Adventists have succeeded in inducing a large number of local unions and at least one international union to accept for members of that religious body a special contract that sidesteps the issue. Under this contract, Adventists may elect not to join the union but to pay the equivalent of union dues, which the union agrees to allocate to the support of welfare activities and to keep apart from funds used to support strikes or other controversial activities.

If this seems to be a compromise that does not dispose of the issue, it is immensely better than throwing a man out of work for no reason but the existence of scruples to which his right to adhere is beyond question. Some unions regard this problem as not serious enough to warrant action; they allow the religious conscientious objector to work in a union shop without a union card. Other unions enforce the rule against him with ruthless thoroughness. National officers of such unions are adamant in their support of such action.[13]

After all extenuating factors have been considered, the assertion that a private agency should have neither power to tax nor power to determine who may work cannot easily be brushed aside. The argument that a union should earn the loyalty of members rather than compel it cannot be countered by a demonstration of employer abuses.

[13] The National Labor Relations Board ruled in 1949 that the discharge of workers who had offered to pay initiation fees and dues, but who refused on religious grounds to take the membership oath, was illegal under the Taft-Hartley Act. It ordered reinstatement and joint reimbursement for lost wages by employer and union. Union Starch Case, 87 NLRB 779. Upheld by the Seventh Circuit Court of Appeals.

Granted that there still exist important industrial areas in the United States where unions are fought with the tools of the 1890s, organized labor in the nation as a whole is very powerful. The Taft-Hartley Act, like the Wagner Act before it, guarantees to all employees the right to join unions of their own choosing, and makes it an illegal practice to interfere with or deny that right. It will require patience and fortitude to insure full obedience to that law in the backwaters of American industry. But the game is worth the candle. It may be that the time has arrived when the unions comprised within the great merged AFL-CIO could reasonably review their policies on union security. Further discussion of this issue appears in Chapter 15 and in Supplementary Notes.

8

Nonbargaining Functions of Unions

When collective bargaining has become an accepted practice and the worker as a result feels reasonably secure in his economic status and as a union member, he feels free to give thought to needs outside the areas of union-employer negotiations. As a result, "the worker, in many unions, has opportunities for education, study classes, lectures, etc. He can participate in the union chorus or orchestra . . . , or in athletic sports. Some unions have art and crafts classes to which the worker can bring his children. . . . His health will be protected by the union clinic, and he can take his holidays at his union's vacation camp. . . . If he is unemployed, the union will help him get his insurance benefits; if he is injured at work, the union will help him to secure his compensation rights." [1]

Cash Benefits

One of the areas in which many unions have provided advantages or benefits to their members is that of assistance in meeting economic hazards. The payment of cash benefits to the families of deceased members is one of the oldest of such practices. In the period 1927 to 1954 inclusive, American unions paid out nearly half a billion dollars for this purpose—an average of over $17 million a year.

Other hazards which many of the stronger unions have assisted their members in meeting include sickness, disability, unemployment, and old age. The total amount paid out for these purposes was as low as $25 million in some of the depression years. In 1954 the amount was $111½ million. Over the years these payments have undoubtedly been helpful to many individuals. In the period preceding the passage

[1] Faulkner and Starr, Labor in America (New York: Harper & Brothers, 1944), pp. 266–267. While the statement quoted is correct, it should be noted that the reference is to "many" unions, not to all. As a matter of fact, with respect to some of the advantages made available by the unions, the word "few" would be more appropriate. Nevertheless, most of the unions provide one or more of the benefits listed.

of the Social Security Law they provided at least a limited stopgap, but they were manifestly inadequate in view of the magnitude of the problem.[2] Millis and Montgomery wrote in 1945:

The total expenditure by trade unions for various kinds of benefits has been small in comparison with the needs of the membership. The inadequacy of the protection furnished is more obvious when it is realized that the bulk of the payments have been made by a few unions, particularly by the Railway Brotherhoods, and that many unions report only insignificant payments and some none at all. It was, indeed, the recognition that their voluntary benefit systems have been at best only a partial success in providing security for their members against the hazards of unemployment, sickness, disability, and old age which caused the unions to develop an enhanced interest in social insurance legislation.[3]

UNION HOUSING

A step beyond the paying of limited cash benefits to help meet economic hazards has been taken in New York City by several important unions. In 1926 the Amalgamated Clothing Workers, whose members work in the factories where men's clothing is made, sponsored a housing project in the Borough of the Bronx. Three years later the union encouraged a similar housing development in the heart of a congested area on New York's lower East Side. Extensive additions were made to the housing project in the Bronx in succeeding years. By 1950, 2,500 units, sufficient to house 10,000 people, had been brought into being by the union, at a total cost of $20 million.

The union assisted in arranging the mortgage financing of these cooperatives. In addition, the Amalgamated Bank helped arrange loans to enable the prospective cooperators to make the necessary down payments on their homes. Through having become stockholders in the cooperative the residents are, in effect, owners of the apartments they occupy.

Soon a number of cooperative activities,—economic, cultural, and recreational—were organized. From the beginning, an Amalgamated publication reports, "the Amalgamated Housing Corporation developed cooperative grocery, vegetable, and fruit stores within the

[2] For further details see Supplementary Notes.
[3] *Organized Labor* (New York: Harper & Brothers, 1945), p. 355.

project. . . . Educational and recreational activities were established," supervised by committees elected by the tenants. A playground, a kindergarten, and a summer day-camp for children were instituted. "Classes in dancing, music appreciation, and dramatics for boys and girls are conducted under the supervision of the Community Activities Department. . . . The auditorium, seating five hundred people, is utilized for lectures, debates, concerts, dances, and a weekly Sunday forum for discussion of current events." [4]

A similar housing cooperative with the International Ladies' Garment Workers' Union as a sponsor-mortgagee was opened in the fall of 1955. In a former slum area on New York's lower East Side, four 21- and 22-story apartment houses were built, with capacity to house over 1,600 families. Built at a cost of $19.2 million, on land purchased with the assistance of the federal government and New York State under slum clearance laws, these apartments represent an equity investment of $4.5 million by the tenant-owners. The union is making low-interest loans to tenants to start them as home owners.

Speaking at the dedication ceremonies in October 1955, David Dubinsky, president of the Union, paid a tribute to other unions that have "pioneered in the field of cooperative housing."

"The true glory of these wonderful structures," said Mr. Dubinsky, "lies in the power of the dream that made them come true—the faith that life in this nation can be something more than a slum. . . . These four structures are the social dividend of our faith in unionism. . . . They are monuments to men and women who believed strongly in freedom." [5]

Besides these developments sponsored by international unions, two local unions have entered the field of cooperative housing in the New York City area. Local 3 of the International Brotherhood of Electrical Workers recently completed a cooperative for 2,200 families. A local of the Amalgamated Meat Cutters has sponsored an enterprise that makes provision for 288 families. Other projects under the supervision of several groups of local unions are in the planning stage. Outside New York, the Automobile Workers Union is concerned in a housing development at Milpitas, California, near San Francisco, where 1,500

[4] Hyman H. Bookbinder and Associates, *To Promote the General Welfare—The Story of the New York Amalgamated Clothing Workers*, 1950, pp. 94–96.
[5] Report of Executive Board to ILGWU convention, May 1956, pp. 192–194.

homes are planned, though only 169 had been completed in early 1957. This is said to be the only sizable union-sponsored housing project outside the New York area.

In New York a privately organized, nonprofit organization, the United Housing Foundation, advises nonprofit organizations interested in launching cooperative housing projects. Through a separately incorporated subsidiary, Community Services, Inc., it gives technical assistance on a moderate fee basis, consistent with the nonprofit status of the Foundation.[6] Members of the Foundation include, among other civic and consumer groups, the unions that have built the cooperative houses referred to above, together with thirteen other union locals which are interested in cooperative housing.

EDUCATION

Organized labor in the United States from its beginnings in the early part of the nineteenth century has been deeply concerned about education. In the 1820s and 1830s when "pauperism was the chief principle" [7] upon which such public schools as existed were founded, organized labor in the Northeastern states was demanding free public schools, open to all. The Workingmen's Party of Philadelphia offered a bill in 1830 for the establishment of free schools, declaring that "its benefits and privileges will not, as at present, be limited as an act of charity to the poor alone, but will extend equally and of right to all classes, and be supported at the expense of all." [8] Organized labor

[6] The president of Community Services is Abraham Kazan, formerly an officer of the Amalgamated Clothing Workers, who has become a leading expert on cooperative housing. He directed the projects of both the Amalgamated Clothing Workers and the International Ladies' Garment Workers' Union, and most of the other important cooperative projects in New York City.

[7] Commons & Associates, *History of Labour in the United States* (New York: The Macmillan Co., 1918), Vol. I, p. 226.

[8] *Documentary History of American Industrial Society*, edited by John R. Commons (and others) (Cleveland, Ohio: Arthur H. Clark Co., 1910), Vol. V, p. 101.

The type of opposition which the advocates of a public-school system had to meet was indicated by an editorial in the Philadelphia *National Gazette* in the summer of 1830: "It is our strong inclination and our obvious interest that literary acquirements should be universal; but we should be guilty of imposture, if we professed to believe in the possibility of that consummation. Literature cannot be acquired without leisure, and wealth gives leisure." The editorial pointed out that the mechanic cannot abandon his work for general studies. If he did, the

continued to stand at the forefront of the advocates of a free public-school system until that battle was won; and ever since it has worked for improvement in the schools. William Schnitzler, Secretary-Treasurer of AFL-CIO, wrote in 1953: "It is the duty of every working man and woman to take a more active and energetic interest in the educational affairs of their communities, by working through parent-teacher associations, by seeking representation on boards of education, by supporting adequate school budgets, and by supporting candidates for office who will work for a stronger educational system." [9]

Labor is not concerned with the public schools alone, however. Because public schools, as a rule, do not supply all the skills and knowledge that the workers need, most unions with varying intensity attempt to provide additional instruction through conferences, institutes, and schools of their own devising. In certain areas there is collaboration between the labor organizations on the one hand and public bodies and employers on the other.

"The educational activities of unions," says Thomas C. Fichandler, "are as old as trade unionism itself. These activities began with the training of apprentices, which the skilled craft unions regarded as one of their major functions." [10] From this they went on to cooperate in the development of vocational schools. A notable example is the school for printers in New York, sponsored jointly by Local 6 of the Typographical Union, the employing printers, and the Board of Education. The Pressmen operate a technical school at their headquarters in Tennessee. Unions in the metal and building trades give much attention to the training of apprentices.

WORKERS' EDUCATION

Apprenticeship and vocational training programs, says Fichandler, are to make better workers; "workers' education [is] designed to make better union members." A study by Joseph Mire, published in 1956,

editorial went on, "most of the conveniences of life and objects of exchange would be wanting. . . . No government, no statesman, no philanthropist can furnish what is incompatible with the very organization and being of civil society." Ibid. pp. 107–108.

[9] Labor and Education in 1953, American Federation of Labor, 1953.

[10] Woytinsky and Associates, Employment and Wages in the United States (New York: The Twentieth Century Fund, 1953), p. 231.

defines the objectives of workers' education as "the improvement of the worker's individual and group competence and the advancement of his social, economic, and cultural interests, so that he can become a 'mature, wise, and responsible' citizen, able to play his part in the union and in a free society and to assume for himself a status of dignity and respect. . . ." [11]

The tremendous influx into the unions in recent years of new workers with no previous trade-union experience and with little knowledge of the method and purpose of trade unions makes it incumbent on the unions to close this gap in information in the interest of their own stability. Most unions do something in this field. Increasingly the internationals are setting up educational departments at union headquarters. Both AFL and CIO maintained agencies to deal with education which are now combined in the new organization. Some of the outstanding unions doing educational work among their members are the United Automobile Workers, the Textile Workers Union of America, the Machinists, the Communications Workers, the Paper Makers, the unions in the clothing trades, and the Steel Workers. Mire lists twenty-nine international unions "with major educational programs served by at least one full-time staff member."

A prominent figure in AFL-CIO summed up the educational activities in the pre-merger CIO, in a letter as follows:

The CIO has given strong emphasis to education from its very beginning, with an active educational department which operates directly in many states and also assists and encourages the international unions to establish their own departments. In the UAW the Education Department is supported by a fixed amount per capita which is determined by the constitution and can be spent only for this department. It has a large staff with field directors and top recognition in union activities. The Textile Workers have considered education as the basis of their entire program. The Steel Workers arrange for different universities to hold educational conferences for their members. The union movement's calendar is studded with one-day educational conferences, 2½ day weekend educational conferences, summer educational conferences of a week, and summer camps which combine education and vacation for their members.

[11] Joseph Mire, *Labor Education* (Inter-University Labor Education Committee, 1956), p. 17.

How this educational work is carried on may be indicated by a few illustrations.[12]

The Telephone Workers

The educational director of the Communications (Telephone) Workers of America plans the union's program, collects teaching material, and directs the work. At a center maintained by the union at Front Royal, Virginia, he trains and certifies union staff members for work as instructors. Ninety or more have been certified to act as instructors at two-day institutes that are conducted at strategic points throughout the country from March through the early fall. In a recent year 212 of these institutes for the training of local officers and stewards were held, with a total attendance of 3,300 persons. The field of study included history of the union, economics of the telephone industry, the work of stewards, preparation of grievance cases, and administration of the local union.

A second educational feature is a series of conferences, including one or two weeks' instruction, held in various sections of the country. Many of them take place at the center in Front Royal; others take place in the South, the Middle West, and the Far West. (It should be remembered that the telephone business is coterminous with the geographical limits of the country). To attend these courses a member must be certified by his local—one member from the smaller locals and an additional member for each 200 members above 100 in the larger locals. The local pays traveling expenses; lodging and board at the conference are provided by the international union. Two types of courses are given at these conferences, sometimes simultaneously: first, a basic course for beginners; second, an advanced training course open to those who have completed the basic course, or to elected officers of locals. The subjects dealt with in the advanced course include administration of the union, industry economics, political action, and leadership problems.

A third type of training course is for local union presidents only. This course deals with leadership problems, collective bargaining, and training in public speaking and parliamentary procedure.

[12] For extended coverage see Mire, op. cit., pp. 37–69.

Steel Workers and Machinists

In contrast to the Communication Workers' program of teaching union philosophy and techniques by qualified members of the union is the plan of the United Steel Workers. Since 1946 this union has been holding week-long classes in the summer on the campuses of co-operating colleges and universities. At the beginning arrangements were made with two universities only. In the summer of 1953 nineteen universities scattered through all sections of the country were cooperating with the union programs. Instruction is given by labor leaders and university professors. The courses include union problems and techniques, but lectures are given on broader subjects also. A three-day seminar on human relations held at Pennsylvania State College in 1951 had as speakers two university presidents, six university professors, two trade unionists, and one spokesman for management. In urging members to attend the classes President David J. McDonald of the international union said that the member would not only benefit himself, "but also aid in strengthening the broad base of our organization in the fields of trade unionism, community development, and political understanding."

The International Association of Machinists uses a different technique and has a somewhat different objective. Instead of all-day sessions of a few days or a week, their institutes are held in the evening after work hours and are generally scheduled for about a week. Everything is geared to suit the needs of the local lodge. Institutes are set up by the international union's education department only when they are requested by the local. Advance planning involves consultation with the local leaders to discover what they believe to be their specific needs. Members of the department then conduct the institutes through the medium of lectures and discussion.[13]

The Ladies' Garment Workers

The pioneer in the field of workers' education is the International Ladies' Garment Workers' Union. Its educational department was established in 1917, and immediately began to organize its work on a broad scale. The chairman of the education committee, Julius Hochman, writing in 1942 of the first twenty-five years of its work, said:

[13] See "IAM Training for Active Participation in Local Lodges," *Monthly Labor Review*, June 1952, pp. 653–657.

"We have attempted to give our members an opportunity to acquire knowledge and understanding of our country and union so as to equip them for better citizenship; as well as an opportunity for cultural development and self-expression through sports, drama, music, art, dancing and singing, and all that goes to make a full life." [14]

The annual reports of the education department give an account of each year's work. In the year ending in May 1953, 1,288 new members attended orientation classes, 2,178 members attended courses in labor problems and trade unionism, over 2,000 were in classes devoted to music and the drama, and nearly 1,200 studied arts and crafts. Language courses were given for some 800 members—French for the English-speaking workers in Montreal, English for Puerto Ricans in New York, and Spanish for the business agents who deal with them. The report lists 1,600 as engaged in "miscellaneous activities." In 1955–56 similar educational and cultural opportunities were taken advantage of by nearly 12,000 members.

A unique feature of the educational work of the Ladies' Garment Workers' Union is the training provided at union headquarters in New York for prospective staff members and officers. Since 1937 members wishing to become candidates in local elections for full-time paid positions in the union, and who have not previously held such offices, have been required to complete the courses offered.

A training institute for prospective staff members opened in 1950 calls for full-time attendance, equally divided between classes and field work, for a twelve-month period. Courses include the economics and the technical aspects of the garment industry, methods of union administration, and collective bargaining. Field work involves assignments to work in the day-to-day activities of union locals. Eligibility requirements include graduation from high school or an equivalent and membership in the age group of twenty-one to thirty-five. Besides these requirements, the most important qualification is "a sense of devotion to trade-union ideals." Preference is given to members of the union and to sons and daughters of members, though other qualified candidates can be admitted. Of 156 students who were accepted in the first six years (1951 to 1956), "49 were members of the ILGWU" and 51 were from families of members; thirty

[14] Report of the Educational Department, ILGWU, 1941–42, p. 3.

were members of other unions and 26 had no union affiliation. Graduates are assigned to staff positions with the union.[15]

American Labor Education Service

An agency outside the ranks of organized labor, but closely associated with it, which has been doing valuable work for thirty years in the field of workers' education is the American Labor Education Service. This organization advises unions about their educational problems, and is constantly engaged in conducting adult-education courses for labor groups and others in various parts of the country. In recent years its energies have been devoted in large part to promoting interest in and understanding of international affairs. Institutes and classes for the discussion of problems in this field have been conducted in industrial centers and in several agricultural states of the Middle West where farmers and wage earners come together for study.

As a result of these efforts, interest among union members in American foreign policy and conditions in foreign countries has been greatly stimulated. The American Labor Education Service has brought trade unionists to New York for guided tours of United Nations headquarters, where they attended sessions of the General Assembly and listened to addresses by delegates, members of the Secretariat, or other experts. Out of such visits developed a "school project," with daily sessions for a period of a week. Students were sent by their local unions, which paid transportation costs, with maintenance in New York provided by the Service. Students on their return home organized week-end conferences where they shared their knowledge with others, or arranged institutes of longer duration with speakers from universities and other persons experienced in inter-

[15] Data derived from interviews, from annual reports of the Education Department, and from the report of the General Executive Board to the 29th Convention of the International Ladies' Garment Workers' Union, May 10, 1956, pp. 195–203. See also "ILGWU Approach to Leadership Training," *Monthly Labor Review,* November 1951. The following announcement concerning the 1957–58 course appeared as an advertisement in the *New Republic,* January 21, 1957: "The International Ladies' Garment Workers' Union Training Institute offers an opportunity to young men and women in the 21-35 age group interested in making service to the trade union movement their life work. . . . All students satisfactorily completing the year's field and class work are guaranteed positions with the ILGWU."

national affairs. The organization promoted a conference in Cleveland in January 1956 on the Social and Industrial Implications of Atomic Energy; it was planned jointly with local trade unions and attended by nearly 500 persons.

Altogether the services rendered to their members by local and international unions outside the scope of collective bargaining is impressive. It ranges from setting up various forms of financial safeguards against industrial hazards through efforts in the direction of cooperative housing to educational activities at technical and cultural levels; finally, it introduces a world-wide view with respect to problems that are of concern to men and women everywhere. Thus steps are taken in the direction of a broader understanding of the issues that confront not only the working people but society itself.

9

The Union and Its Members

Most competent observers agree that labor organizations have improved the lot of their members. There are some outstanding economists who hold that labor's share in the national product has not been influenced to any great extent by the unions, but that is far from saying that the member derives no benefit from his membership. Indeed, Professor Kenneth Boulding—who holds that there is "no evidence whatever" that unions have had much effect on wages, and that "with the exception of the monopolistic corners, the strictly economic gains of unionism are what workers as a whole would have got anyhow"—still regards the labor movement "as an enormously important and necessary force in Western society, which has performed the almost miraculous achievement of virtually abolishing the proletariat. . . ." [1]

Union members generally would heartily agree with the latter conclusion, as would most nonmember observers, except the die-hard opponents of organized labor. Evidence in support of that belief is readily available. Members of the Ladies' Garment Workers' Union, now fully protected by collectively bargained contracts, remember not only the sweatshop days of their fathers but the Triangle fire of 1911 and the locked door which brought death to more than a hundred women. The Amalgamated Clothing Workers, one of the strongest unions in the country, recalls its struggle in the Hart, Shaffner and Marx strike of 1910 to win from employers the right to bargain about their wages, and then the further struggle within the labor movement itself to maintain their organization.

When the railroad men established their Brotherhoods, the purpose at the outset was to provide for themselves the life and casualty insurance that they could not get from the existing insurance companies because of the hazards of their employment. Later, under the

[1] *The Organizational Revolution* (New York: Harper & Brothers, 1953), pp. 43, 94, 263.

urging of the unions, federal legislation was enacted requiring the use of safety devices in railway service.

Similarly, the United Mine Workers has obtained legislation requiring safety precautions in the operation of mines. The latest important action in this field was a federal law authorizing the United States Bureau of Mines to close down a mine that disregarded the safety code. In other respects the coal miners have through their union come a long way since 1902, when the president of a railroad serving the anthracite region justified his refusal to confer with union representatives on the ground that the welfare of the workers was safely in the hands of the "Christian gentlemen to whom God, in his infinite wisdom, has entrusted the property interests of the country."

Reference is made in the Preface to the study of labor conditions in the steel industry made many years ago under the direction of Professor Commons and the able leadership of Paul Kellogg, editor of the *Survey*.[2] The practice referred to there as to the almost incredibly long working hours was modified somewhat as the years passed. A stockholders' movement in 1911 initiated by Charles M. Cabot of Boston led to a lessening of the 7-day requirement in mills of the United States Steel Corporation. In 1923, the steel companies generally, under political pressure and after an extraordinary manifestation of public opinion led by religious organizations, formally abandoned the 12-hour day.

It remained, however, for the union-organizing campaigns of the early 1930s, following the enactment of the Recovery Act in 1933 and the Wagner Act of 1935, to bring about thoroughgoing changes. Under the protection of these laws the CIO Steel Workers' Organizing Committee was formed and led a campaign that launched the United Steel Workers, which now has over a million members. The first union contract in twenty-eight years was signed in 1937 by officers of United States Steel, and later by all the leading steel companies. Shortly before it was signed, the spy system was abolished. The contract ended the unilateral settlement of grievances and established the 8-hour day. The 40-hour week then followed.[3]

[2] John A. Fitch, *The Steel Workers* (New York: Charities Publication Committee, 1910).

[3] The above data relating to hours refer to production workers only. The average

I asked a man who had had many years' experience as union organizer, as minor and major executive, and as director of union activities over a wide geographical area to tell me what benefits union organization had brought to the workers during his long term of service. This was his answer: "When I began as organizer I was assigned to an industry in which the labor force consisted largely of young girls. They were paid about $5 a week, on the average. They couldn't live on it. Some of them lived with their parents who supplemented their earnings and thus subsidized the industry. The bosses in the plants took advantage of their helplessness. Many of them turned to prostitution from economic necessity. Now the wage level in this industry is still low, but it is seven to eight times what it was a generation ago and, despite the increased cost of consumers' goods, it provides a living. The increased wage brought about by the union and the very existence of the union protects them from the moral hazards of the pre-union days, and promotes their comfort and well-being."

This man had had a good deal of experience organizing and administering union activities in the textile industry in the South, and I asked him about that.

"When I went to that job," he said, "the workers were shabby and poor. You could always tell cotton mill workers on the street by their clothes—the same cheap cotton attire that they wore in the mill. The factory girls were easily distinguished by their unattractive clothing and their unkempt hair. Now, in the same towns, after twenty years of trade unionism, you can't tell the difference between the girls from the mills and the others. They have the same attractive clothes and the same permanents.

---

length of the work week for all employees of the United States Steel Corporation was on the indicated dates as follows:

Date		Hours
1912	When the 7-day week requirement was modified	69.0
1924	After the practical abolition of the 12-hour day	52.8
1920–29	Average for the decade	55.6
1930–36	Depression years' average	33.9
1937	When the first union contract since 1909 was signed	37.6
1938–55	Average	37.5

SOURCE: *Annual Report*, U. S. Steel Corporation, 1955, p. 30.

"Standards have been raised all along the line. Illiteracy is being wiped out. When our organizing campaign began, a majority of the workers, white and black, couldn't sign their names. Applications for union membership were signed with an 'X.' Children were taken out of school at an early age to help out the family income by working in the mills. Now they are going through High School. Adequate diets are wiping out TB which used to be prevalent. The workers are taking their part in community affairs."

There are other areas in which unions have made a valuable contribution to improvements in working conditions. Perhaps few examples are more impressive than the case of the Red Caps and the Pullman porters.

Red Caps and Pullman Porters

Prior to 1938, when the Red Caps formed their union (The United Transport Service Employees) these men, who carry luggage on and off trains, were not on any payroll. They were independent enterprisers, receiving no wages and dependent exclusively on tips. Their first act as a union was an appeal to the Interstate Commerce Commission to declare them to be "employees," and so to be protected in their right to organize and to bargain collectively under the guarantees of the Railway Labor Act. Having won this appeal in September 1938, they became entitled at once to the wage of 25 cents per hour under the original requirement of the Fair Labor Standards Act, which became law in the same year. After representation elections held in 1939 by the National (RR) Mediation Board, which the union won by a vote of 85 per cent of those participating, contracts were negotiated with ten railroads.[4] Beginning with the 25 cents hourly wage in 1938, a series of contract negotiations brought this rate to $1.16 in 1949. In 1951 the figure was $1.39 and the agreement negotiated as of March 1, 1956, brought the hourly wage to $1.63, or approximately $65 for a 40-hour week.[5]

The Brotherhood of Sleeping Car Porters came into being in 1925. At that time the minimum rate of pay for Pullman porters was $67 a

[4] Since then the area of negotiation has been widened, and bargaining is now conducted on an industry-wide basis.

[5] Data from "thumb-nail" history published in connection with the 8th Biennial Convention of United Transport Service Employees, 1952; and conference with J. K. Mebane, Recording Secretary, New York City Local.

month. The Pullman Company had set up a company union, through which a series of wage advances was negotiated. These brought the minimum monthly wage to $77.50 in 1935. Two years later the first contract between the Pullman Company and the Brotherhood of Sleeping Car Porters was signed. Minimum pay was increased to $89.50. Further negotiations brought the minimum to $113.50 in 1941 and to $137.50 in 1943.[6] In 1956 the minimum monthly rate for Pullman porters was $326, and the maximum, based on length of service, was $336.[7] At all times the basic pay of sleeping car porters is enhanced by tips, the average amount of which is not generally known.

Wage increases are the result of many pressures such as competition and the cost of living as well as trade-union activity. They are made possible by increased productivity arising frequently from more skillful management and technological advance. Without challenging here the judgment of the economists who agree with Professor Boulding, the experience of the railway station and Pullman porters is convincing evidence of the importance and effectiveness of a union where substandard conditions have prevailed.

The limited illustrations given above, which are believed to be typical, demonstrate the type of service that unions can and do render their members.

But this is not the whole story of the relation of the union, and particularly the leadership, to the rank-and-file. Questions are frequently asked about this relationship. In the rendering of service, is the union an agency for carrying out the will of the members, specifically and authoritatively expressed, or is it a master, benevolent probably, but still a master? In other words, are the unions democratically run? Does power emerge from the ranks, or is it a function of office holding?

CENTRALIZATION OF AUTHORITY

The tendency over the years has been in the direction of centraliza-

[6] Brailsford R. Brazeal, The Brotherhood of Sleeping Car Porters (New York: Harper & Brothers, 1946), p. 219. See also Spero and Harris, The Black Worker (New York: Columbia University Press, 1931).
[7] Letter to author from A. Philip Randolph, President, Brotherhood of Sleeping Car Porters, March 1, 1956.

tion of authority. The usual pattern of organization includes a president, a secretary-treasurer, and several vice-presidents, who together constitute an executive board. These officers are elected, either by the convention, consisting of delegates from the various local bodies, or by referendum vote of the entire membership. When the latter is the practice, candidates in some unions are nominated by the conventions. The more usual practice, however, in referendum elections, is for nominations also to be made by referendum. The names of candidates submitted by the required number of locals—the required minimum is reasonably low—are printed on ballots which are then distributed by the headquarters office to the membership.

This is a democratic procedure, insuring an opportunity for full expression of preference by the qualified voters. Unless, therefore, there is fraud in the counting of the ballots—and seldom has such a charge been made—the officers so elected are obviously the real choice of the membership, even though the number of members who vote in such elections may be relatively small.

When the convention elects the officers, as is the practice in the great majority of the unions, there is less certainty of rank-and-file approval. This is the case not only because the delegates are a step removed from the membership, but also because most of them are far from home and because deals are possible when a few hundred voters come together for the sole purpose of transacting the business of the union. Moreover, the delegates are usually the most active members of the locals and often are ambitious for advancement in the union. Some of them, also, are paid organizers appointed by the international president, and thus constitute a patronage group loyal to the administration.

For these reasons—the small number voting in the referendum and the existence of mixed motives among the convention delegates—the officers when elected seem to constitute a body of considerable independence, existing at some distance from the membership. It is this factor that gives special importance to the powers vested in the national officers by the union constitutions.

Presidential Authority

Some of the powers that may be exercised by international presidents are worth mentioning here. Typical of union constitutions generally are the provisions in the constitution of the Bricklayers, Masons and Plasterers Union. The president is given general control over the local bodies of his union. In exercising this power, he may visit the locals, inspect their books, require observance of the laws and rules of the parent body, and, "in the event he shall find that in his judgment" any local or its officers are failing to comply with the rules and usages of the union, "in his discretion he may appoint a receiver" for the local who is to "take full charge of and manage the affairs" of the local "with all the power of a receiver in a court of law" and continue to do so until the local is in full compliance with the constitution and rules.

Similar authority is vested in the president by nearly all the unions. In most cases, but not in all, his actions are subject to the approval of the executive board. Other powers possessed by the president usually include the appointment and removal of organizers and other subordinate staff members and the fixing of their salaries, sometimes subject to the approval of the executive board and sometimes without requiring such approval.

Less typical are certain extraordinary presidential powers listed in the constitutions of some organizations. An example is a clause in the constitution of the former AFL Automobile Workers—now known as the Allied Industrial Workers of America—which gives the president power to "summarily expel" a member for violation of the constitution or local by-laws or for such other causes as are "deemed sufficient by him to require prompt and immediate action on his part." An added clause, following this grant of power, reads: "The power herein conferred upon the International President is an emergency power, to be used sparingly."

The constitution of the United Textile Workers of America contains the following provision: "When in the opinion of the International President any affiliated organization, any officer thereof, or any member or group of members . . . act, have acted or contemplate or threaten to act, in violation of the constitution or against the policies or best interest of the International Union, he shall declare an emergency to exist" and after such a declaration "he shall have full and complete power and authority to suspend the charter of any local union" or other affiliate, remove officers, "suspend from membership any member . . ." and "assume all power and authority hereinbefore vested in the International Executive Council." Action under this provision is subject to appeal to the next meeting of the Executive Council, which meets every three months, and from there to the convention, which meets every two years. Meanwhile, "in any event . . . the emergency action of the International President and the subsequent decision of the International Executive Council upon same shall remain in full force and effect until a final decision has been made on any appeal taken from such action or decision to the International Convention."

In no other union, so far as a rather extensive examination of constitutions reveals, is such extraordinary power given to a president as is done by the American Federation of Musicians (AFM). Robert D. Leiter in a book dealing with that union quotes Article I, Section 1 of the by-laws as follows: [8]

Duties of President . . . It shall be his duty and prerogative to exercise supervision over the affairs of the Federation; to make decisions in cases where, in his opinion, an emergency exists; and to give effect to such decisions he is authorized and empowered to promulgate and issue executive orders, which shall be conclusive and binding upon all members and/ or locals; any such order may by its terms (a) enforce the Constitution, By-laws, standing Resolutions, or other laws, resolutions or rules of the Federation, or (b) may annul or set aside same or any portion thereof, except such which treat with the finances of the organization, and substitute therefor other and different provisions of his own making. . . . (Constitution, By-laws, and Standing Resolutions, 1947, p. 20).

The following is Mr. Leiter's comment on the above:

These vast powers have been assigned to the President of the AFM since 1919, and, although they never have been utilized to the disadvantage of musicians, the president has no clear check on his discretion. In almost all cases where the president has had to make hasty decisions he has consulted and received the unanimous approval of the executive board.

DISCIPLINE AND PENALTIES

Union constitutions generally provide certain limitations on the activities of members, under the general head of "discipline" or

[8] Robert D. Leiter, *The Musicians and Petrillo* (New York: Bookman Associates, 1953), p. 77.

"offenses" or "penalties." The forbidden activities generally include such offenses as would be outlawed in any organization of sensible persons. They include violations of the union constitution and all sorts of misconduct ranging from drunkenness at a union meeting to felony. Other restrictions have to do with behavior involving the particular relationship of the member with his union. The constitutions forbid revealing to outsiders the affairs of the union.

Other prohibitions, however, are of wider scope, including distributing circulars attacking any officer of the union, making false accusations against an officer or a member, or "impugning the motives or questioning the integrity" of an officer. In many constitutions members are forbidden to discuss union affairs anywhere but at a regularly-scheduled meeting in the meeting hall.

The following is a list of acts subject to penalty, excerpted from a union constitution:

Resorting to a court of law [without first exhausting remedies provided by the union].

Violating any provision of this constitution.

Obtaining membership by fraudulent means. . . .

Publishing false reports among the membership or making false statements about the union to public officials or others.

Creating or attempting to create dissension [among members or local unions].

Working in the interest of any organization or cause detrimental to or opposed to [the union].

Slandering or otherwise wronging a member.

Attending union meetings when intoxicated.

Making known the business of a local union to persons not entitled to such knowledge.

Fraudulently receiving or misappropriating the money of any local union.

Attending or participating in any gathering or meeting whatsoever, held outside meetings of a local union at which the affairs of the union are discussed, or at which conclusions are arrived at regarding the business and the affairs of a local union or regarding officers or a candidate or candidates for local union office.

Mailing, handing out, or posting cards, handbills, letters, marked ballots or political literature of any kind, or displaying streamers, banners, signs or anything else of a political nature, or being a party in any way to such being done in an effort to induce members to vote for or against any candidate or candidates for local union office, or candidates to conventions.

Absent from the above list are some of the more vaguely-phrased offenses that appear in many constitutions. The vaguest term of all— and it appears in the great majority of union constitutions—is "conduct unbecoming a member." Many of the constitutions contain no definition of this term. Some recognize the difficulty involved by requiring the complainant to specify in writing the nature of the conduct to which objection is made.

A few of the unions are more meticulous. The National Association of Broadcast Employees and Technicians requires all charges to be in the form of affidavits which must "recite clearly and concisely the offense charged . . . particulars with respect to the violation or conduct complained of," the sections of the constitution involved, and the names of witnesses. The constitution of the International Association of Machinists sets forth with precision the offenses that are to be considered conduct "unbecoming a member." The Typographical Union requires that any charge brought against a member "must be signed by the complainant and shall be sufficiently specific as to the provisions of union law violated, and the alleged acts which constitute the basis of the charges, to permit the defendant to prepare a proper defense." Both of these unions require that a vote by a local on the question of guilt of a member shall be by secret ballot.

When a union member is charged with an offense under the constitution, he is usually tried by the local body of which he is a member. The procedure is much the same in the different unions. First, the complaint is lodged with the local president. It is read at a meeting of the local and the president appoints a committee to investigate. The committee holds a hearing, collects evidence, and reports back to a meeting of the local, indicating its opinion with respect to innocence or guilt, and in case of the latter makes a recommendation with respect to a penalty. The local then votes to approve or reject the report of the committee. Usually an appeal may be taken to the president of the international union or to the general executive board, and from these officials to the convention, which has the final word.

CENTRALIZATION—A CRITICAL VIEW

Some competent observers see in the trend toward centralization and the limitations on members' activity merely sensible arrangements making for efficient administration. Others consider the trend little less than a betrayal of democracy. A few excerpts from the writings of some of these observers may serve to point up the divergence of opinion.

Kermit Eby, formerly director of Research and Education for the CIO and now a professor at the University of Chicago, wrote a few years ago that "the power structure of the labor movement . . . is hierarchical, monolithic, and guilty of persistent top-level policy decisions." [9]

Some years earlier, Will Herberg, then educational director for the Dress and Waist Makers local of the Ladies' Garment Workers' Union in New York, wrote a challenging criticism of union bureaucracy.[10] "The rank-and-file union members," he wrote, "frequently enjoy less freedom in relation to their own union leader than they do in relation to their employer." In the administration of his union "he sometimes has less to say than, thanks to collective bargaining, he has in the affairs of his shop or factory."

Mr. Herberg called attention to the dual role of the modern labor organization. Unions are "business-like service organizations . . . which require efficient bureaucratic administration, very much like a bank or insurance company . . ." and at the same time "an expression and vehicle of the historical movement of the submerged laboring masses for social recognition and democratic self-determination. . . ." As such, it is "an idealistic, quasi-religious collectivity . . . a crusading reform movement of which the members . . . and their democratic self-expression are the very essence."

[9] "A Critical Look at Labor," *Labor & Nation*, Fall 1951.
[10] "Bureaucracy and Democracy in Labor Unions," *Antioch Review*, September 1943.

In the early days of union development, Mr. Herberg said, the latter spirit was dominant. But with growth and power "the businesslike service aspect comes to the fore," and then the exercise of power becomes a function of top leadership. Even an idealistic administration becomes inevitably "practical" and "realistic." This arises "out of the very nature of large scale organization." Bureaucracy becomes essential to efficient, sustained administration. "Legislative power gradually passed from the membership meeting, first to the executive board and then, by a further remove, to the paid officials ('the office')." The office rules. "Membership meeting becomes a mere plebiscitary body . . . also a medium through which the directives of the leadership are transmitted to the masses of members."

This whittling down of democracy, Mr. Herberg suggests, is a gradual thing, coming into being almost imperceptibly. Eventually the members get used to it and even like it. The member "doesn't want self-government. . . . What he wants is protection and service, his money's worth for his dues." Thus the officials become members of "a privileged caste, devoted to keeping themselves in office."

The thing needed to change this trend, Mr. Herberg concludes, is "a profound transformation in the moral atmosphere. What is needed is the creation of a labor conscience"—a "labor civic morality" among the masses. Among the leaders "what is fundamentally needed is a powerful social idealism capable of mitigating, controlling, and transcending the crudities of personal ambition and power politics."

Clyde Summers, Professor of Law at the University of Buffalo, is a severe critic of the trend toward centralization of authority in the unions. While conceding that the number of discipline cases in which power is abused is "probably very small," he is of the opinion that "the problem of union discipline . . . is important because it involves the individual rights of a member within his union. It is a problem of civil liberties." [11]

In a paper presented at the Fifth New York University Conference on Labor, in 1952, Professor Summers discussed further the civil liberties aspect of union discipline. Citing constitutional provisions that he considers a threat to the individual, he pointed out that fifteen international unions have provisions prohibiting the issuing of

[11] *Industrial & Labor Relations Review*, July 1950, pp. 486, 487.

any circular among the membership without the consent of the international officers; nine unions prohibit the organizing of any group within the union whose purpose is to shape its policies or influence the choice of officers . . . seventy-four unions have clauses . . . which limit the criticism of officers and fellow members. . . . Closely akin are the clauses that prohibit the filing of "unfounded or malicious charges," which appear in thirty-five constitutions.

Beyond these more specific clauses, almost all unions have vague and general catch-all clauses . . . which prohibit "any act or conduct in violation of their obligation or anything detrimental to the union." These clauses, by their very vagueness, are particularly susceptible to abuse.

After citing a number of cases before courts and administrative agencies involving penalties against members for various acts in opposition to the union leaders,[12] Professor Summers continued:

The instances of political discipline which have been cited do not represent normal union practices, for these clauses customarily lie dormant. . . . This, however, does not lessen the relevance of these cases, for they do represent the potential danger. . . . Almost every union has some clause (in its constitution) which can be readily used to curb those who seek changes in policy or leadership. The very presence of these provisions creates an atmosphere of caution, and only occasional use of them can produce a paralyzing fear. The reported cases make clear that these clauses have been used repeatedly against political dissenters. . . . Thus a dangerous shadow of fear is cast over the political freedom of union members.

A More Favorable View

A different view is expressed in a book [13] by Professor Philip Taft of Brown University. He reviews the policies which, according to Herberg and Summers, lead to autocracy and suppression of the rank and file. He does not deny the existence of these policies, but he explains them and points to counteracting forces which, in his opinion, modify the results.

"It is necessary," says Professor Taft (p. 35), "to keep in mind the

[12] Proceedings of the New York University Fifth Annual Conference on Labor, 1952, pp. 443–480.
[13] *The Structure and Government of Labor Unions* (Cambridge, Mass.: Harvard University Press, 1954).

difference between a labor union and society at large. A union, unlike civil society, is a single purpose organization," its principal objective being "the protection of the economic interests of its members." The importance of this objective is such that "a union must be prepared to take defensive or offensive economic action involving discipline and sacrifice by its members." A hot election campaign for union offices, "or even the building up of a following in order to challenge a general officer may tend to undermine the cohesiveness upon which a union's existence depends."

Then, too, since "an opposition must raise issues, attack established policies, and attempt to discredit the incumbent officer," an adverse effect on employer-union relations may be engendered. "How are unpalatable compromises to be made and how are contracts . . . to be enforced when the intelligence or integrity of the leaders are questioned?"

As to the alleged invasion of the rights of individual members that may be inferred from many of the prohibitory clauses, both Summers and Taft point out that the rule does not always reveal the practice. As Professor Taft puts it, "the constitutional powers granted are not an adequate guide to the realities of union political life." He states that union presidents seldom exercise the right to take over the administration of locals, and, when they do, it is usually necessary to prevent disregard of union contracts, misuse of funds, or maladministration by the officers.

Professor Taft believes that curbs on membership activity are essential safeguards of union integrity and strength in the economic struggle in which the union is engaged. The implication is that the union is like an advancing army, the members of which simply cannot be permitted to attack their leaders, or go off on individually-planned forays of their own. He concedes that "the prohibitions contained in most union constitutions against issuing circulars without approval of the officers, or against undermining the union or defaming officers, would hinder the formation of formal and organized opposition to chief officers," but for the reasons cited he does not consider this an evil.

In contrast to Professor Summers' contention that charges against union members are tried by the very officers who have been offended by the activities complained of, Professor Taft states that more often than not the defendant is acquitted by the local body having original jurisdiction, regardless of the evidence; and that appeals to the higher echelons are necessary to insure an objective examination of the evidence.

SOME CONCLUSIONS

What shall be said of this conflict of opinion among the experts? A defense of the practices discussed here that is offered by responsible union leaders is the alleged precarious position of the unions. These leaders believe that powerful antagonistic forces are still plotting the destruction of the unions. It is easy, they say, for an "enemy" spy to get a job, join the union, and become a leader of an opposition within the ranks. The members of this group may be sincerely desirous of promoting the best interests of the union, while their leader is intent on creating confusion and weakness. In the light of this possibility, the union that tries to operate on the basis of a New England town meeting, these leaders believe, is doomed.

Another factor deserving of careful consideration is the size of present-day unions and the character of their membership. When unions were in their infancy they were the outgrowth of grass-roots activity. The "self-organization" referred to in the Wagner and Taft-Hartley laws was an actuality—the workers organized themselves and every member knew that he was a part of the whole. Now, even the smaller unions—say of 10,000 to 25,000 members—are the result of the work of salaried organizers following a more or less elaborate technique. When new groups of workers are organized, the impetus and direction come from the top. This is the result of the complexity of organization of industry as well as that of the union, and it makes an important difference. The membership includes a very considerable proportion who are newcomers both to industry and to unionism, such as recent high school graduates, recruits from rural areas, and housewives. They have not participated in the formation of the union; they have found it already functioning when they got their jobs. They join because it is the thing to do; some of them because, as in a union shop, they have to join to hold their jobs. These workers are not acquainted with labor history and have a middle-class outlook. They are neither pioneers nor agitators; they pay their dues and hope not to be disturbed. Their presence creates a problem of considerable magnitude for the union leaders and for the hard core of convinced and enthusiastic members.

If this is a problem for the small unions, it is greater in the unions that bargain not for tens of thousands but for hundreds of thousands of members. A member of a relatively small union told me of attending a meeting of the Detroit local representing the Ford workers. He was greatly impressed with the attendance: three or four hundred were there. Later he learned that the local had 60,000 members.

When the present scene is viewed as a whole, it is possible to understand the feeling of responsible union leaders that a powerful bureaucracy is essential to the proper functioning of a union. It is possible to see the logic of Professor Taft's position. But there is danger, it seems to me, that logic and understanding may lead, however inadvertently, toward condoning abuses when they do occur.

Professor Summers describes an episode involving the Operative Potters Union [14] which has received considerable publicity elsewhere.[15] The officers "voted themselves" an increase in salary early in 1947. A group in the union claimed the increases were illegal in that the officers had usurped a power that under the union constitution belonged only to the membership or to the convention, and they campaigned against the re-election of the officers. The latter were successful, however, and the convention which met in June of that year amended the constitution to provide that a member convicted by the convention of "false accusations," or the use of "degrading literature," could be punished. The recalcitrant group continued its attack both by publishing leaflets criticizing the officers and by a successful appeal to the courts to enjoin the officers' salary increase. After the 1948 convention had amended the constitution again to provide penalties for this sort of conduct, the rebels were fined $50 apiece and barred from holding union office for a term of years.[16]

"This episode," writes Professor Summers, "does not depict the normal use of union discipline. It does, however, reveal some of the most critical aspects of union discipline and dramatically illustrates its potentiality for destroying union democracy."

[14] Proceedings of the New York University Conference on Labor, 1952, p. 45.

[15] Jack Barbash, The Practice of Unionism (New York: Harper & Brothers, 1956), pp. 70–71.

[16] According to Barbash, op. cit., "The opposition again turned to the courts and the disciplinary action was revoked."

We may agree with Professor Taft that a union cannot be run like a high school literary society, and still find logic in Professor Summers' position. It is reasonable to expect the unions to put up barriers against the abuses cited; in fact, it seems imperative that they should. Even one such case is a challenge to the whole structure.

A weak point in the appeals procedure provided for in union constitutions is that which makes the convention the final arbiter. If the conventions are held at reasonably frequent intervals, the appellant may not have to wait an unreasonable time for a final hearing. An interval of one year between conventions seems reasonable. But some unions meet in convention at intervals of two or three years, or even longer. A publication of the United States Bureau of Labor Statistics [17] reports, among other items, prevailing practices of unions with respect to the time of holding conventions. The report shows that of 206 unions answering questionnaires (including departments of some unions), 16 gave no information on the subject of conventions and ten reported that no conventions are held. All of these 26 unions are small.

Of the 180 unions reporting on this point 39 hold conventions annually and 70, biennially; nineteen unions, every three years; 27, every four years; and there are 12 unions whose conventions take place only in every fifth year. The remaining 13 unions (or departments) reported various or miscellaneous practices. All of these are small unions except the Hod Carriers, Building and Common Laborers Union, which reported 433,000 members and which holds a "membership referendum every five years" on the question of holding a convention. Thus nearly two-thirds of all unions reporting hold conventions at intervals of two years or more—a long time for a suspended or expelled member to wait for a final adjudication. The problem is intensified by the provision in most union constitutions that makes it an offense to appeal to the civil courts before exhausting all the remedies provided by the union. The Upholsterers Union has met the situation by setting up a board of appeals having authority to make final decisions and consisting of neutral outsiders, not members of the union. The Automobile Workers at their 1957 convention took similar action.

[17] *Directory of National and International Labor Unions in the United States, 1955*, Bulletin 1185.

The union that has gone farthest in attempting to assure fair procedure in trials and appeals is the International Typographical Union. This union is frequently cited as the most democratic of American unions. It does not try to prevent the development of opposition within its ranks. In fact, it has long harbored two recognized "political" parties which regularly nominate candidates for office and campaign vigorously in their behalf. The practice of this union with respect to trials and appeals as outlined in the constitution is worth noting in some detail.

When a member is charged with an offense against the union, two copies of the charges are delivered to the president of the local, one of which is sent to the accused member. At the next meeting of the local the charges are read and discussed, after which "the following question shall be put to a vote by secret ballot: 'Shall the charges as presented be cognizable?' " If the vote is affirmative, the presiding officer appoints a committee of five members (three in the smaller locals) to investigate the charges. This committee reports its findings at the next meeting of the local and the members then vote, again by secret ballot, on whether the charges are serious enough to justify a trial. If the vote is in favor of a trial, the presiding officer appoints a committee to conduct it. But if either party objects to the personnel selected, the committee is to be drawn by lot from the members present.

At the hearings before this committee both parties are entitled to counsel who must be members of the union, and either party may demand that witnesses be sworn. At the next meeting after the trial committee has reached a decision, its report is read to the members and the accused may defend himself before the union. After consideration and debate the members vote by secret ballot for conviction or acquittal. If the vote affirms the guilt of the accused, another secret ballot is taken on the penalty to be imposed. It takes a two-thirds vote to convict and a three-fourths vote of members present to impose a penalty of suspension or expulsion. Thus three secret votes by the members of the local are essential for conviction and a fourth vote is required before the heaviest penalty can be imposed. An appeal may be taken to the higher officers of the union, and for a final decision to the convention, which meets annually.

The facts presented in this chapter reveal two seemingly contradictory trends. On the one hand the unions provide services of utmost value to their members and thus invite their loyalty; on the other hand, centralization of authority and rules that restrict—in some cases practically destroy—the independence and initiative of the rank-and-file member encourage indifference or, at the worst, disaffection. These rules have emerged, in part at least, from the precarious hold on the right to exist that has been the lot of many of the unions in the past; they are relics of a period of struggle and are now defended as essential to effective administration. In their extreme application, however, they create an elite power group capable of exercising such firm control over the membership as in some cases to encourage corrupt practices.

The experiences and practices of the Typographical Union indicate that it is possible for efficient administration and adherence to democratic principles to go hand in hand. Yet nothing is more important from an ethical point of view than recognition that human beings of whatever class or station are susceptible to corruption by the lure of power, prestige, and financial advantage and must be held strictly accountable to those from whom their authority derives.

10

Inter-Union Relations

The constitution of the American Federation of Labor as adopted at its founding in 1886,[1] and as it stood in 1955 before merging with the CIO, contained a declaration that one of the objects of the Federation should be "the establishment of National and International Trade Unions, based upon a strict recognition of the autonomy of each trade. . . ." This assurance was emphasized by a declaration in a later clause of the constitution that "we recognize the right of each trade to manage its own affairs. . . ." However, the word "autonomy" in AFL discussions has often been used to refer to a union's range of jurisdiction as well as its self-government. Throughout the history of the American labor movement the effort to set boundaries to the area of activity of the different unions has caused many a headache.

In 1900 a clause was added to the AFL constitution which declared that in the future any organization seeking admission to the Federation must present "a positive and clear definition of the trade jurisdiction claimed," and if it should appear that the claim constituted "a trespass on the jurisdiction of existing affiliated unions," a charter of affiliation should not be granted.

These two concepts, self-government and exclusive jurisdiction, are doubtless among the essentials that helped to make possible the development and continuity of federation in the American labor move-

[1] The American Federation of Labor from 1889 on has considered 1881 as the year of its founding. Its 1955 convention, consequently, is listed in its records as the "74th Annual Convention." The body that was created in 1881 was officially named "Federation of Organized Trades and Labor Organizations of the United States and Canada." Its activities were almost wholly devoted to legislative objectives. In 1886 it met as an organized body with a group of delegates from trade unions which had not joined the 1881 federation. Together they created a new organization which they named the American Federation of Labor. This federation after three years voted in 1889 "that the continuity of the American Federation of Labor be recognized and dated from the year 1881 in all future documents issued."

ment during its early years. Nevertheless, they have been the source of embarrassment and conflict almost from the beginning, and at times both have been disregarded in the interest of expediency.

Autonomy

The right of each affiliated national or international union to govern itself has seldom been challenged in either the AFL or the CIO, though the latter was never as positive in the assertion of the right as the AFL. The word "autonomy" so carefully proclaimed in the AFL constitution did not appear anywhere in the corresponding CIO document. When the CIO was formed, self-government was taken for granted in the older unions; but the recently organized unions and those just coming into being under the leadership of "organizing committees" were without experienced leadership within their own ranks and looked to the older unions for guidance. For a number of years, therefore, some of the newer unions were not self-governing in the fullest sense of the term. The very organizers who did the most effective work in setting them up were frequently men from other industries. The president of the CIO sometimes presided over meetings of constituent unions and to some extent directed their affairs.

A group of experienced organizers most of whom were members of the United Mine Workers led in organizing the steel workers. The chairman of the organizing committee was Philip Murray, then a vice-president of the United Mine Workers. John L. Lewis, its president and first president of CIO, negotiated the first agreement for the Automobile Workers in 1937, and performed the same service that year for the Steel Workers Organizing Committee. When the latter became the United Steel Workers, Philip Murray was elected as its first president, and continued in that office until his death in 1952. As the newer CIO unions gained strength and experience they began to develop their own leaders and have now become as autonomy-conscious as the others.

To what extent the doctrine that each union is master in its own house has been disregarded by the federations is uncertain. At times small unions have been subjected to pressure from more powerful unions without interference from Federation officialdom. Both AFL and CIO at times took action that curtailed or denied the freedom of affiliated unions. Usually this took the form of requiring small unions to disband, and their members to join larger unions.

In the AFL for many years the independent status of affiliated unions was regarded as a bar to action against unions that tolerated racketeering or other forms of misconduct among their officers. When examples of such behavior were brought to the attention of Federation officials, it was explained that the unions in question were supreme over their own internal affairs—"sovereign entities," Samuel Gompers called them—and that the Federation had no authority in such matters. It was apparently overlooked that lack of power to force an affiliate to mend its ways did not require the Federation to continue to associate with it. When George Meany became president of the AFL that sort of evasion was not resorted to in the case of the International Longshoremen's Association, which, having become notorious for its failure to rid itself of gangster leadership, was expelled from the Federation.

The CIO, a newer body less bound by tradition, expelled ten affiliated unions in 1949 and 1950 under charges of Communist domination. The charge as presented to the convention was that "the policies and activities" of the offending unions "are consistently directed toward the achievement of the program and purposes of the Communist Party rather than the objectives set forth in the Constitution of the CIO." This action did not necessarily constitute a precedent for expelling member unions tolerating gangsterism or racketeering. Yet when Walter Reuther, as president of the CIO in 1954 demanded action from the Retail and Department Store Workers Union against racketeers in their membership, he cited the expulsion of the Communist-dominated unions as evidence that the CIO was not without power to deal with the situation.

JURISDICTION

The problem of jurisdiction or, as the British term it, "demarcation," has been one of the most difficult and vexing of issues that the American labor movement has had to cope with. The twenty-year split that was brought to an end by the merger of AFL and CIO in December 1955 had its origin in large part in differences over jurisdiction. A brief statement of the development of the problem over the years is essential to an understanding both of the breach and of the steps taken toward its healing.

The men who organized the AFL in 1886 were not actively conscious of the problem. The constitution provided for the "establishment" of trade unions, but it contained no specifications that would prevent overlapping jurisdictions. Some of the charters issued to the older unions could be interpreted as covering all occupations within an industry.

Moreover, in its early history the Federation itself sometimes created problems by chartering more than one union in the same trade. In the period just prior to the start of the present century the AFL was harboring two coal miners' unions, two of boot-and-shoe workers, three of machinists, three of carpenters, and in addition a directly affiliated local carpenters' union. This caused difficulty within the trades, and soon there began to be trouble between unions in different trades, at least one of which had organized on a broad industrial basis. The United Mine Workers was taking into its membership all workers "in and around" the mines. This was objected to by the craft unions, particularly the Blacksmiths and the Firemen.

As a result of growing dissatisfaction a special "committee on autonomy" [2] was created at the 1901 convention at Scranton, Pennsylvania. This committee made a report that has been referred to ever since as the "Scranton Declaration." After stating that the craft form of organization should be adhered to as closely as "the recent great changes in methods of production and employment make practicable," the report made an exception of isolated industries in which the overwhelming majority of the workers "follow one branch thereof," and where only a few members of other crafts are employed. In such cases the committee believed that "jurisdiction by the paramount organization would yield the best results to the workers therein." [3]

The adoption of this report had the effect of authorizing the United Mine Workers to continue to function broadly as an industrial union. No further deviations from the craft principle were implied, since no important industry but coal fitted the terms of the definition. Nevertheless for many years thereafter all attempts to extend the principle

[2] Using the word to mean jurisdiction.
[3] AFL Convention Proceedings, 1901, p. 240.

of industrial unionism to other areas were defeated in Federation conventions on the ground that the Scranton Declaration already permitted organization on an industrial as well as on a craft basis.

The most ambitious attempt, prior to the 1930s, to commit the Federation to industrial unionism was led by the Mine Workers at the Convention of 1912. After a prolonged debate, participated in by the heads of very nearly all the leading unions, the proposal was defeated by a majority of about 60 per cent of the votes cast. Twenty-three years passed before the subject again assumed so important a place in convention proceedings; and then, in 1935, the proposal was again voted down by a majority slightly larger than in 1912.

Opposition to the industrial form of organization was due to a number of causes. In the earlier years the opposition was in part ideological. The movement for industrial organization within the Federation was at first led by Socialists, a fact that in itself made the proposals unpalatable to a majority of convention delegates and particularly to the Federation president, Samuel Gompers. But Mr. Gompers' opposition was due also to a profound conviction, manifest throughout his life, that organization by craft groups was the only sound policy for a labor movement.[4]

THE PROBLEM OF ORGANIZING

As time went on, however, it became evident that the practice of organizing by crafts was ill-adapted to the situation existing in the rapidly-growing mass-production industries. The attempt to organize the steel industry in 1919–20 was hampered by bickering in the organizing committee, which consisted of representatives of twenty-four craft unions, each of which claimed jurisdiction over some segment of the industry.

[4] In his report to the 1903 convention, under the caption "Hew to Trade Union Lines," Mr. Gompers expressed himself with characteristic vigor: "The attempt to force the trade unions into what has been termed industrial organization is perversive of the history of the labor movement, runs counter to the best conceptions of the toilers' interests now, and is sure to lead to the confusion which precedes dissolution and disruption. It is time for the American Federation of Labor to solemnly call a halt. It is time for our fellow-unionists entrusted with grave responsibilities to help stem the tide of expansion madness, lest either by their indifference or encouragement their organizations will be drawn into the vortex that will engulf them to their possible dismemberment and destruction." AFL Convention Proceedings, 1903, p. 15.

In 1914 and again in 1926 efforts by a group of craft unions to organize the automobile industry failed. In 1927 the Executive Council of the American Federation of Labor reported to the convention that the "second" among outstanding problems confronting the Federation (the "first" being the legal status of the union) was "How to Organize Highly Mechanized Industries."

"The use of mechanical power and machine tools," the report stated, "is characteristic of quantity production and also of the still more highly specialized methods called mass production. These methods mean . . . subdivision of the work previously done by craftsmen into repetitive operations performed by a number of workers. This production technique . . . requires new kinds of skill and new group bases for organization of the workers into unions. In practically none of these industries are the workers organized. . . . There must be a new basis of appeal." [5]

However, all efforts to organize in mass-production industries were along craft lines. The baffling experiences with automobiles and steel brought no changes in organizing methods, nor did the plea of the Executive Council in 1927 for a "new basis of appeal" lead to its formulation.

At the end of the first World War, in 1920, AFL membership had reached a previously-untouched peak of four million. As a result of the open-shop drive and the recession of 1920–21, approximately a million members were lost in those two years, and few new members were won in the prosperous years extending to the 1929 financial crash. The depression years depleted the membership rolls still further. In 1933, the American Federation of Labor had approximately 2,127,000 members—the smallest membership since 1916.

It was the National Industrial Recovery Act of 1933 that revived the spirit of organization. Section 7-A of that Act established for the first time in any federal law the principle that workers had a right to organize in unions. The law declared "that employees shall have the right to organize and bargain collectively through representatives of their own choosing, and shall be free from the interference, restraint or coercion of employers . . . in the designation of such representatives or in self-organization or other concerted activities. . . ."

[5] AFL Convention Proceedings, 1927, pp. 40–41. (See also p. 317.)

Though enforcement of the new law was doubtful, organizing spirit in the unions revived and the unorganized workers in the mass-production industries—relieved of the fear of employer reprisals—began to manifest a desire for organization. Total AFL membership increased in 1934 by nearly half a million. Company unions began cautiously to develop independence.

But the craft unions were fearful. Many of the new members had been recruited into so-called federal locals—plant locals organized on an industrial basis. This had long been the policy of the Federation for organizing workers in unorganized areas; later it would cull out the craft workers and assign them to the affiliated internationals which they were eligible to join. The policy often resulted in destroying the plant locals, as the president of the Metal Trades Department had reported more than once. When the AFL convention met in 1933, many of the leaders were concerned about these developments. The convention voted to ask the Executive Council to call a conference of interested internationals to "consider the entire subject."

Such a conference was held in January 1934, attended by delegates from seventy-five unions and five AFL Departments. The report that emerged from the conference emphasized the desirability of taking advantage of the prevailing situation to extend the area of organization but "bearing in mind that . . . the present structure, rights, and interests of the national and international unions must be followed, observed and safeguarded." [6]

The final sentence appeared to leave the problem unsolved, and with craft unionism still in the ascendency. This was the situation when the delegates assembled for the convention which met in San Francisco in October 1934. But here, for the first time since 1912, there was present a strong integrated bloc of delegates committed to the idea of industrial unionism, and determined that the mass-production industries should be organized. Unlike the 1912 procedure, however, the debate over the issue took place behind closed doors in the committee on resolutions, and a unanimous report was presented to the convention. That report seemed to indicate willingness to accept a change in policy. The committee had considered

[6] AFL Convention Proceedings, 1934, pp. 40–42.

fifteen resolutions that were offered on the subject of organizing methods, most of them favoring industrial unionism; two of them, sponsored by high officials in the metal trades, were opposed.

The committee report, offered as a substitute for the resolutions, called attention to certain "new methods" that had brought about changes in the work of "millions of workers in industries" in which organization into craft unions had been "most difficult or impossible." In these industries the new legislation protecting the right to organize had resulted in "freeing the flood of organizing sentiment." It was "to meet this new condition" that the report proposed to direct the Executive Council to "issue charters for national or international unions in the automotive, cement, aluminum, and such other mass-production and miscellaneous industries as in the judgment of the Executive Council may be necessary," and to inaugurate a campaign of organization in the steel industry.

After some discussion, consisting largely of questions from leaders of craft unions, whose fears were apparently allayed by the explanations offered by members of the resolutions committee, the report was adopted by unanimous vote. The advocates of industrial unionism left the convention hall convinced that their battle had been won.

During the succeeding year the Executive Council issued charters to newly created unions in the automobile and rubber industries; but it reported to the convention of 1935 that it had taken no steps toward organizing the steel industry, because internal strife in the only existing union of steel workers had made it impossible for a campaign of organization to be conducted.

The charters issued were at least quasi-industrial. They included all semi-skilled workers and some of the skilled. Although they excluded a limited number of highly skilled machinists, in the industries concerned they represented a striking advance over the older craft limitations. But this did not satisfy the industrial unionists, who believed that the Council had been ordered to issue unrestricted charters, and they were outraged over the failure to attempt an organization in steel. John L. Lewis, president of the United Mine Workers, called it "a breach of faith and a travesty on good conscience." The resolutions committee presented two reports. The majority report was a defense of the action of the Executive Council. The minority report called for the issuance of unrestricted industrial charters in the mass-production industries. The minority report was defeated by a heavy vote, and the majority report was adopted.

RISE OF THE CIO [7]

A few months before the 1935 convention Congress had passed the Wagner Act. It reaffirmed the right to organize that had been asserted by the Recovery Act, and strengthened it by provisions for its implementation. The opportunity thus presented seemed to the industrial unionists too good to be lost. Moreover, they were convinced that the issue was no longer solely a question of craft unionism versus industrial unionism. They doubted that the majority of the craft-union leaders were really concerned about organizing the unorganized. They thought that if these leaders were left to themselves, no effective movement to bring in the millions in automobiles, steel, and other mass-production industries would be launched. They decided that the action of the convention did not constitute a bar to proceeding on their own. A few weeks after the 1935 convention, eight presidents of AFL unions, led by John L. Lewis of the Miners and Sidney Hillman, president of the Amalgamated Clothing Workers, met and organized the Committee for Industrial Organization and began to organize workers in the mass-production industries on an industrial basis.

This behavior was regarded by the AFL as treason. The unions that had endorsed the actions of the eight presidents were suspended and later expelled. These unions, joined by others, then (in 1938) formed the Congress of Industrial Organizations as a rival federation.

The years since then have been years of further change. The loss of a million members to the CIO and the rapid growth of that organization left the AFL, for a time, inferior numerically. But the older body was stimulated into organizational activity. Almost at a single bound it retrieved its losses and soon surpassed the CIO in membership—a relative position that has widened over the years. Sensing the new situation, the AFL in a few years was condoning the action of affiliates which were transforming themselves into industrial unions.

---

[7] For an informed discussion of the split in the labor movement and the circumstances leading to the merger, see Jack Barbash, *The Practice of Unionism* (New York: Harper & Brothers, 1956), pp. 113–121.

Soon AFL leaders were appealing to the CIO to "return to the house of labor" on the ground that there were no longer any differences between the two federations. Joint unity committees were set up which conferred and disbanded; the CIO first sought "functional unity," while the AFL urged "organic unity" at once. Meanwhile rivalry and memories of bitter opposition made agreement difficult.

At the end of 1952, a new situation developed with dramatic suddenness. Within a month of each other, William Green and Philip Murray, presidents of the two federations, died. New men took their places. Neither George Meany nor Walter Reuther had participated actively in the struggle of 1935. Most of the leading actors in that controversy had passed from the scene through either retirement or death. John L. Lewis, who had fought with both federations, had withdrawn to the sidelines. The slate was clean for the cooperation that Meany and Reuther both desired.

THE MERGER [8]

Early in 1953 a new joint unity committee was set up. In June of that year it drafted an anti-raiding compact which was agreed to by most of the unions in both federations. In February 1954 a merger agreement was drawn up and in May a proposed constitution for the merged body was made public. Steps were taken by rival unions toward amalgamation. Friendly conferences were held between former opponents.

On December 1 and 2, 1955, the two federations met separately and ratified the new constitution. Then, with obvious consciousness that they were making history, the delegates from the two final conventions met in a joint convention and created a new federation to be known as the "American Federation of Labor and Congress of Industrial Organizations."

They ratified a constitution that in specific terms declared the conflict of 1935 at an end. Not once but three times the constitution states that both craft and industrial unions in the new body are "equal" and that both are "appropriate and necessary." The constitu-

[8] An especially valuable discussion of historical background, development, and significance of the merger by competent authorities appeared in *Industrial and Labor Relations Review*, April 1956.

tion created an Industrial Union Department with which are now affiliated most of the former CIO unions and the AFL unions that had been organized in part or wholly on industrial lines.

Whether, in fact, the conflict that came to a head in 1935 is a thing of the past remains to be determined. The matter of union jurisdiction was in about as chaotic a state in 1956 as it was in 1900, before the "no trespass" rule was adopted. Many unions, regardless of defined areas of jurisdiction, have for some years been taking into their membership any group of workers, as convenience dictated. The Teamsters organized hat-check girls; the Machinists admitted industrial nurses; the Mine Workers have set up a roving, nongeographical arm known as District 50 which takes in anybody from chemical workers to dairy farmers. In the very week that the new federation was set up, the National Labor Relations Board announced representation elections in which deck hands and cooks were to vote for or against representation by the Machinists Union; employees of a clock company were to decide whether or not to be represented by the Automobile Workers; truck drivers and a "part-time janitor" were to vote for or against the Meat Cutters; stock clerks and sign painters working in a Coca-Cola plant were to weigh the merits of the Teamsters Union. Elections or certifications were reported in which from two to four AFL unions were to compete against each other for representation rights, or had so competed.

The word "trespass" does not appear in the new constitution, but it does declare that each affiliated union "is entitled to have its autonomy, integrity, and jurisdiction protected and preserved," and new charters are not to be issued "in conflict with the jurisdiction" of already-affiliated unions. Each affiliate must "respect the established collective-bargaining relationship of every other affiliate" and "no affiliate shall raid the established collective-bargaining relationship" of any other. Any alleged violation of the foregoing may be dealt with by the president, the executive council, and the convention, in that order. The action of the convention apparently is final and binding.

District 50 of the independent United Mine Workers is not obligated by anything in the AFL-CIO constitution. Whether the new federation will be able to settle existing conflicts between some of its own affiliates or curb the roving tendencies of others is a matter for speculation.

THE NEW FEDERATION

The constitution of the AFL-CIO is in many respects a unique document in American labor history. The anti-employer spirit manifested by the preamble of the old AFL constitution, dating back to 1881 [9] is lacking. There are indications of an attitude of cooperation and good will.

"The establishment of this Federation," the Preamble declares, "is an expression of the hopes and aspirations of the working people of America," the fulfillment of which is to be sought "through democratic processes within the framework of our constitutional government and consistent with our institutions and traditions."

The "hopes and aspirations" find expression in a pledge to secure to the workers "the rights to which they are justly entitled . . . , higher standards of living and working conditions . . . , the leisure which their skills make possible," and the "strengthening and extension of our way of life and the fundamental freedoms which are the basis of our democratic society." Further, and beyond the particular interests of the workers as such, "at the bargaining table, in the community, and in the exercise of the rights and responsibilities of citizenship, we shall responsibly serve the interests of all the American people. . . . We shall strive always to win full respect for the dignity of the human individual whom our unions serve."

"With Divine guidance," the preamble concludes, "grateful for the fine traditions of our past, confident of meeting the challenge of the future, we proclaim this constitution."

Among the "Objects and Principles" set forth in the new constitution is the expression of a purpose "to protect the labor movement from any and all corrupt influences and from the undermining efforts of communist agencies. . . ." Further on we read: "It is a basic principle of this Federation that it must be and remain free from any and all corrupt influences and from the undermining efforts of communist, fascist, or other totalitarian agencies who are opposed to the basic principles of our democracy and of free and democratic trade unionism."

In order to establish this principle, the Executive Council is given power, whenever it is advised that a member union is guilty of any

[9] See Chap. 12.

such dereliction, to investigate the charges. If it finds any truth in them, it may "make recommendation or give directions" to the union in question, and it may by a two-thirds vote suspend any union "found guilty of a violation of this section." The union may appeal this decision to the convention, but it is to be effective at once and "remain in full force and effect pending the appeal." To support the Executive Council in this procedure, and to assist it in the implementation of the constitutional requirement, a permanent Committee on Ethical Practices was created by the constitution.

Thus, for the purpose of dealing with corruption and with totalitarian heresies, the new federation comes into possession of a degree of authority previously unknown to the AFL, and more extensive than the powers set forth in the constitution of the CIO.

At the meeting of the Executive Council in June 1956 the Committee on Ethical Practices was provided with staff assistants and given authority to proceed "upon its own motion" to make preliminary inquiries in order to ascertain "whether any situations exist which require formal investigation." At the request of the president or any member of the Executive Council a formal investigation may be made of any situation in which "there is reason to believe an affiliate is dominated, controlled, or substantially influenced in the conduct of its affairs by any corrupt influence. . . ." The committee was further directed "to develop a set of principles and guides for adoption by the AFL-CIO in order to implement the constitutional determination that the AFL-CIO shall be and remain free from all corrupt influences." [10] Action in accordance with this direction is reported in Supplementary Notes.

As stated in a previous chapter, this constitution contains a declaration of racial equality, and provides for a standing committee on civil rights whose duty is to "assist the Executive Council to bring about at the earliest possible date the effective implementation of the principle . . . of nondiscrimination in accordance with the provisions of this constitution."

Another declared objective is "to give constructive aid in promot-

[10] The Committee on Ethical Practices, as organized in 1956, consisted of A. J. Hayes, president of the International Association of Machinists, Chairman, and the following presidents of international unions: George M. Harrison, Railway Clerks'; Joseph Curran, National Maritime Union; David Dubinsky, International Ladies' Garment Workers; Jacob S. Potofsky, Amalgamated Clothing Workers.

ing the cause of peace and freedom in the world," as well as to aid and cooperate with "free and democratic labor movements throughout the world." A standing committee on international affairs is to give attention to these objectives.

A continuance of efforts to improve intra-union relationships and to lessen the danger of jurisdictional disputes is assured by a clause that extends the "no-raiding" agreement entered into between AFL and CIO unions before the merger.

Before the merger each federation had set up an agency for dealing with disputes among its own affiliated bodies. The new constitution provides for the creation of a joint committee to work out a plan for incorporating these two agencies and the no-raiding agreement into a combined "no-raiding and organizational and jurisdictional disputes agreement."

Provision is made for a standing committee on legislation and another on political education. There are a half dozen or so other standing committees whose titles indicate their functions, such as education, research, social security, community services, housing, safety, and occupational health.

The constitution of the merged body does not, however, solve all the problems mentioned in this chapter. The selfishness implicit in the struggle over jurisdictional claims cannot be wiped out by a clause written into a document. The notion that a certificate of affiliation assigning an area for organization activities constitutes something like a deed to acres of land—to be improved or allowed to lie fallow at the owner's choice—has not been rendered nonexistent by the merging of two rival federations. The struggle between craft unions and industrial unions over possession of segments of industry is not over.

But the work of the joint committee that sweated over these and other matters, the new insight gained through the efforts toward the composing of differences, the resulting educational influence upon the whole labor movement—all these are factors that may create a new atmosphere within organized labor. Steps have been taken toward a lessening of internal strife. Leaders have emerged to whom the new situation is an affirmation of principles to be respected and made effective. The road toward the development of a more responsible trade unionism has been opened.

11

Union Policy on Membership

Throughout trade-union history in the United States it has been possible to discern two attitudes with respect to nonmembers. One suggests that every effort should be made to bring all wage earners without exception into the unions. The other position is represented by those who would organize only certain segments of a trade or industry, or exclude from membership certain specified groups. There are graduations of opinion and practice in between, but it will be helpful to keep these two extremes in mind.

The belief that a trade union should be all-inclusive has been held as a matter of course by all adherents to a class-conscious philosophy. Such a point of view is not limited, however, to believers in the class struggle as a concomitant of an inevitable antagonism between capital and labor. It is held by those who believe with something like missionary zeal that the labor movement should include all wage earners, and that the strong among them should help the weak. It includes also those with the hard-headed, pragmatic view that the labor movement as a whole is weakened if any considerable number of workers are unorganized, and, conversely, that its strength grows as progress is made toward 100 per cent union organization. The movement for industrial unionism was led primarily by these pragmatists.

The purpose of a limitation on union membership within a trade is also pragmatic; it seeks regularity of employment for the limited number who are members of the union. This is one of the features that have come to be associated with the term "business unionism." The purpose is most effectively achieved when a closed union is party to a closed-shop agreement. The term "closed union" is applied to a local union which for a period of greater or lesser duration refuses to admit new members—thus guaranteeing to the existing union membership first chance at available work. This practice, which if effective creates an unhealthy monopoly for the benefit of a privi-

116

leged group, may develop into something even more questionable when job opportunities exceed union membership. Under such circumstances the local union sometimes issues "permits" to non-members (or even to members from out of town) enabling them to work in closed-shop areas, charging a fee considerably in excess of union dues, and frequently amounting to several dollars a week. This system has lent itself to abuse and has come under the condemnation of the national unions generally. Professor William Haber (in a book published in 1929) reported that the New York local of the Electrical Workers Union, at a time a few years earlier when 18,000 electricians "were needed in the New York building market," refused to admit new members beyond the 6,000 who then belonged to it. More than 5,000 electricians had applied for membership. "Permits were issued to nonunion men when all union electricians had work, and were withdrawn in favor of the latter when they were unemployed. The permit men were charged $2.50 a week, and helpers $1.00 a week." [1]

The permit card system has sometimes become a prolific source of graft, with corrupt union officials pocketing the fees instead of turning them over to the union treasury. In addition, it has sometimes defeated its intended purpose—job insurance for the members. "The union officials become interested in issuing as many permit cards as possible," wrote Professor Sumner Slichter in 1941, "with the result that permit card holders may be working while good union members may be idle." [2]

The permit system, according to Professor Haber, "is not widely prevalent and its effect is much overrated." Professor Slichter stated that it was "pretty much confined to the building trades" and that "the national unions invariably" oppose it. It has been vigorously opposed by officials of some of the building trade unions. With reference to the Electrical Workers in New York, Professor Haber wrote that the international union "waged an aggressive campaign against the practice," ousted the local officials, and "completely reorganized the New York locals." [3]

[1] William Haber, *Industrial Relations in the Building Industry* (Cambridge, Mass.: Harvard University Press, 1930), pp. 203-4.
[2] *Union Policies and Industrial Management* (Washington, D.C.: The Brookings Institution, 1941), p. 70.
[3] William Haber, *op. cit.*, p. 549.

The practice, moreover, is illegal under certain provisions of the Taft-Hartley Act and court rulings relative to that law. The reasons for referring to it here are that it is a part of union history, and that there is evidence that to a certain extent it still obtains.[4]

The more important aspect of trade-union exclusiveness, which has been greatly modified, especially in recent years, involves either indifference about extending organization, or arbitrary refusal to admit certain groups to membership. The former was manifested by a reluctance to organize outside the ranks of skilled workers, which was referred to in the preceding chapter. The practice of discrimination has involved women to a certain extent and, to a very great extent, Negroes. These policies call for discussion.

The Unskilled

It is not surprising that when union leaders were groping toward an acceptable form of organization seventy-five to a hundred years ago little attention should have been given to organizing the unskilled. It was an era of small shops, and the practice of handicraft was dominant. The importance of the craftsman—the man of manual skill—was everywhere recognized as the indispensable core of industry. It was assumed, and undoubtedly with justification, that stable trade unions could be built only by such men. In 1881, when the forerunner of the American Federation of Labor was established by a group of craftsmen led by the skilled cigar maker Samuel Gompers,

---

[4] The Senate subcommittee that investigated union welfare funds in 1955 and 1956 reported that the permit system was being practiced by a local of the Plumbers Union, although it is forbidden by the constitution of the parent union. This local at Knoxville, Tennessee, had been charging fees for permits to work since "about 1942 or 1943." Members of the Plumbers Union who came from outside the area to work on construction jobs in connection with atomic energy installations or TVA activities were required to obtain permits from the local union before going to work, for which they paid one dollar a week and later two dollars. This practice, which brought in large sums to the union treasury—over $57,000 in the ten months ending April 30, 1955—was camouflaged after July 1952 as contributions to a "sick and welfare fund," although "no welfare benefits are paid from the sums accumulated." The practice is commonly referred to as "doby," which, the committee report stated, is a "colloquial contraction of 'give me the dough, boy.'" A similar practice by the local at Houston, Texas, was terminated in 1954 under instructions from the international union. Final Report of Subcommittee on Welfare and Pension Funds of the Senate Committee on Labor and Public Welfare, April 1956, pp. 287–292.

there was discussion concerning the name that should be given the new organization. At the initial convention, Mr. Gompers, as chairman of a committee on organization, brought in a report recommending that the new movement be called the "Federation of Organized Trades Unions of the United States of America and Canada." Some of the delegates objected that this name was too exclusive. A Pittsburgh spokesman for the Knights of Labor, referred to in the report of the convention as "the colored delegate," wanted the plan of organization to be broad enough to include common laborers. After a prolonged debate the words "and Labor Unions" were inserted. Yet, a half dozen years later an AFL document declared that trade unions were established "to prevent the skilled labor of America from being reduced to beggary and to sustain the standard of American workmanship and skill. . . ." [5]

Toward the end of his career Mr. Gompers wrote in his autobiography that the Federation which he led had been needed in order to promote "organization of all workers of America, skilled and unskilled." Nevertheless, the Federation continued to be an association of craft unions as long as Gompers lived, with little infiltration from the unskilled.

The situation as it was a half century or more ago was realistically described by Valentine Reuther, father of Walter Reuther, at the last convention of the CIO before it merged with the AFL. Mr. Reuther said he went to work in a steel mill "in the late nineties." He worked first as an unskilled laborer, but later was promoted to "a job at the furnace." When that happened, an organizer appeared and told him that as a skilled worker he was now eligible for union membership. He joined, but at the union meeting he did not see any of his former associates on the laboring job. When he made inquiries they told him, "Oh, we don't want those men. Most of them are Polacks and Hunkies and Dagoes, and we just want the skilled men." [6]

Some concern about the unskilled workers manifested itself in AFL conventions in the decade of 1910 to 1920. At this time the

[5] Samuel Gompers, *Seventy Years of Life and Labor* (New York: E. P. Dutton & Co., 1925), Vol. I, p. 261.
[6] Proceedings, Seventeenth Constitutional Convention, CIO, December 1, 1955, pp. 255–256.

IWW (Industrial Workers of the World) with its industrial union philosophy was giving considerable attention to the unskilled and the migratory workers on the West Coast. This fact may have aroused the interest of California delegates, who attempted for several years to induce the AFL to attempt to organize such workers. Little action resulted. Some organizing work was done, but it was not until 1946 that a charter was issued to an organization consisting largely of migratory workers. In general, no marked change in the AFL attitude toward organizing the unskilled was manifest until the 1930s [7] when there was a general revival of organizing activity. Millis and Montgomery, in their authoritative text dealing with the history and practices of unions, had this to say, referring to 1936 and 1937: "Prodded into more vigorous activity by the organizational efforts of the CIO, the AFL assumed leadership . . . in campaigns to organize the unorganized industries. International unions at the same time increased their organizational staffs, extended their jurisdiction, and received with open arms unskilled and semi-skilled workers previously not welcomed." [8]

At the present time, therefore, the unskilled employed in manufacturing industries have been taken into the unions by all the true industrial (plant-wide) union organizations. Since the trend in general is toward industrial unionism, the unskilled are seldom left without a union which they would be considered eligible to join.

WOMEN

A former prejudice against the admission of women to unions, never general, has now almost disappeared. In the early period of union organization—in the first half of the nineteenth century—workingmen were frequently concerned about the employment of women in factories, considering their employment hazardous both physically and morally, and offering at the same time a dangerous competition with men. The earlier unions frequently barred women

[7] An interesting comment on AFL attitude toward the unskilled, which differs in part from the views expressed above and in part supports them, appears in Labor Movements, Vol. IV, History of Labor in the United States (New York: The Macmillan Company, 1935), pp. 628–629, by Perlman and Taft.

[8] Millis & Montgomery, Organized Labor (New York: McGraw-Hill Book Co., 1945), pp. 195–196.

from membership by constitutional limitations. As women increasingly came into industrial employment, however, the barriers began to come down. "At the beginning of the first World War the doors of a considerable number of unions remained closed. By the end of the war period (1919), however, all but a few of the internationals with jurisdiction in trades and industries in which women had found employment had opened their doors to them." [9] At the beginning of 1955, there were nearly 3 million women in American trade unions.[10] A random sampling of union constitutions has revealed no discriminatory clauses based on sex except in the case of the railway brotherhoods. These organizations specify that applicants for membership must be of the male sex.

RACIAL DISCRIMINATION

We turn now to another discriminatory practice, more persistent than any other though now on its way out: the exclusion of Negroes from union membership or their relegation to a limited and secondary role.

AFL Policy

The story of the development of policy within the American Federation of Labor with respect to Negro membership is long and involved, and can be dealt with only briefly here. First of all, a distinction must be made between Federation policy and that of the constituent unions. The Federation as such in 1890 adopted a declaration that it "looks with disfavor upon trade unions having provisions which exclude from membership persons on account of race or color" and "most respectfully" requested the Machinists Union to "remove from their constitution" such a provision.[11] The AFL convention of 1893 adopted a resolution declaring that "we here and now reaffirm as one of the cardinal principles of the labor movement that the working people must unite and organize, irrespective of creed, color, sex, nationality, or politics." [12]

9 Millis & Montgomery, op. cit., p. 262.
10 Directory of Labor Unions in the U.S., p. 12. Bulletin 1185, U. S. Bureau of Labor Statistics.
11 AFL Convention Proceedings, 1890, p. 31.
12 AFL Convention Proceedings. 1893, p. 56.

Thereafter the convention repeatedly announced its adherence to the principle of nondiscrimination on grounds of race or color. There can be no doubt that this was and continued to be the official position of the Federation.[13] Nevertheless, it is also beyond doubt that there has been through the greater part of the life of the Federation a considerable amount of deviation from the principle on the part of affiliated unions. When such deviations were brought to the attention of Federation conventions, no action was taken against the offending unions on the ground that the principle of autonomy made intervention impossible.

Policy of Affiliates

A study of union policy toward Negroes revealed the following variations in AFL unions in 1944: one union excluded Negroes by "provision in ritual." Six unions excluded them by constitutional provisions. Six excluded them by "tacit consent," and other unions dealt with the problem by setting up auxiliary locals composed of Negro members only.[14]

That the last arrangement did not involve equality of rights between white and colored workers is made clear by some of the constitutional provisions creating the auxiliary locals. In the Brotherhood of Railway Carmen separate locals of Negro workers were to be "under the jurisdiction of and [be] represented by the delegate of the nearest white local in any meeting of the Joint Protective Board Federation or convention where delegates may be seated." The constitution of the Maintenance of Way Employees provided that Negroes in separate local lodges "shall be entitled to all the benefits and protection guaranteed by the constitution to its members and shall be represented in

[13] In his annual report to the AFL Convention in 1900 (Proceedings, p. 23), President Gompers said: "Realizing the necessity for the unity of the wage-earners of our country, the AFL has upon all occasions declared that trade unions should open their portals to all wage workers irrespective of creed, color, nationality, sex, or politics. . . . Unless we shall give the Negro workers the opportunity to organize, and thus place them where they can protect and defend themselves against the rapacity and cupidity of their employers; unless we continue the policy of endeavoring to make friends of them, there can be no question but that they will not only be forced down in the economic scale and be used against any effort made by us for our economic and social advancement, but race prejudice will be made more bitter, to the injury of all."

[14] Herbert Northrup, *Organized Labor and the Negro* (New York: Harper & Brothers, 1944).

the Grand Lodge [i.e. convention] by delegates of their own choice selected from any white lodge on the System Division."

The constitution of the Boilermakers' Union, as amended in 1937, provided for auxiliary locals of Negroes which, according to Herbert Northrup, could be set up only in localities where a white local existed and had no voice in national union affairs. They were "dependent on the business agent of the 'supervising' white local for job assignments," and although they paid the same dues as white members they rated "only half as much in death and disability benefits." Northrup summed up the situation as to auxiliary locals as follows: "Nine [unions] . . . permit Negroes to join [and pay dues] but limit their participation to Jim Crow auxiliary bodies which in one way or another prohibit them from having a voice in the affairs of the union, from negotiating their own agreements, or from having an opportunity to advance in the occupational hierarchy." [15]

Northrup's study indicated that twenty international unions affiliated with the AFL in 1944 either excluded Negroes altogether or permitted them only a severely truncated form of membership. Since that time many changes have taken place. One of the most significant is the development of a new attitude in affiliated unions with respect to racial discrimination. By 1955 all but one of the AFL unions had stricken from their constitutions the "all-white" clauses,[16] but some of them still retain the practice of maintaining separate, auxiliary locals.[17]

The Laggard Brotherhoods

In one area the earlier prejudices remain. In all four of the railway operating Brotherhoods [18] the door is closed against Negroes. The membership clause of the Brotherhood of Railroad Trainmen reads: "The applicant [for membership] shall be a white male. . . ." Simi-

[15] Herbert Northrup, op. cit., pp. 2–5.

[16] Statement by National Urban League. The one exception was the Wire Weavers' Protective Association with 403 members in 1954.

[17] Jack Barbash, The Practice of Unionism (New York: Harper & Brothers, 1956), p. 73.

[18] Commonly so called because three of them, Engineers, Firemen and Trainmen, have the word "Brotherhood" in their titles. The fourth, the Order of Railway Conductors, being closely allied with the others in type of employment, is also generally referred to as one of the Brotherhoods.

larly worded membership clauses appear in the constitutions of the other Brotherhoods.

The railroad operating unions are older than all but a small handful of other unions now in existence. The Engineers' Brotherhood dates back to the period of the Civil War, and the Conductors' and Firemen's organizations were established soon afterward. The youngest of these bodies, the Trainmen, was organized in 1883. Perhaps the persistence of the anti-Negro policy of these unions stems in part from a prejudice inherited from the period in which they had their origins. Northrup, in the study mentioned above, stresses the fact that the Brotherhoods, except the Trainmen, "were founded as fraternal and beneficial societies rather than as trade unions," and that the "social features" thus implied are still emphasized. "To admit Negroes, the Southern members declared, would be tantamount to admitting that the Negro is the 'social equal' of the white man." [19] Northrup makes it clear, however, that competition for jobs lay at the root of the determination not only to keep the Negroes out of the unions but if possible to eliminate them from railway employment. Even the American Railway Union, founded by Eugene V. Debs in 1893 to supplant craft unionism with an all-embracing industrial union, wrote a "white only" clause into its constitution.[20]

New Developments

The constitution of the merged AFL and CIO bodies, adopted in December 1955, sets forth as one of its objectives the encouragement of "all workers without regard to race, color, or national origin to share in the full benefits of union organization." [21] It further provides

[19] Herbert Northrup, op. cit., p. 50.

[20] At the first convention of the American Railway Union, held in 1894, a proposal was made that the clause in the constitution providing that "all employees of white parentage shall be eligible . . ." should be amended by striking out the words "of white parentage." After debate lasting nearly an entire day a roll call vote was taken. The proposal was defeated by a vote of 112 to 110. Somewhat later the following resolution was adopted: "That the American Railway Union . . . recommend to the colored railway employees that they organize in a protective order similar to the American Railway Union, and in the event of such organization be it further resolved that we tender them our sympathy and support."

[21] The CIO in its constitution adopted in 1938 declared as its first object: "To bring about the effective organization of the workingmen and women of America regardless of race, creed, color or nationality. . . ."

for a standing committee on civil rights, whose "duty and responsibility" will be to aid in bringing about "at the earliest possible date the effective implementation of the principle stated in this constitution of nondiscrimination."

A somewhat stronger statement is to be found in the Merger Agreement which was drawn up by the Joint Unity Committee before the constitution was drafted. Paragraph (f) of Section 2 of that agreement is as follows: "The merged federation shall constitutionally recognize the right of all workers, without regard to race, creed, color, or national origin to share in the full benefits of trade-union organization in the merged federation. The merged federation shall establish appropriate internal machinery to bring about, at the earliest possible date, the effective implementation of this principle of nondiscrimination." The Merger Agreement was ratified by both the AFL and the CIO Conventions and it is apparently as completely a part of the basic principles of the merged body as is the constitution itself.

It is not to be supposed, however, that either the abolition of discriminatory clauses from union constitutions or the affirmations of the new Federation will of themselves bring about complete interracial justice within organized labor. Many of the international unions permit their locals to control admission to membership. Many locals —not all of them in the deep South—maintain barriers against Negro membership as high and as strict as if "white only" clauses were still in the constitutions of the major bodies. In areas where prejudice is persistent, discriminatory practices may continue for some time.

Evidence of this possibility appeared in the first reaction of many trade unionists in Southern states to the Supreme Court decision on segregation in public schools. In some localities, unions revolted against the policy of their parent organizations. There was even some agitation, which has now subsided, for the creation of a Southern Federation of Labor. A different attitude is manifest in several Southern states where AFL and CIO state bodies have merged. The constitutions of each of these new state organizations contains a nondiscrimination clause as strong as that of the parent AFL-CIO.

However, because acceptance of the official policy of nondiscrimination is not universal, Negro trade unionists are not entirely satisfied with the relevant clauses of the AFL-CIO constitution. A. Philip Randolph, president of the Brotherhood of Sleeping Car Porters, made an effort to have the merged federation take as definite a stand against such discrimination as it does against corruption and Communism. Mr. Randolph offered a resolution proposing that "racist" agencies "opposed to the basic principles of our democracy" be brought under the same condemnation as Communist or Fascist organizations, and that unions practicing discrimination based on race or color be subject to suspension by the Executive Council, equally with unions guilty of corrupt practices or controlled by Communists.

This resolution was not acted upon either by the AFL Convention which preceded the joint convention, or by the AFL-CIO convention. It was referred to the twenty-nine-man Executive Council of which two Negroes, Mr. Randolph and Willard S. Townsend, president of the United Transport Service Employees (Red Caps), were members. It is understood that before the next convention meets (December, 1957), the Executive Council will study the question and make a report.

Despite lack of unanimity the outlook for the elimination of racial inequalities in the unions seems greatly improved. The clauses in the AFL-CIO constitution just referred to are one of the signs. No such declaration of principle appeared in the old AFL constitution. The election of two Negro labor leaders as vice-presidents of the merged Federation is another sign.

Governmental Action

Governmental actions, federal and state, are contributing toward an improved outlook. Executive orders issued by Presidents Truman and Eisenhower forbid discrimination in government employment and in private employment involving government contracts. To police the latter, Executive Order 10479 (1953) created a Committee on Government Contracts which receives complaints concerning discriminatory practices and refers them to the federal agencies involved for investigation and action.

Fifteen states have enacted laws forbidding discrimination in employment by either employers or labor organizations, although in three of these provision for enforcement is lacking. The effectiveness of these laws in important industrial states was a factor in leading unions which had followed discriminatory practices to abandon them by constitutional amendment.

Eighteen railroads, including the New York Central and the Pennsylvania, and an equal number of airlines, after conferences with the New York and New Jersey agencies that administer the nondiscrimination laws of those states, have announced their adherence to a policy of nondiscrimination in hiring.[22]

Decisions by state courts and by the United States Supreme Court have contributed further to the building of a body of law to which some of the discussed practices are repugnant. Two notable decisions having this effect were handed down in December 1944: one by the Supreme Court of California, the other by the Supreme Court of the United States.

The California decision [23] upheld an injunction issued by a lower court against the discharge of Negro employees of a shipbuilding company. The union, a local of the Boiler Makers, had a closed-shop agreement with the employers, and it maintained an auxiliary local for Negro members. The employees who sought the injunction had refused to join the auxiliary local and so were discharged, in accordance with the terms of the closed-shop agreement. The court found that membership in the auxiliary local did not accord to its members the same rights as those possessed by members of the "supervising" [white] local, from which Negroes were excluded.

"The fundamental question in this case," the Court declared, "is whether a closed union coupled with a closed shop is a legitimate objective of organized labor." Closed-shop agreements were legal in California, the Court conceded, but "it does not follow that a union may maintain both [24] a closed-shop agreement or other form of labor monopoly together with a closed or partially closed membership." A union that has "attained a monopoly of the supply of labor by means of closed-shop agreements occupies a quasi-public position," and may not "claim the same freedom from legal restraint enjoyed by golf clubs or fraternal associations." And, finally, "the discriminatory practices involved in this case are . . . contrary to the public policy of the United States and this state."

The case before the United States Supreme Court [25] in the same

---

[22] *The New York Times*, December 11, 1956.
[23] James v. Marinship Corporation, 25 Calif. 2nd 329, Dec. 30, 1944.
[24] Italics as in original.
[25] Steele v. L. & N. R. R. 323 U. S. 192, Dec. 18, 1944.

month involved discrimination of an even more drastic character. The Brotherhood of Railroad Firemen and Enginemen, which had always excluded Negroes from membership, had recently evolved a plan to end the employment of Negro firemen on the southeastern railroads. Having established the practice that only white firemen could be promoted to positions as engineers, the Firemen and some twenty southeastern railroads entered into an agreement in February 1941 which provided that only "promotable" men should be assigned to new runs, or selected to fill vacancies. This meant that within a few years all firemen's jobs would be held by white men.

A Negro fireman brought suit, asking for an injunction against carrying out the agreements, for a declaratory judgment as to their rights, and for damages. Having failed in the state courts, he appealed to the United States Supreme Court. The case turned upon the interpretation of certain clauses of the Railway Labor Act. Just as in the Wagner and Taft-Hartley Acts, the Railway Labor Act provides that "employees shall have the right to organize and bargain collectively through representatives of their own choosing," and "the majority of any craft or class of employees shall have the right to determine" who their representatives in negotiating with the employer shall be. It is the "majority of the craft or class" who select these representatives.

"We think," said the Supreme Court, "that Congress . . . did not intend to confer plenary power upon the union to sacrifice, for the benefit of its members, rights of the minority of the craft without imposing on it any duty to protect the minority." When the majority of a craft has made its choice of a representative, it has an obligation to represent "all of its members, the majority as well as the minority and it is to act for and not against those whom it represents. . . . While the statute does not deny to a . . . labor organization the right to determine eligibility to its membership, it does require the union . . . in making contracts with the carrier, to represent non-union or minority union members of the craft without hostile discrimination, fairly, impartially, and in good faith."

In these developments the leadership in organized labor is moving with the dominant forces in society itself toward a broader recognition of human rights. The new organizing efforts of AFL-CIO are accompanied by no talk of skilled versus unskilled workers. The barriers against the inclusion of women in labor unions have practically disappeared. Despite setbacks here and there racial discrimination is being eliminated from trade unionism.

Here is an area in which progress is being made. At the same time, action taken by the Executive Council of AFL-CIO in August 1956 has disturbing implications. The Council "stretched its constitution," Joseph A. Loftus reported in *The New York Times*, "to admit a union that discriminates against Negroes." This was the Brotherhood of Locomotive Firemen, which "had done nothing about ceasing discrimination." President Meany was quoted as saying: "We feel that by getting them into the combined labor organization we are quite confident that can be accomplished." [26]

[26] *The New York Times*, August 28, 1956.

12

Unions and Management

During the first third of the present century a spirit of friendliness and goodwill was not a marked feature of union-management relations. Even before the turn of the century the American Federation of Labor had put at its masthead this declaration:

A struggle is going on in all the nations of the civilized world between the oppressors and the oppressed of all countries, a struggle between the capitalist and the laborer, which grows in intensity from year to year and will work disastrous results to the toiling millions, if they are not combined for mutual protection and benefit.

At the convention of the Federation in 1916, President Gompers issued a challenge to allegedly hostile management: "You men of wealth, be careful how far you go, for there is a limit to human endurance. You throw down the gauntlet, and we will accept the challenge! And when it comes we will quote from the greatest bard the world ever had—'Lay on Macduff, and damned be he who first cries Hold! Enough!'" [1]

In 1922 *The New York Times* published a signed article by Mr. Gompers, in which he charged that a conspiracy existed to destroy the trade-union movement—"a concerted movement on the part of the employers to restore and maintain autocratic control of American industry." In support of this charge he cited the activities of employers' associations to promote the open shop; the refusal of Judge E. H. Gary of the United States Steel Corporation to bargain with a union of his employees about the twelve-hour day; and the anti-union attitude of the railroads of the country in the shopmen's strike of that year. [2]

Two weeks later the *Times* published a reply to the Gompers charges by Samuel Harden Church, president of the Carnegie Institute in Pittsburgh and a former official of the Pennsylvania Railroad.

[1] AFL Convention Proceedings, 1916, p. 293.
[2] *The New York Times*, September 17, 1922.

Mr. Church denied that a conspiracy existed. The "expressions of protest" cited by Mr. Gompers were "the simple and natural voice of a nation whose endurance has been overstrained, and whose patience has been exhausted." "The American people," Mr. Church asserted, "do not like things that are too big. Our people have always restrained business when it would grow too big. And now they are face to face with an organization more powerful, more merciless, and more dangerous than anything that has ever existed in this country—the American Federation of Labor." [3]

CHANGING ATTITUDES—LABOR

Over the years, the attitudes of open conflict have undergone significant changes. There are no references to class struggle in the constitution of the AFL-CIO. The convention speeches of the leaders of the merged bodies were spirited, but contained no specific challenge. At the end, however, President Meany took cognizance of the criticism, in some quarters, that "what we are doing . . . is inimical to the welfare of the country." These criticisms, he said, "will not turn us aside from our chosen paths." He warned: "This is not going to be any milk-toast movement. We are going to seek these things in the militant manner in which our organization was founded. We are going to use every legal means at the command of American citizens to organize the unorganized, to bring the benefits of the trade union movement to the millions who lack those benefits today. No little men with loud voices in either political or industrial life are going to turn us aside."

Following this challenge, Mr. Meany went over to the meeting of the National Association of Manufacturers and offered a program of cooperation and good will.

Organized labor's less truculent attitude toward management is due in part to its sense of security under the legislation of the 1930s. These laws—the Norris-La-Guardia Anti-Injunction Act of 1932, the Recovery Act of 1933, the Amendments to the Railway Labor Act in 1934, the Wagner Act of 1935, and finally the Supreme Court decision in 1937 upholding the Wagner Act—all tended in the direction of a new status for the unions. The right of a worker to join a union

[3] *The New York Times,* October 1, 1922.

had existed before, in the sense that there was nothing illegal about it. The new laws of the 1930s, and particularly the Railway Labor Act and the Wagner Act, protected him in the exercise of that right. It was now illegal to interfere with efforts to organize and bargain collectively, and union membership grew apace. Before the decade of the 1930s was over membership rolls had risen more than 200 per cent—from just under 3 million in 1933 to nearly 9 million in 1939.[4] Thus to a sense of security under the laws there was added a consciousness of greater strength.

CHANGING ATTITUDES—MANAGEMENT

Growth in union membership has been due not only to the new laws, but in part also to management attitudes that have been undergoing developmental changes since the mid-1930s. Where there had been almost total hostility [5] to unions in the major industries there is now general acceptance of unions and collective bargaining. To be sure there are areas where managerial hostility is as manifest today as in the earlier period, and where opposition takes as crude a form as any made use of in the 1920s, but in the leading or major industries unionism is now taken for granted and in some industries even welcomed. There are three major factors that account for this change. First, as noted above, the legislation of the 1930s gave governmental support to union organization and collective bargaining. Obedience to the law—by no means general at first and not universal now—led to more or less reluctant acceptance of unions by leading and influential employers. Mr. Carroll E. French, a spokesman for management, outlined the situation in an address before a university audience as follows:

It is a matter of record that industry generally . . . for many years looked upon the movement for the organization of labor and the spread

---

[4] The latest available report on union membership—AFL-CIO and independent—in continental United States, puts the figure at 16,718,000 in 1954. Directory of National and International Labor Unions in the United States, 1955. Bulletin 1185, U. S. Department of Labor, p. 9.

[5] An exception should be noted in the case of the railroads, which had recognized the operating Brotherhoods and dealt with them for many years before the legislation of the 1930s. Their acceptance of unionism did not extend to the non-operating employees, however, until the passage of the Railway Labor Act in 1926, which received strengthening amendments in 1934.

of collective bargaining with suspicion, fear, and even outright hostility. However, once the will of the public was clearly made known and the rights of workers with respect to organization and collective bargaining safeguarded and assured as a matter of national labor policy, industry was realistic enough to set about making whatever adjustments were necessary.[6]

The second factor was the increase in union membership. As unions grew and extended themselves over wider industrial areas, their bargaining strength made acceptance a virtue of necessity. This factor is implied in the words of Mr. French quoted above, and its existence is so obvious as to require no elaboration.

The third factor was the growth of mutual understanding resulting from experience with collective bargaining. In the long run, and in the main, neither party to the labor contract has found the other as difficult or as unreasonable as had been anticipated. A notable example of the growth of understanding over a period of years, which started with mutual distrust and hostility and ended with mutual confidence and goodwill, is set forth in a report of a searching investigation of developments in a single plant by Professor William F. Whyte of Cornell University.[7]

Perhaps nothing in our industrial history illustrates the third point better than a comparison of two industrial conferences, one of which was initiated by President Wilson in 1919 and the other by President Truman in 1945. The 1919 conference broke up over the question of collective bargaining. The employer group (there were three groups in the conference, designated respectively as labor, employer, and public) refused to accept a resolution which recognized the right of wage earners to organize and bargain collectively through "representatives of their own choosing," even though an added clause read: "This must not be understood as limiting the right of any wage earner to refrain from joining any organization or to deal directly with his employer if he so chooses." The employer group offered instead a resolution recognizing the right of workers to join unions or "shop industrial councils" and to bargain collectively, but declaring the "right of an employer to deal or not to deal with men or groups who

[6] Carroll E. French, Director of Industrial Relations Division, National Association of Manufacturers. Address delivered at University of North Carolina, May 12, 1949.

[7] *Patterns for Industrial Peace* (New York: Harper & Brothers), 1951.

are not his employees." The labor group rejected this proposal and the conference came to an end.[8]

At the conference called by President Truman in 1945, labor and management representatives again failed to agree on many proposals. The report on collective bargaining was not acted on for that reason. But what the record shows they did agree on, even though it never was "officially" adopted, is very impressive in comparison with the record of the earlier conference. "Collective bargaining," they said in identical statements, "is required by law. It is approved by the public. It is and must be accepted by employers, employees, and their representatives in every instance where workers choose to organize to bargain collectively on questions of wages, hours, and working conditions." [9]

Evidences of improved relations between management and labor are easy to find. Thousands of union-management agreements are renewed every year without flurry or suggestion of conflict. There is evidence, moreover, not only of management's acceptance of unionism, but even of cordial and willing acceptance. Steel, earlier in the forefront of opposition, is a leading example of the new trend. A spokesman for a large independent steel company told me that management "would be lost" without the union—a statement that was interpreted as meaning that with the thousands of workers in a

[8] *Monthly Labor Review*, November 1919, p. 43 ff.

[9] *President's National Labor-Management Conference, November, 1945*, U. S. Department of Labor, Division of Labor Standards, Bulletin No. 77.
There were several other paragraphs in the report on which labor and management representatives were in full agreement. The principal differences were over three clauses which management wanted included, and which labor representatives would not accept. One of these called for including in labor contracts a ban on strikes, lockouts, or boycotts. Another pointed out that management had been subject to government controls for a long time and stated that labor organizations should be equally controlled and made equally liable for breach of contract.
A third clause proposed by the management men was as follows: "The voluntary and just settlement in collective bargaining issues is impossible under conditions of force, regardless of its source or nature. Voluntary negotiation or free collective bargaining is not possible except under conditions of law and order and the absence of force. Management and labor are but a part of the public. The public has the right to insist that management and labor at all times practice collective bargaining with full regard for protection of individuals and property against unlawful acts." This was objected to by the unions as lacking definiteness and subject to misinterpretation.

modern steel plant, the union is an essential agency for communication between management and men.

The United States Steel Corporation, which started in 1901 with a pronouncement against extension of unions, celebrated its fiftieth anniversary in 1951 with a historical volume in which it noted as one of its achievements the establishment of collective bargaining.[10] There have been notable strikes in the steel industry, but there has also been considerable evidence of mutual goodwill. After the 1952 strike, arrangements were made by the late Philip Murray, president of the union, and Benjamin Fairless, president of the Steel Corporation, to make a joint tour of the corporation's plants, to meet the local officials and rank-and-file workers. Mr. Murray's death in 1952 postponed the project, but it was carried out later by Mr. Fairless and David J. McDonald, Mr. Murray's successor.[11]

At a dinner in Pittsburgh honoring Mr. McDonald, Mr. Fairless made the following comment:

. . . earlier in this century labor fought an all-out war to establish the right of American workers to organize and to bargain collectively. . . . That war ended more than twenty years ago, and labor won it decisively. . . . I happen to think that labor's victory in that cause was a fine thing for America. Today union representation is not only an accepted part of our industrial system—it is, I think, a very necessary one. . . . I firmly believe that if union representation were to disappear entirely, enlightened management in many industries would quickly welcome its revival in the interest of orderly and organized bargaining in the plants.[12]

[10] In a chapter entitled "The Human Element," reference is made to a clause in the 1947 contract with the union; this, said the writer, "is a landmark of enlightened thinking. It means turning to a fresh page where the writing should be inspired by mutual good will, trust, and respect free from recrimination and name-calling. It means that prosperity is indivisible and that the well-being of one party cannot be jeopardized without detriment to the well-being of the other." *Steel Serves the Nation* (U. S. Steel Corporation, 1951), pp. 71–72; 75–78.

[11] Commenting on these visits, John A. Stephens, U. S. Steel vice-president in charge of industrial relations, said in a speech at a meeting of the American Management Association in September 1955: "I'm not sure we can yet measure results. . . . [but] the visits have put to rest one basic influence against better relations—a belief among union officials, employees, and, to a degree, supervision, that United States Steel had never fully accepted the union and, should a propitious time arrive, might seek its destruction."

[12] *Monthly Labor Review*, January 1954, p. 67.

Whether the sort of relationship suggested by this address has suffered damage by the development of the 1956 strike may be questioned. In the course of the strike President McDonald of the union spoke of "deceit and lies" and "five years of concentrated greed," in referring to the steel industry leaders.

A team of investigators from the Chicago University School of Business made a study in 1953 of the reaction of management to union activities in a steel plant employing 14,000 workers. They interviewed all members of top management and supervisors down to the foreman level. "Overwhelmingly," they reported, "the management group as a whole believes that the union has made an important contribution toward the well-being of the employees, the company, or both. Fewer than half of those interviewed held the union responsible for actions detrimental to the welfare of the company or its workers, with almost all of these giving the union credit for desirable changes as well."

Among the achievements for which the union was given credit "by various management officials" were raising wages, reducing inequities, improving working conditions, establishing a grievance procedure, improving the safety program, inducing the company to improve plant sanitation and other housekeeping practices.

A "top" management man said "it [the union] has forced management to do many things that management should have done anyway. . . . The union has forced management to be a damn-sight better management. Anybody can yell at people and get something done by force. A supervisor today has to be twice as good a man as 20 years ago." [13]

A marked decline in the proportion of strikes to attain union objectives provides further evidence of lessened tension. Official reports on the "major issues" involved in strikes reveal significant trends. During the half-dozen years prior to the application of the labor pro-

[13] On the other hand, the spokesman quoted was "unhappy about the 'hostile' and 'uncooperative' attitude of some leaders of the local union." Management officials criticized the seniority rule, claiming that it was a "brake on employee incentive" and forced the retention of "lazy and incompetent" workers. In general, however, the view "that the union has been of benefit to the company as well as the men was encountered at all levels of management." *Management Views the Local Union*, by Joel Seidman, Richard Hammett, Jack London, and Bernard Karsh. *Journal of Business*, April 1953, pp. 91 ff.

visions of the Recovery Act—1928 to 1933 inclusive—strikes for such objectives as recognition of the union, closed or union shop, "strengthening bargaining position," etc., averaged about 31 per cent of all strikes. The next eight years were devoted to struggle to take advantage of the new laws. The percentage of strikes called to promote union organization jumped from 32 in 1933 to 45 in 1934. The average for the period 1934 to 1941 inclusive was over 49 per cent. In 1942, with union membership at approximately 10½ million, the proportion of strikes for "union organization" dropped abruptly to 13 per cent. It has remained fairly close to that figure ever since.[14]

CONTINUING PROBLEMS

The developments of the last fifteen or twenty years, with which our discussion here has been concerned, indicate gratifying progress in human relations. It is not intended, however, to convey the impression that there are no longer problems to be thrashed out in the labor-management field. Even where mutual respect and confidence prevail there is no assurance of agreement on particular issues. There is no sure barrier against strikes and lockouts. At a conference of clergymen and Christian laymen held in the summer of 1955, a member of the management group remarked, half humorously, to a union official: "We're brothers here, but that doesn't mean that we won't be as tough as ever the next time we meet at the bargaining table."

Underlying all the new attitudes are memories of another day. Despite all that has been learned in the recent past, the time has been too short to erase the effect in men's minds of the hostilities of a generation ago. To cite extreme examples, Herrin is remembered as against labor; and Ludlow is a symbol of capitalist terror.[15] Even after men are no longer alive who remember the scenes of violence sug-

[14] U. S. Bureau of Labor Statistics, Bulletin 651, *Strikes in the United States, 1880–1936. Handbook of Labor Statistics*, 1950 edition, p. 146. *Monthly Labor Review*, May, 1952, 1953, 1954, 1955.

[15] The Herrin affair occurred during a coal-mine strike in southern Illinois in 1922. Sixteen or more strike breakers were killed by union sympathizers when marching away from a struck mine under promise of safe conduct. During another strike of coal miners at Ludlow, Colorado, in 1914 two women and twelve children were killed as a result of an attack by militiamen and mine guards on a tent colony occupied by strikers and their families.

gested by these names, their stories will doubtless live on as myths or legends and have their effect on labor and management attitudes.

As pointed out earlier, the belief that management would, if it could, revert to the tactics of an earlier period and wipe out unionism, root and branch, is probably held by most labor leaders. Their fears are strengthened by occasional expressions of opinion emanating from management organizations. A pamphlet published in 1954 by the Chamber of Commerce of the United States contained the statement: ". . . however authentic the original employee needs and drives behind the development of a labor union may have been, at times the need diminishes or disappears. . . . To a substantial degree, much of the original basis of unionism has disappeared. . . ." [16]

Management, on its part, even while disclaiming the existence of any sound basis for labor's fears, is itself distrustful of labor's attitudes. This distrust is contributed to by an occasional militant voice, like that of a resolution adopted in a recent union convention declaring: "In every sound union man's heart down through the years has been a hope for a greater unity of all labor to fight the Boss." It is fostered also by such minor incidents as the not uncommon publication in labor papers of cartoons depicting employers as stupid, or avaricious, or unjust.

It is not these union pin-pricks, however, that mainly account for management's distrust. It arises rather out of occurrences here and there of picket-line tactics or of bargaining-table pressures that are believed to be uncooperative, or undemocratic, or to involve interference with the legal rights of individuals.

Elsewhere we have discussed the controversy over the union shop.[17] The practice on the part of some unions of taking strike votes just prior to the opening of contract negotiations or resorting to slowdowns or stoppages during negotiations seems to many employers to be a negation of good-faith bargaining. However, a 1955 decision of the United States Court of Appeals for the District of Columbia held (two to one) that "harassing tactics" during contract negotiations, which included among other things "slowdown" and "unannounced

[16] *Labor and the American Economy* (Chamber of Commerce of the United States, 1954), p. 19.
[17] Chap. 7, "Union Security."

walkouts," did not constitute refusal to bargain in good faith under the terms of the Taft-Hartley Act.[18]

Whether or not this was a correct interpretation of the law, such action on the part of the union seems to raise an ethical question not decided by the court. To be sure, a strike vote before negotiations begin is routine practice in many unions. Even without such a vote both sides know that a breakdown of negotiations might result in a strike. The case before the court, however, involved "harassing tactics" *during* negotiations, having as their purpose pressure on management to meet the union's demands. A common-sense view, as distinguished from a technical interpretation of a law, seems to put such tactics outside the realm of good-faith bargaining.

Violence in labor disputes is another factor having important repercussions on labor-management relations, whether caused by the strikers or by the employers. This is a matter of concern to the public also, and is discussed in the following chapter.

THE OUTLOOK

If what is said here about the continued existence of a certain amount of mutual distrust seems in any sense to cancel out the earlier evidence indicating the emergence of better relations, such an implication is neither intended nor justified. An appraisal of attitudes in labor-management relations that did not take into account adverse as well as favorable aspects would be less than realistic. It would do no good to ignore the fact that under the best of conditions labor and management sometimes view each other's acts in a spirit of protective skepticism, and that there are still areas where unions or management, or both, act on occasion as if the rejected tactics of an earlier period were still justifiable and expedient.

But, taking all the evidence into account, the favorable trends are more impressive and more general than the reverse. Clinton Golden commented on these trends in his introduction to a summary of the reports of a body of experts who had engaged in a "seven-year search for the causes of industrial peace." Out of the fullness of his long experience as worker, labor leader, and director of the Trade Union Program at Harvard University he wrote:

[18] Textile Workers Union, CIO v. NLRB, 227 F 2nd. 409.

. . . a remarkable change in the climate of industrial relations has occurred over the past eighteen years. There has been a steady growth of mutual confidence between management and organized labor coupled with the discovery of new techniques for peaceful settlement of disputes.

Beginning in 1937, thousands of collective-bargaining agreements were negotiated for the first time. . . . In spite of the heritage of fears and suspicions and the unpreparedness on both sides, with notable exceptions, agreements were reached without interruptions to production. As time passed, management and union representatives were brought into closer personal contact and gradually faced their new responsibilities.

Many newly negotiated agreements covered a comparatively short period —usually one year. In retrospect, it is obvious that management had not yet come to believe that the unions would be enduring and permanent institutions. And union leaders, particularly in the new and rapidly expanding organizations, were not too confident of the cohesiveness and solidarity of their own organizations or of the good faith of management in the new relationship.

. . . Nevertheless the frequently unwilling partnership continued. Expiration dates of the initial agreements, although approached with apprehension on both sides, did not terminate relationships. In most instances contracts were renewed and continued on the basis of mutually acceptable revisions and with a minimum of interruption to production. [Even in 1946,] when the American public heard or read about more strikes than ever before in our history, more than nine out of every ten contracts between employers and unions were negotiated peacefully.

We must not, however, expect too much. "There are relative degrees of industrial peace," says Mr. Golden. "These range from a precarious equilibrium of mutually hostile forces for a stated period of time—the life of an agreement—to an enduring, harmonious, and cooperative relationship of a really creative character. Under present conditions, neither extreme represents the typical. There is some evidence, though, that we are moving from the first *in the direction of* the second, which may be thought of as the ideal." [19]

[19] Clinton S. Golden and Virginia D. Parker, *Causes of Industrial Peace* (New York: Harper & Brothers, 1955), pp. 3, 4, 5, 8. Italics in original.

13

Organized Labor and the Public

There is a tendency to speak of "labor and the public" as separate entities. Here it is assumed rather that the "public" consists of the people who live at any time within the confines of any particular geographical or political area. Therefore "labor" is always a part of the public, and is no more to be distinguished from the mass than any other definable group within it. There is, however, a sense in which any group within the public may be set off from the total for examination. That is, it may be so treated if it has some special characteristics not shared by others—in addition to the characteristics or interests common to all. In this sense we may with propriety speak of "management and the public," or "doctors and the public," or "ministers and the public." With equal propriety we may speak of "labor and the public."

Labor—A Part of the Public

The members of organized labor are distinguished first by the fact that they earn a living by working for wages (or salaries) and second that they organize in order to protect and improve their economic status. Since, however, they continue to be citizens with concerns and interests that they hold in common with others outside their ranks, they tend, especially as they grow more secure in their ability to deal with the economic problems of their members, to deal also with matters of general public concern. A sense of economic security seems to be the essential element preceding any considerable union activity in public affairs as distinguished from matters of concern to the members strictly as members. This is indicated by the fact that it is only in comparatively recent years that the labor movement generally has taken serious action toward promotion of a variety of objectives involving public affairs.

To be sure, the promotion of free public education has been one of the objectives of organized labor in the United States from its beginnings more than a century ago. Opposition to child labor has also been one of the outstanding planks in labor's platform for many years. The first convention, in 1881, of the federation that was the forerunner of the American Federation of Labor took action favoring compulsory education and the prohibition of the employment of children under fourteen "in any capacity." But it was long before organized labor bodies began to express themselves with respect to a broad area of public affairs.

It is interesting to contrast the AFL convention of 1933, meeting in the midst of the depression and representing slightly over two million members, with the first convention of AFL-CIO in December 1955, representing 15 million trade unionists. The 1933 convention adopted, or referred to the Executive Council for action, 96 resolutions. Of these, 22, approximately 23 per cent, dealt with public affairs and 74, 77 per cent, with matters of primary or exclusive concern to trade unionists. The 1955 convention adopted 55 resolutions, 29 of which dealt with public affairs.

The primary purpose of the labor movement continues to be, of course, the protection and advancement of the interests of its present and prospective members. Its growing sense of responsibility in the field of citizenship is an impressive aspect of its development in recent years. But the existence of these two objectives sometimes creates a problem for the leaders who attempt to give public expression to labor's aims. It is an example of the universal ethical problem of reconciling self-interest and social obligation. George Meany, in his address before the AFL-CIO convention on December 5, 1955, accepting the presidency of the merged body, gave evidence of the conflict in union thinking between purely parochial aims and a broader concern in which self-interest is merged with public interest.[1]

"The Kind of World We Live In"

Mr. Meany declared that the trade-union movement "has for its sole, definite, and single purpose the advancement of the welfare and interest of the great mass of workers who are part of this movement," that it has "no other reason for existence than the job . . . of advancing the interests and welfare of its members." Further along,

[1] Proceedings First Constitutional Convention AFL-CIO, December 5, 1955, p. 26.

however, Mr. Meany was saying: "As we face the future . . . we should give some sober thought to the kind of world that we live in, to the problems we have at home and the problems that we have abroad. . . ." Nothing could better illustrate the ethical dilemma confronting all economic groups.

"We have come a long way," he continued, "in building up the standard of life and of work with the people of this great nation, but we can't say we have come all the way. . . . We still need better schools and more schools for the children of America. . . . Then we have housing which is still a problem. . . . We still have thousands and thousands of people who are living in slums. . . . We need better roads. We need to improve our social security system. We need to bring about a system of medical care that will take care of the health of the nation as a whole."

Racial discrimination, Mr. Meany implied, constitutes a rejection of American tradition and a violation of the Bill of Rights. Christians, he said, "should remember that the words 'and thy neighbor as thyself' are still an integral part of the Ten Commandments.[2]

"Then we have to give some sober thought to our duties as citizens . . . , making our contribution to good government. . . . As workers we have a special interest in the foreign policy of our government. We have a special interest in seeing to it that our government makes its full contribution to the preservation of human freedom everywhere on this earth where it is possible to make a contribution.

"In meeting these problems at home and abroad," Mr. Meany asserted, "we must be mindful of our duty to the nation as a whole. . . . We must show the American people that this movement, this organization, is dedicated to the good of our nation, to the good of all the citizens of our nation . . . ," for, "after all, the American worker is just a part, . . . one segment of this great big family we call the United States. . . ."[3]

[2] In the enthusiasm of extemporaneous speech, Mr. Meany forgot that these correctly quoted Biblical words are not a part of the Decalogue.

[3] In his address Mr. Meany spoke also of intra-union affairs and objectives: autonomy for affiliated unions within the new federation, extending organizing activities, opposition to anti-union employers, political action to counteract reactionary legislative proposals, and the use of our "economic weapon" if necessary "to get a fair share of the wealth that we jointly produce with management."

The constitution of AFL-CIO contains frequent avowals of union responsibility in the broader areas discussed by Mr. Meany. How much influence these declarations may have on the future of the labor movement we cannot foretell, but what organized labor has done and is now doing in matters that concern the public may offer some basis for judgment. Whether we agree with Mr. Meany that the advancement of the interests of its members is the sole purpose of unionism, or believe (also with Mr. Meany) that unions must give "sober thought to the kind of world we live in," we may reasonably consider the impact of union objectives and activities, past and present, on the general welfare.

STRIKES AND THE PUBLIC

Most strikes inflict some economic loss on some part of the public, ranging from a small segment to a large proportion of the total as when a strike is nationwide in scope and affects such necessities as fuel, food, or transportation. In such a case the affected public consists of all consumers of the goods or services in question, including wage earners.

On the other hand, in the long run many strikes cause little or no economic loss. While they are in progress, however, losses are incurred by both strikers and employers—the losses being heavy or light according to duration and other factors.

Discussion of the effect of strikes on society at large is often as uninformed and as exaggerated in tone as popular ideas about their extent.[4] In addition to the mistaken belief about the frequency and magnitude of strikes, and the notion that unions and their members are ever eager to strike—which is refuted by the roadblocks set up in union constitutions—there is a tendency in some circles, remote from the actualities, to think of all strikes as constituting some degree of menace to public welfare. Under some circumstances a strike could present such a threat. That was recognized at the outset of World War II when nearly all of the international unions in the United States pledged the Government that they would forego the calling of strikes for the period of the war.[5]

[4] See Supplementary Notes.
[5] With few exceptions, they kept their word. Such strikes as did occur were mostly wildcat strikes called locally and against the will of the top officials.

It should be noted also that the practice of computing the cost of a strike by estimating the value of goods not produced and the amount of wages not earned because of the strike is based on an erroneous assumption. Such a calculation would be correct only if the industry or the concern affected were operating at full capacity, month in, month out. Actually, the loss in production and in wages due to a particular strike may merely take up the slack resulting from seasonal shutdowns or curtailments due to market recessions.

Under ordinary circumstances strikes fall into several categories, according to the degree to which they affect the public. The areas in which strikes may occur range from those affecting products, whose absence from the market causes inconvenience to few and hardship to none, to stoppages of the production of goods or services that are of extraordinary value in terms of human welfare or even essential to life itself. Strikes in the latter category may do great harm to all, or nearly all, of the population in the areas affected.

Strikes in industries on which other industries depend are apt to have wide repercussions. As supplies of raw materials diminish, dependent industries begin to curtail operations or close down, handicapping retailers and consumers and throwing additional employees out of work. Such a train of events often creates hardship to many workers not concerned with the original dispute, as well as to suppliers, retailers, and business generally. It was estimated that the 34-day strike in the steel industry in 1956 caused 125,000 additional workers to be laid off.

Strike Violence

Another occasional aspect of strikes in which the public has much at stake is the emergence of violence. Reference has been made to the attitude of strikers toward nonstrikers and strike breakers, and the explosive possibilities of mass picketing. It is generally agreed that violence in labor disputes occurs less frequently nowadays than was the case some years ago. Where an industry is fairly completely organized, or where management has a keen desire to maintain as good labor relations as possible, a plant is usually closed down during a strike, thus precluding clashes between strikers and strike breakers. In such circumstances the pickets have no incitement to violent action. There have even been instances of a benevolent (or shrewd) management providing facilities to promote the comfort of the pickets. In some outstanding strikes in the last few years, however, there have been scenes of violence reminiscent of an earlier day, not only in parts of the country where unionism has not yet been accepted by either management or public authorities but also in regions where labor organizations have been taken for granted for years.

Nothing short of a detailed study of each case would suffice to justify an apportionment of blame for these outbreaks. One suspects—and some of the known facts tend to support the suspicion—that in some of these cases the employer, or his representative, was as much responsible for the violence as the union.[6] In one recent strike, in which there was violence, there was apparently sincere conviction on both sides that the other party was the greater, if not the sole, offender.

In trying to discover truth in this matter it is important to keep in mind the fact that a strike is an emotion-laden affair. When a thousand men are on strike, there are a thousand wills involved working under varying degrees of self-control. The impetuous acts of a few are often sufficient to create a situation that tends to bring the whole union under public condemnation. In the nature of the case the leaders may be incapable of preventing "incidents" from occurring.

After allowing for all of that, as well as for the possibility of employers' participation, it should be pointed out that in these more recent strikes there is lack of evidence that the union leaders have been seriously engaged in efforts to prevent the commission of illegal acts. In the absence of such evidence in the case of a few unions the basis is laid for distrust of all unions, however unjust such general condemnation may be.

Public Intervention in Strikes

The public, in the broadest sense of the term, is affected by strikes and is justified in its concern. However justifiable the strike, it usually affects the public in ways that seem adverse, for the time being at least, despite the fact that in the long run a strike for a justifiable purpose is likely to have consequences that benefit the public as well as the workers. At best, while it is going on, it present aspects that call

---

[6] In the earlier "hostility" period there was much evidence of employer-induced violence.

for serious consideration on the part of the nonparticipating public. At worst, it may have grave consequences for community welfare. In considering it as a public phenomenon, it is important to keep in mind the fact that the public is concerned with something more than the suppression of disorder. Before acting the public has an obligation to be informed; and when acting it has an obligation to seek justice. A further obligation is to attempt to discriminate between danger and inconvenience. No one has a vested right to immunity from inconvenience.

In view of the undoubted losses caused by strikes, it is significant that there is no general demand for their prohibition. The belief is generally held in democratic countries that strikes are a wholesome safety valve and that in many cases strikes or potential strikes are essential for the maintenance of bargaining power. Nor is there much support for compulsory arbitration, except on the part of some railway officials who are already under compulsion, on the income side, by public regulation of rates. There is from time to time considerable pressure for the limitation or regulation of strikes involving public utilities. In 1947—the same year that Congress passed the Taft-Hartley Act—laws were enacted in nine states providing for some form of compulsory arbitration of disputes in such industries when collective bargaining fails.[7] Section 206 of Title II of the Taft-Hartley Act deals with "national emergency" strikes. It outlines a procedure to be followed when "in the opinion of the President . . . a threatened or actual strike or lockout affecting an entire industry or a substantial part thereof" imperils the "national health or safety." The procedure includes investigation of the dispute, a possible injunction against the strike or lockout, continuance of bargaining—assisted by the Federal Conciliation and Mediation Service—and a secret ballot (if the dispute is not settled earlier) on the employer's last offer. This is the full procedure. If the dispute is not settled earlier, the injunction is terminated at the end of eighty days, and the parties are then free to settle or continue the dispute as they see fit.

This procedure has been invoked in a dozen cases since the law was

[7] These states were Florida, Indiana, Massachusetts, Missouri, Nebraska, New Jersey, Pennsylvania, Virginia, and Wisconsin. See Charles C. Killingsworth, *State Labor Relations Acts* (Chicago: University of Chicago Press, 1948), pp. 293–98.

enacted in 1947, with dubious results.[8] In every case where a ballot on the employer's last offer was taken, the employees have rejected it. In a few cases the issues have been settled by collective bargaining after the injunction was lifted; in a few other cases the strike has been resumed at the end of the eighty-day period.

The Taft-Hartley Act forbids strikes by employees of the federal government and provides penalties in the form of immediate discharge, loss of civil service status, and ineligibility for re-employment for a period of three years. Similar laws have been enacted in certain states. The Condon-Wadlin Law in New York imposes even more drastic penalties, with the result that enforcement has been lax or, in some cases, even totally lacking. These laws share with unmodified compulsory arbitration laws the injustice of depriving the employees of their final means of protest against injustice. Without a quid pro quo the workers affected are denied rights that are possessed by all others. What might be a reasonable substitute for the right to strike is a question about which there are differences of opinion. A very suggestive proviso was inserted in a bill introduced in Congress in 1947—among a host of other bills that finally led to the Taft-Hartley Act. This bill, which called for compulsory arbitration as a preventive of strikes vitally affecting public welfare, called upon the arbitrators to "take into consideration" the fact that the employees affected are engaged in an essential industry and that "by reason of being so employed their right to strike has been limited . . . and that in view of the foregoing, such employees ought to have, in relation to others not so situated, at least as favorable a status in the matter of the terms and conditions of their employment."

It is obvious that the last word on the subject of emergency strikes has not been spoken. There are activities of such vital importance to human well-being that a stoppage would constitute a public disaster of startling proportions. Perhaps the extreme example would be the shutting down of a city water supply. There are areas of lesser importance in which a strike, if prolonged, could constitute a menace

[8] "The best case that can be made for the national emergency section of the Taft-Hartley Act is essentially a negative one; that is, viewing the record overall, the Act's effects do not appear to have been unduly harmful." Frank C. Pierson, *Emergency Disputes and National Policy* (New York: Harper & Brothers, 1955), p. 132.

to public health. Under such conditions the demand for a curb on union action is bound to gather strength. A drastic remedy which has been tried more than once is seizure by governmental authority. The results have not been very reassuring, partly because the penalties of seizure have not always been obvious. Indeed, one party or the other might benefit from seizure. An interesting proposal to make seizure unpalatable to both employer and union has been made by a New York lawyer and legislator. If the employer were deprived of profits during seizure, the union deprived of the right to collect dues or to enforce a union shop, and the striker deprived of the right to build up credits toward a pension, all parties might be impelled toward a settlement.[9]

Whatever the merits of such a proposal, the burden of finding a way to protect the public against the dangers inherent in emergency strikes rests heavily on the shoulders of labor and management. It is in their interest to discover a just and practicable solution of this problem.

Labor and Public Affairs

More than half of the resolutions adopted by the AFL-CIO convention in December 1955 were devoted to matters affecting the general public. Some of the more important of these resolutions call for brief presentation.

Housing

"One-third of the nation," the convention declared, "is still ill-housed. More than 10,000,000 dwellings are so dilapidated that they should be torn down and some 5,000,000 more require major overhaul to make them fit places in which to live. Each year more homes are added to these categories than are torn down or adequately overhauled. . . .

"We believe the very foundations of our private enterprise system and our democratic way of life require that our people be properly housed. We believe this can be achieved in a manner fully consistent with our economic system; in fact, an adequate housing program will greatly enhance the basic strength of our economy."

[9] Ludwig Teller, "What Should be Done About Emergency Strikes?"; *Labor Law Journal* January, 1950, pp. 263–277.

The situation calls, the resolution declared, for "two million new housing units a year, a major portion" of which "should be constructed and marketed at cost within the reach of low and moderate income families with incomes below $5,000 a year, most of whom are now priced out of the private housing market." The plan proposed "low interest, long amortization loans for cooperative nonprofit rental and sales housing," with mortgages "on a 40-year term with nominal down payments" and a National Mortgage Corporation to make loans "not to exceed four billion dollars a year."

Community Services

From 1941 to 1955 the AFL "Labor League for Human Rights," later renamed the "Community Relations Committee," and the CIO "Community Services Committee" were active in the field of health and welfare. The permanent national committee on Community Services provided for in the AFL-CIO constitution insures the continuance of the work. The original committees were established for purposes of war relief, but at the end of the war they turned to activities involving civilian needs. At that time officers of Community Chests and Councils—the national coordinating agency for similarly named local bodies—succeeded in effecting a joint relationship with the two labor committees making possible cooperation between the public and private social agencies and the unions.

As a result unions and social agencies have been working together on both the national and local levels for social betterment. Both AFL and CIO had members serving on boards of community chests and social agencies all over the country, and on committees of such bodies. At the end of 1955 it was estimated that as many as twenty-five to thirty thousand union members were serving in this manner. Both federations regularly assisted in the raising of funds. Of the more than $300 million raised for community chests in 1955 about a third came from individuals, a third from employer organizations, and the remaining third from employee groups, including organized labor.

One of the activities of the CIO Community Services Committee was the development of a union counseling program. Individuals working in the shops who volunteered to act as counselors were given training by union leaders and social workers to acquaint them with the purposes and methods of the social agencies, public and private, of the community. These counselors assisted their fellows who might be in need of advice with respect to personal or family problems by acting as referral agents, sending the applicant to the specialized local agency best equipped to deal with his problem. This committee also provided special services for union members who were unemployed or on strike. Problems that could be lived with under normal circumstances tend to become more acute when regular income stops. Besides screening applicants for financial assistance, and referring those qualified to the local welfare agencies, they stepped up other phases of the program to make sure that they met the various problems as they arose.

The resolution on community services adopted at the merger convention declared that "members of the AFL-CIO function first and foremost as citizens of their communities." Their objectives "in the area of community organization for health, welfare, and recreation" were set forth as including the encouragement of "equitable labor representation on agency boards and committees" and "labor participation in formulating agency policies and programs," the interpretation of such agency programs for union members, and the assistance of "union members, their families, and other citizens in time of need." The program further includes helping in the "development of health and welfare services" and cooperation with other agencies "in dealing with and solving social and health problems."

International Affairs

In 1913 the AFL convention created, at the suggestion of President Samuel Gompers, a Committee on International Relations, later to become the Committee on International Labor Relations. Each year from 1913 to 1954 the convention received a report from this Committee on international activities of concern to labor. In the earlier years the reports dealt mostly with the activities of the trade unions of the different countries, organized as trade "secretariats"—international federations of unions in a particular trade or in allied trades—or with the International Federation of Trade Unions, a loose federation of national federations which ceased to function with the onset of the second World War.[10]

[10] During the Versailles Peace Conference in 1919, Samuel Gompers played an important role in setting up the International Labor Organization, an agency of

In 1920, under the sobering shadow of World War I, the AFL Executive Council included in its report to the convention the following statement:

"There cannot be during the coming year, nor probably ever again in our future, a restriction of our interest and activity in relation to the work and the welfare of the rest of the world. Whatever may be our desires, the fact is that the course of events and the needs of people have woven our destinies into such a relation with the peoples of the world that our attention can not be withdrawn from what is happening in other countries and on other continents." [11]

Despite these manifestations of interest American labor for some time continued to show little concern about matters involving international policy at the government level. The Convention of 1933 condemned Hitlerism and favored affiliation with the ILO, but took no other action with respect to international affairs. But as Italian fascism developed and as Nazi Germany continued to expand its power, both AFL and CIO began to take notice. Both established permanent committees, each with a full-time staff, to study and deal with international affairs. Both sent labor representatives abroad after the war to assist in rebuilding the labor movements in Europe and in establishing free trade unions in Asian countries. Under the combined leadership of AFL, CIO, and the British Trade Union Congress, the International Confederation of Free Trade Unions was organized in London in 1949. In 1953 this organization had 102 affiliates representing some 54 million workers in 77 countries and territories.[12] Its purpose is to improve standards of living "for working people everywhere"; to promote world peace; "to strengthen free trade unions in the struggle against totalitarianism . . ."; to oppose colonialism, and "to protect and strengthen workers' rights everywhere."

From minor concern with international affairs a score of years ago American labor has moved on until in the half-dozen years preceding the merger of AFL and CIO the two federations were giving a degree of attention to that field fairly comparable to their concern over

---

the League of Nations through which member nations conferred on international action with reference to labor conditions. It continued as an independent body after the breakdown of the League and is now a part of the United Nations.

[11] AFL Convention Proceedings, 1920, p. 131.
[12] *Monthly Labor Review*, November 1953, p. 1911.

strictly labor affairs. This was made manifest at the final conventions which took place in December 1955, and even more impressively at the merger convention itself. At the final CIO convention the Department for International Affairs reported that "CIO has worked closely with labor in other parts of the world—through the International Confederation of Free Trade Unions—and has acted on matters of foreign policy within this country, in both cases with the firm determination of furthering peace, security, and increased well-being." At about the same time the executive council of the AFL was reporting to their delegates that it had been "mindful of the responsibilities that American labor must meet in this critical period of world history. Today our duty goes far beyond the building of a powerful trade-union movement in our own country. Today, our tasks go far beyond those of strengthening our trade-union movement as a dynamic voluntary organization, as a pivotal force in, of, and for our free society and American way of life. Even our basic task of promoting and protecting the interests and rights of the working people, of constantly improving their conditions of life and labor, is part of the complex international situation. It is subject to and greatly affected by the strains and stresses of the world scene and the role our country plays therein."

The merged body, in the convention immediately following, declared it to be its purpose to continue and enlarge the program that the preceding federations had been following. "We . . . have," the convention said, "three main areas of activities in our efforts to aid our country in the fulfillment of its new historic role. These are: (1) Through our trade-union strength and political actions, to help build an ever better and stronger America, a prosperous and progressive land free from economic and social inequity and all racial and every other form of discrimination. (2) Through democratic processes, to help our nation evolve and execute an effective democratic foreign policy. (3) Through cooperation with and assistance to the International Confederation of Free Trade Unions, to aid free labor everywhere in becoming a most powerful force for furthering social justice, national and human freedom, economic well-being and world peace."

After presenting details on twenty-two points, in which the above purposes were spelled out, the resolution concluded: "In this spirit, we shall encourage a greater knowledge of and a greater interest in international affairs among our membership, toward the end that the wage earners' great stake in our country's foreign policy will be more clearly recognized and reflected in its formulation and conduct." [13]

Other Areas of Concern

Other resolutions adopted at the 1955 convention of AFL-CIO covered many subjects of public interest and called for action by unions and by the Government. These include support of child-labor laws and other measures in the interest of childhood and youth; federal aid to medical schools, hospitals, and medical research; health insurance; improved facilities for the handicapped; federal aid to education; "revision and liberalization" of the McCarren-Walter Immigration Act; amendment of the Refugee Relief Act to insure admission of the full number of refugees authorized in the law; provision for federal flood insurance; enactment of a fair employment practices law; approval of the Supreme Court ruling on segregation in schools; and provisions for peace-time use of atomic energy.

The fact that the resolutions were adopted in most cases without comment or debate is not in itself evidence of lack of genuine approval on the part of the delegates. In general, one can rely on vigorous support for measures that have long been a part of the program of the merged bodies, as well as for other proposals more recently espoused, notably those relating to international affairs.

THE PROBLEM OF "BIGNESS"

A discussion of organized labor and the public would be incomplete without adverting to questions that have long been raised about the significance for the general welfare of growing labor power. Since the merger the tempo of such discussion has been notably stepped up. Henry G. Riter, president in 1955 of the National Association of Manufacturers, is reported to have said two days after the AFL-CIO merger convention: "Within the last 48 hours, we have seen the amassing in the hands of a few men of the greatest potential economic, and possibly political power, in the history of this country." [14]

[13] Proceedings of the First Constitutional Convention, AFL-CIO, December 1955, pp. 101–104.
[14] Quoted by Peter Henle in address before Industrial Relations Research Association, New York, December 28, 1955, p. 222 of Proceedings.

The fear manifested in this statement is based, at least in part, on a misapprehension: the merger in itself has not altered the picture in the manner suggested. Before the merger there were two federations of national and international unions; now there is one federation of the same unions. AFL-CIO is a larger federation than either of its predecessors, but the affiliated unions were not thereby increased in size or strength, and these affiliated unions are the agencies that deal with the employers. Neither AFL nor CIO engaged in collective bargaining and the merged body is likewise in no position to do so.

Let us turn, then, to a consideration of the extent to which the affiliated unions as separate bodies may be thought to have it within their power to endanger the public in the manner suggested.

The view is often expressed that a powerful union, by reason of its size or strategic position, might be termed a monopoly. In Chapter 7 it was suggested that a union with a closed-shop contract that "closes its books" and permits no further entrance of new members has something like monopolistic power in the area affected. But this is far from saying that unions in general are monopolies. Even in the area where such practices have been most prevalent—the building trades—there has been a notable lack of ability to control labor competition in the industry generally.

In considering this matter we are confronted with the question whether labor unions, by reason of their size or their practices, may properly be considered monopolies in the sense in which the term might be applied to a corporation controlling the entire output of a particular commodity. It seems obvious that there are significant differences: commodities are inanimate things. They can be stored and withheld from the market, or shipped hither and yon at the will of an owner. Obviously there could be no such control over human beings in a democratic society. "Labor" is not an entity, like a ton of coal. It is potential energy, stored up in a man. It is inseparable from its possessor and can be delivered to an employer only as the possessor delivers his own person at the same time. The delivery of labor, therefore, is not at the will of an agency, such as a union, but only at the will of as many individuals as are in possession of the kind of labor required.[15]

[15] In a paper read at a meeting of the Industrial Relations Research Association in December 1955 entitled "Labor Monopoly and All That," Professor Edward

It is likely that those who fear a "labor monopoly" are actually fearful of "big unionism," whether a monopoly or not. The question then appears to be: "Can a big union, because of the power engendered by its bigness, become a public danger?" And here we may take reasonable, but not exaggerated, cognizance of the merger. While that development has not in itself made the constituent unions any bigger, its influence will be in that direction, both because of the prospective mergers of AFL and CIO unions and because of the anticipated drive on unorganized territory. This, if successful, may bring large numbers of new members into the existing unions or may create some new unions. Which course is taken, as well as the extent of success of the project, will determine whether any contribution to bigness in a significant sense has been made.

As to present examples of bigness, there are in AFL-CIO three unions with more than a million members each, and two or perhaps three with a membership of 800,000 or more. At the start of 1955, according to the Bureau of Labor Statistics,[16] 3 unions had between 300,000 and 400,000 members, and 13 unions (out of 199) had altogether nearly half of the total of nearly 18 million members.[17]

These larger unions are doubtless strong enough to cause trouble if they wish to do so. The Bureau report has a cautionary statement that should be taken into account. "Sheer size," it says, "is not necessarily the key index to union strength that it appears to be. The larger international unions can, of course, muster greater support, financial and otherwise, to help their affiliated locals. However, smaller unions organizing in industries with a smaller labor force . . . have an inherent strength not readily apparent from membership figures." [18]

Circumstances more than size tend to determine the degree of power that a union exercises. The history of the movement for the "guaranteed annual wage" illustrates the point. The Automobile

---

S. Mason, who considered it axiomatic that labor unions are monopolies, pointed out, nevertheless, that "whatever else it may be, a trade union is not a seller of labor services." Proceedings, p. 192.

[16] Bulletin 1175, op. cit., p. 11.

[17] The total membership of American unions as given by the Bureau was 17,757,000. Of these, 16,718,000 were in continental United States, slightly over one million in Canada, 933,000 in Hawaii; the remainder were scattered among territories and possessions. Bulletin No. 1185, p. 9.

[18] Bulletin No. 1185, p. 11.

Workers and the Steel Workers, two of the million-member unions, had been trying for at least ten years to get this question on the agenda at bargaining conferences before they succeeded in having it accepted for serious discussion. In 1955 the Automobile Workers obtained an agreement for a limited guarantee to cover six months in each year, if certain conditions were met. The Steel Workers succeeded in gaining, in 1956, a similar though more extensive guarantee. One might deduce from these developments that big unions do not always get their own way with ease, at any rate not when dealing with employers that also are big.

In the automobile industry the smaller manufacturers sign agreements having marked similarity to those signed first by the "Big Three." It is not without significance that in both automobiles and steel bargaining with the smaller units follows the approach to the big manufacturers. In large industries with some large and some small employers the small ones may be under compulsion to accept the conditions agreed to by the large industrial units.[19] On the other hand, they may be protected by the bargaining power of the big employers.

In any case, the most important question concerns the use of power. Aside from the bargaining power of the employers, there are two other factors that offer promise of protection against possible dangers arising from the power of big unionism. One is the moral strength within the labor movement itself. The AFL-CIO, under the leadership of George Meany, stepped in to curb irresponsible behavior on the part of the biggest union of all, the Teamsters. It prevented the consummation of a proposed loan of $400,000 to the Longshoremen and forced the abandonment of the Teamsters' plan for a "mutual-assistance" pact with that union.

At the convention of his union in May 1956, David Dubinsky, president of the Ladies' Garment Workers Union, denounced union officers who engage in business activities in the same field as that covered by their own unions' jurisdiction. He called such leaders "immoral, unethical, and unfit to serve the labor movement." [20] Mr. Dubinsky is a member of the AFL-CIO Committee on Ethical Prac-

---

[19] See Chap. 5, pp. 39–40, for comment on the position of the small employer under a contract negotiated with an association.
[20] The New York Times, May 11, 1956.

tices. The next day President Meany endorsed the position taken by Mr. Dubinsky. This policy, as A. H. Raskin said in his dispatch in *The New York Times*, "would hit key leaders of the International Brotherhood of Teamsters and smaller unions in which officials have profited by running businesses themselves or by selling services to employers under contract with their organizations." [21]

The other factor is the diversity of interest among the unions themselves. "Labor," even organized labor, does not speak with a single and united voice. There are approximately 200 national and international unions in the United States, whose interests range from piano playing to the operation of bulldozers; 57 of the 200 unions with about 2 million members are outside the fold of the AFL-CIO. In addition there are in the neighborhood of 300 local unions—single plant unions mostly—that are unaffiliated with any other labor group and represent altogether a half-million workers. There are about twice as many nonunion wage earners in the country as there are union members.

While all aggregations of power have in them an element of social hazard, the threat of bigness in labor unionism is clearly reduced by important factors. One is the tendency of union members to behave independently as human beings, resisting any attempt at regimentation by their leaders. Another is the check upon labor power by "countervailing" power in the hands of management. A third is the great diversity of interests and aims among the unions themselves. Not only are they very numerous but many of them are independent.

Finally, if the new Federation tends toward an increase of power, its increased concern for social and moral discipline gives promise of wholesome restraint.

LABOR AND POLITICS

Another question that the merger has brought into the foreground of public discussion concerns the participation of labor in politics. To be sure, organized labor in the United States has always been in politics. Independent political action, from the local labor parties of the 1830s to the Conference for Progressive Political Action of 1924, which rounded up nearly five million votes for Robert M.

[21] *The New York Times*, May 12, 1956.

La Follette, Sr., for President, has usually been short-lived. But labor activity in politics is a different thing. Samuel Gompers and his associates launched an appeal to trade unionists in 1906 to "reward our friends and defeat our enemies"—a slogan which has influenced organized labor ever since.

It was not, however, until the period of the New Deal that the non-partisan political movement began to take more definite organized form. The CIO was first in the field with its "Labor's Nonpartisan League" in 1936, and later its Political Action Committee organized in 1943.[22] The AFL Labor's League for Political Education was launched shortly after PAC. These two are now joined in one body in AFL-CIO—the Committee on Political Education, which is usually abbreviated to "COPE."

Under these bodies the unions have been active as never before in the attempt to influence voters to support candidates favorable to the aims of organized labor. Because of their activities and particularly since the merger, they have been subject to criticism and attack. The chief points of criticism appear to be the following:

1. Organized labor in politics is a menace to democratic institutions since it endangers the freedom of the union member, whose vote may be subject to the control of dictatorial leaders.
2. Union members are Democrats, Republicans, or independents. It is unfair and dishonest to use their dues to help elect to public office persons whose political views differ from those of individual members.
3. Organized labor has no right to engage in political activity.

The first criticism requires little comment. It assumes that the labor leader has unquestioned control over the voting habits of union members. If such power existed, it would be serious indeed, but the supposition is denied by both theory and practice. With the secret ballot, the voter can disregard with impunity the commands of any boss, whether he represents labor, employer, or a political party. The election returns from heavily populated industrial districts frequently indicate the reverse of labor-union dictatorship. The United Automobile Workers, despite its efforts, has not been able to elect a mayor

---

[22] PAC actively supported Franklin D. Roosevelt in 1936 and was joined in later campaigns by the AFL body. Nationally speaking, therefore, they were not exactly nonpartisan.

of Detroit. Industrial Ohio voted to return the late Senator Taft to office in 1950 although the leadership of organized labor fought him. In 1954 in Ohio the CIO failed to influence enough labor votes to win a referendum on an amendment to the unemployment-insurance law.

The second criticism presents a different problem. Whenever union funds are used to pay the expenses of political campaigns it is practically certain that some of the members will thus involuntarily be helping to elect to office some persons whom they would prefer to see defeated. The Taft-Hartley Act forbids the use of union funds in connection with federal elections. Funds for PAC or COPE have therefore been raised by appeals for voluntary contributions. But this does not make it certain that union funds will not be used for political purposes under any circumstances. The situation is somewhat confused. The Supreme Court dismissed a case against Philip Murray, who as president of the CIO had published a statement of his preferences in a Congressional election in the CIO News. In a recent campaign the Automobile Workers used union money to pay for a television broadcast in behalf of a candidate. The union and its officers were indicted, charged with a violation of the Taft-Hartley Act. The indictment was dismissed by the Federal District Court in Detroit, but on March 11, 1957, the Supreme Court sent it back to the District Court for trial.

Unions are free to spend money in state elections unless forbidden by state law. Bills to accomplish that end were introduced in several state legislatures in 1955 and 1956, and one became law in Wisconsin. Prohibitory laws of this sort were enacted a few years ago in Delaware, Pennsylvania, and Texas.

The political activities of the unions are as a rule nonpartisan, in the sense that endorsement is given to a candidate on the basis of his record rather than of his party. Nevertheless there are doubtless some union members who are sufficiently devoted to party to feel imposed upon when a candidate of an opposing party is favored.

In Great Britain the problem was solved for a time by legislation enacted in 1913 requiring unions, if they wished to engage in political action, to set up a special fund for that purpose. Members could be required to pay dues to this fund unless they filed formal notice of unwillingness to do so. This was called "contracting out." In 1927, the Conservatives having come into power, the rule was reversed, and a member could not be asked to pay political dues unless he "contracted in"—that is, filed formal notice of his willingness to contribute. In 1946 the Labor Government repealed the 1927 law, thus reinstating the contracting out features of the 1913 law.

It is a question whether in most unions in this country the issue is numerically important. Indeed, if a poll were taken among union members, such as the elections originally required under the Taft-Hartley Act to determine preferences regarding the union shop, it would not be too surprising if the vote should be as overwhelmingly in favor of the union leadership as it was in the matter of the union shop. The Executive Council of AFL-CIO voted 17–5 on August 28, 1956, to endorse Adlai Stevenson and Estes Kefauver for President and Vice-President of the United States—an action that was approved by the Executive Board two weeks later, with a half-dozen dissenting votes out of 145 members present.

There is, however, a moral issue here. Unions could help to resolve it by voluntarily adopting a rule similar to the present law in Great Britain. The problem has something in common with that involving religious conscientious objectors to the union shop. Unions could afford to deal with it as realistically as some of them have done in the latter case.[23]

The Right to Political Action

Those who contend that unions because of their nature have no right to engage in political action overlook the fact that governments are deeply, if not chiefly, concerned with the making of economic decisions. It has never been said, so far as I know, that farmers have no right to be in politics. Economic groups of all sorts maintain lobbies in Washington and at the state capitals. Businessmen are organized in various ways to protect their interests against what they consider political attacks. The situation was well expressed a number of years ago by a senator, who doubtless was not aware of the full implications of his utterance. It was suggested that he represented

[23] A respected critic writes me: "Use of union dues [for political purposes] is one of the strongest arguments against any form of compulsory union membership."

the United States Steel Corporation in Congress. He denied it, insisting that he represented the smaller steel companies there—not Big Steel!

I am not suggesting here that there is anything wrong about businessmen and farmers favoring the election of candidates who understand their problems. Indeed, I believe it is necessary that they should do so in order to make sure that no legitimate economic interests are overlooked in the conduct of public affairs, though I should have liked the senator's statement better if he had mentioned the people of his state, as well as the steel companies, as coming within the sweep of his concern. It follows that organized labor also has a right to be in politics if it, too, has economic interests that come under consideration by agencies of government. That organized labor does have such interests is so obvious as to require no argument.[24] The situation may be illuminated, however, by two examples.

Eighteen state legislatures, influenced by organized groups, have enacted "right-to-work" laws. A national organization led by former Congressman Fred Hartley of New Jersey is now engaged in an effort to secure the adoption of such laws in other states. These organized groups and Mr. Hartley's national committee are presumably spokesmen for employer groups, since both the Chamber of Commerce of the United States and the National Association of Manufacturers are strong supporters of the legislation.

As stated earlier, these laws assure to no one a right to a job. They forbid employers and unions to enter into union-shop or other union-security agreements. Now, whether they are correct in this opinion or not, union spokesmen without exception believe these laws will be injurious to organized labor. It would seem to be their right, therefore, to oppose them just as the employers' organizations have a right to attempt to secure their enactment.[25]

[24] A team of investigators from the faculty of Wayne University, after a study of union voting in Detroit, concluded: "The fact and the prospects of restrictive legislation almost compel unions to enter seriously into politics to combat policies which, as they see it, would cripple union organizations and undermine their effectiveness. . . . Unions, like other groups, employ their political strength to defend themselves . . . and to move toward their own organizational objectives." Kornhauser, Sheppard, and Mayes, When Labor Votes (New York: University Books, Inc., 1956), p. 271.

[25] See Supplementary Notes.

The Taft-Hartley Act

The other example to be cited here is the Taft-Hartley Act. This law, passed by Congress in 1947 as an amendment to the Wagner Act but in reality a thorough revision of it, retains most of the basic rights accorded labor in the earlier enactment. Additional clauses spell out more definitely what is involved in "genuine" collective bargaining. It requires unions, as well as employers, to bargain collectively. It brings up the lagging rear of trade unionism by requiring all unions to keep accounts and make them available to their members. It requires unions and employers to notify each other of a desire to change an existing contract well before its expiration, and to give similar notice to public mediation agencies. It also includes some features that the unions regard as injurious to their movement.

These are matters that lie at the heart of labor's interests, and so justify a concern that can manifest itself effectively only through some form of political action. This would be true even if organized labor approved in general of the law as passed. The fact is, however, that from its enactment the unions have found it unacceptable, and consider it as a whole a threat to their stability—a hostile move by a hostile Congress, the only true remedy for which is total repeal.

The earliest reaction was expressed in exaggerated predictions of the evils that would be worked by the new law. As time has passed, the tone of the attacks has tended to become less extreme, and the demand for total repeal has become less insistent. The fact remains, however, that leaders of organized labor regard the law as designed to work injury to their movement, and it continues to be the number-one legislative enemy as they plan political strategy.

We may review briefly, some of the provisions of the law that have aroused the most antagonism.

The unions are wary of the provisions in the Taft-Hartley Act opening the door for the use of the injunction. The Norris-LaGuardia Act of 1932 almost completely prohibited the federal courts from issuing injunctions in labor disputes, but the Taft-Hartley Act permits use of injunctions to enforce NLRB orders. This is a limited breach, not only because it applies only to procedure under the Taft-Hartley Act itself but because the injunction can be sought only by NLRB officials, not by employers. But the history of "government by injunction" has been such as to make the very word anathema to the unions. Moreover, the unions see one-sidedness in the provision that makes the seeking of an injunction against unfair labor practices "permissive" in every situation but one. It is "mandatory" in the case of a suspected secondary boycott. There is no such requirement with respect to any unfair labor practice by an employer.[26]

The unions complain also of the scope of the anti-boycotting provision. This, in one of its aspects, makes it an unfair labor practice for union workers to refuse to work on orders transferred from a shop where a legitimate strike is in effect, thus requiring union men, they assert, to "scab" on fellow trade unionists.[27]

Another objection is to the provision that bars strikers not "eligible for reinstatement" from voting in a representation election. This means that when an employer has filled the strikers' places he may petition for an election to determine their preferences as to representation. With the strikers barred, the strike breakers may vote for "no union." This is the provision that President Eisenhower during his 1952 campaign denounced before the AFL convention as a "union-busting" device which he opposed.

The "states rights" clause in the law is also objectionable to the unions. Taft-Hartley permits the union shop, but allows the states to nullify this aspect of the federal law by enacting such measures as "right-to-work" laws. Curiously, the Congressional policy thus set forth is the opposite of the policy of the Railway Labor Act, which also permits the union shop but declares its precedence over state laws having the contrary provisions.[28]

There are many other areas of governmental activity in all its branches that profoundly affect the basic and legitimate interests of the unions. It is the existence of these areas that makes inevitable the entrance of labor organizations into political activity.

The facts presented here indicate not only that organized labor is a part of "the public," but that its members and leaders are becoming

[26] For a statement setting forth more explicitly some of the features of the Taft-Hartley Act, see Supplementary Notes.
[27] See Supplementary Notes.
[28] This provision of the Railway Labor Act was upheld by the Supreme Court May 21, 1956, Railway Employees Department v. Hanson, 76 Supreme Court Reporter 714.

increasingly aware of their position, and of their responsibilities as citizens. As union members they have economic objectives not shared by everyone outside their fellowship and are therefore confronted at times with the dilemma of dual loyalty resulting from the fact that they are citizens as well as trade unionists. In this respect they are in no sense different from other groups in society. The conflict between self-interest and concern for others is one in which every human being is involved as a member of a group and as a person.[29]

[29] For discussion of many of the subjects considered in this chapter, see Arthur J. Goldberg, *AFL-CIO United* (New York: McGraw-Hill Book Company, Inc., 1956).

14

Malpractice in Unions

Newspaper readers during the last half-dozen years have been impressed by a series of exposures of various forms of corruption in unions, involving racketeering, extortion, and welfare-fund abuses. Grand juries and other agencies, state and federal, have done some probing in these areas but no exhaustive studies have yet been made, and there is no reason to suppose that all of the diseased spots have been discovered. At the same time the known facts support the general belief that instances of corruption are exceptional. A subcommittee of the Labor Committee of the United States Senate, reporting in 1956 on welfare-fund abuses, stated that "the great majority of welfare and pension programs are being responsibly and honestly administered." Some of the outstanding evidence concerning various forms of malpractice will be summarized in this chapter. We start with the cases before the federal courts in 1955.

CONVICTIONS OF INDIVIDUALS IN 1955

Thirty-four individuals, mostly officers or business agents of local unions, were found guilty in 1955 of violations of one or the other of two federal statutes: the anti-racketeering or Hobbs Law, and a section of the Taft-Hartley Act dealing with payments to employee representatives. One person was convicted under both laws. In addition, one employing corporation and two local unions were found guilty under the Taft-Hartley Act.[1]

The Hobbs Law [2] declares it to be a felony to use physical violence (or threaten its use) in furtherance of a plan to accomplish "robbery or extortion." Twenty-four union representatives were convicted

[1] Information received from the Department of Justice.
[2] The Hobbs Act was enacted in 1946 as an amendment to the anti-racketeering act of 1934. The Supreme Court had held that the language of the earlier law had been such as to exempt trade-union representatives from its penalties. (U.S. v. Local 807, 315 U.S. 521; 1942).

under this law in 1955—a number comparatively so small as to seem to contribute practically nothing to our knowledge of trade-union practices. There may be some significance, however, in the incidence of the several cases, as respects union affiliation. Three international unions, Painters, Plumbers, and Structural Iron Workers, were represented by one conviction each. Three convictions were of representatives of the International Longshoremen's Association; five involved the Hodcarriers, five the Operating Engineers, and eight of the twenty-four convicted agents were members of locals of the Teamsters Union.

In a speech prepared for delivery at the law school of Southern Methodist University in April 1955, Attorney General Herbert Brownell explained one of the cases referred to above. Evan Dale, an officer of the Hodcarriers Union, and an associate, were found guilty of attempting to compel a contractor who was building a power plant for the Government at Joppa, Illinois, to pay them one per cent of the contract price "as the price of labor peace," a demand that was said to involve a sum exceeding one million dollars. "When the money was not forthcoming, Dale plagued [the contractor] with eighteen months of jurisdictional strikes, sabotage of equipment, violence to workers, and every conceivable kind of intimidation." The men were each sentenced to pay a $10,000 fine, and to serve a fifteen-year term of imprisonment. The cost to the Government of the "campaign of sabotage and terrorism" was "estimated at the trial to be $51 million." [3]

The other federal statute under which there were convictions in 1955 is a section of the Taft-Hartley Act which makes it unlawful for an employer to pay "to any representative of his employees," or for any representative to accept, "any money or other thing of value" unless it involves an obligation in a legitimate transaction. The maximum penalty for violation is a fine of $10,000 or imprisonment for one year, or both. This section of the law is intended to forbid bribery or extortion.

In 1955 ten individuals, one employing company, and two local unions were found guilty of violations under this statute. Of the locals, one was an affiliate of the Building Service Employees Union

[3] Department of Justice, press release, April 23, 1955.

and one of the Teamsters Union. Of the individuals, one was the former president of the Longshoremen's Union and one was vice-president of the convicted employing company; one was secretary-treasurer of a District Council of the Painters Union; one was a business agent of a local of the Operating Engineers; and six were officers or business agents of the Teamsters' Union.

Combining the record under these two statutes, and referring to each conviction (of an individual or a local) as a "case," we find that altogether eight international unions were involved. Three of these unions, the Building Service Employees, the Plumbers, and the Structural Iron Workers, were involved in one case each. The Painters were represented in two cases. The Longshoremen were involved in four cases, the Hodcarriers in five, the Operating Engineers in six, and the Teamsters in fourteen. In addition one employing company and its vice-president were found guilty.[4]

THE INTERNATIONAL UNIONS

Of some two hundred national or international unions in the United States, four have figured prominently in the news either because of alleged violation of law or because of conduct not necessarily criminal but of such a character as to raise suspicions concerning the moral scruples of the leaders. The cases of two of these unions are presented below. The other two are dealt with in connection with the discussion of welfare funds.

The Longshoremen

The International Longshoremen's Association was expelled from the American Federation of Labor by action of the 1953 convention. The resolution of expulsion declared: "The ILA has permitted gang-

---

[4] In view of the fact that the Taft-Hartley Act makes bribe giving and bribe taking equally illegal, it seemed odd that only one employing concern was included among those found guilty of violating the statute. An inquiry on this point addressed to the Department of Justice elicited a reply which noted that six of the labor men in the list were employees of the convicted employer. As to the others, the reply stated: "We cannot categorically answer your question as to whether for every guilty representative under this Act there would be a guilty employer or vice versa. In the prosecution of every criminal case there are a multitude of factors which give rise to the ultimate conclusion of guilt. The amount of available admissible evidence determines whether we indict any one defendant."

sters, racketeers, and thugs to fasten themselves to the body of its organization, infecting it with corruption and destroying its integrity, its effectiveness, and its trade union character." The resolution emphasized the "autonomous responsibility" of a union to deal with its "own internal problems," but it affirmed the "right of the American Federation of Labor to refuse to associate with those who fail to meet the standards of good citizenship and sound trade unionism." [5]

The events leading up to this action have been widely publicized and need not be set forth in detail here. A brief summary of the findings of a board appointed by the Commissioner of Labor of New York to investigate a waterfront strike will be sufficient as an outline of the major aspects of the picture. This Board of Inquiry was appointed in November 1951 to investigate a wild-cat strike that had "paralyzed" the Port of New York. The Board reported on the circumstances of the strike in January 1952, and stated that it was "an outbreak of a long-festering accumulation of complaints and dissatisfaction." It found, among other things, that some locals had failed to hold elections of officers "for a period of ten years or more," that some locals kept no financial records, and that some had no bank accounts, although they handled large sums of money. Business agents of some locals designated themselves as delegates to the wage-scale conference, which acted as the bargaining agent for the union, without holding the election required by the union constitution. The Board found that some of the union officers were acting as employers, thus creating a situation whereby "the same man is both the employer of labor and the union representative of labor he hires."

The Board found evidence of criminal activities, including "pilferage, extortion, 'kick-backs,' and 'loan-sharking'." It found that "a number of organizers, public loaders, hiring bosses, and others in the International Longshoremen's Association have criminal records." These conditions could not prevail, the Board believed, "unless condoned by the business interests involved." They constituted a "sad commentary not only on the business and labor organizations . . . but on the governmental and community forces which have permitted them to exist." [6]

[5] AFL Convention Proceedings, 1953, p. 486.
[6] Final Report to the Industrial Commissioner, State of New York, from Board

The first reaction to these disclosures by the leaders of the American Federation of Labor was marked by skepticism and a defensive attitude. At the request of Joseph P. Ryan, president of the Longshoremen's Union, William Green, president of the AFL, appointed a committee consisting of a vice-president of the AFL and four New York labor officials to evaluate the report of the Board of Inquiry. This Committee made a report to President Green in August 1952, in which it ignored the charges brought against the union, and criticized the Board of Inquiry for going beyond the strict limits of the terms of its appointment which authorized it merely to inquire into the "causes and circumstances" of a strike. It called the report "biased and dangerous."

It was after reports had been made by two more official bodies [7] that the AFL, under new leadership, expelled the Longshoremen's Union.

This action marked a new departure in AFL policy. It was the first time that any affiliate of the American Federation of Labor had been disciplined on grounds of misbehavior. The time-honored doctrine of autonomy had been thought to forestall any such action by the Federation. On previous occasions officers of the Federation had explained their tolerance of unsavory elements on the ground of lack of power to act against them. Now, under the leadership of George Meany in the first year of his presidency of the Federation, this subterfuge was swept away. In a letter to the officers of the Longshoremen, dated February 3, 1953, the Executive Council announced a new concept. "The exercise of autonomy by affiliated units in an organization such as ours presupposes the maintenance of minimum standards of trade-union decency. No affiliate of the American Federation of Labor has any right to expect to remain an affiliate on the grounds of organizational autonomy if its conduct, as such, is to bring the entire movement into disrepute. . . . AFL affiliates have autonomy in the conduct of their affairs, but it must be conceded by all that there is an unwritten law that this freedom of action must be used to advance the interests of labor, not to exploit the workers." [8]

---

of Inquiry on Longshore Work Stoppage October-November 1951. January 22, 1952.

[7] See Supplementary Notes for summaries of these reports.

[8] AFL Convention Proceedings, 1953, p. 55.

The Teamsters

The International Brotherhood of Teamsters, Chauffeurs, Warehousemen and Helpers of America, commonly referred to as the Teamsters Union, is noteworthy in many respects. It came into the American Federation of Labor in 1899 as the Team Drivers International Union, with 1700 members, being at that time forty-third in membership rank among Federation affiliates. In 1955 it reported to the AFL a membership of over one and a quarter million and was, presumably, the largest union in the world.[9] Its constitution defines its jurisdiction so broadly as to suggest the absence of any limits.[10] Under this broad concept, which derives both from its constitution and from the inclination of its leaders, the Teamsters have been carrying on aggressive organizing campaigns. They have refused to join the "no-raiding" pact that has been signed by most of the other unions in AFL-CIO.

Dave Beck, who was elected president of the Teamsters Union in 1952, has played several contradictory roles since taking that office. He was active in 1953 in connection with the expulsion of the Longshoremen's Union from the AFL. He was one of five trustees appointed to assist in the establishment of a new AFL union to take its place. Nevertheless, as reported in the press, shortly after this action, leading figures in the Teamsters Union were holding conferences with the old ILA and sending a delegation to intercede with George Meany to take this racketeering union back into the AFL.

On the eve of the consummation of the merger of AFL and CIO the Teamsters Union signed a "mutual-aid and assistance" compact with the Longshoremen, and its Western Conference signed a similar agreement with the Mine, Mill and Smelter Workers. The latter union had been expelled from the CIO in 1950 because of alleged Communist domination. Later the Teamsters entered into an agreement with the expelled Longshoremen for a joint organizing campaign.[11]

[9] In December 1955, President Beck announced that the membership of his union had reached the figure of 1,449,000. *The New York Times*, December 7, 1955.

[10] See Supplementary Notes for text of clause in the union constitution which outlines jurisdictional claims.

[11] *The International Teamster*, May 1956. In this issue President Beck de-

The Teamsters Union withdrew from these agreements after President Beck had had a conference with President George Meany of the AFL-CIO, in which Mr. Meany, presumably, called attention to a clause in the constitution of the merged body which provides in part that "no organization that has seceded or has been suspended or expelled" by the AFL-CIO or by either of the federations that preceded the merger or by any of their subordinate bodies shall be "allowed representation or recognition in the Federation or in any subordinate body" or affiliate "under penalty of suspension."

A further strange chapter in the story of the Teamsters was written in 1954. The Union and several of its locals were charged before the National Labor Relations Board with having engaged in an unfair labor practice under the terms of the National Labor Management Relations Act (Taft-Hartley) by discharging some of their clerical employees for union activities. The trial examiner who conducted hearings found the union guilty, but on appeal the Board in a 3–2 decision dismissed the case "in its entirety" on the ground that a union, even when acting as an employer, being a nonprofit organization is not subject to the jurisdiction of the Board.[12]

THE HANDLING OF WELFARE FUNDS

Organized plans in accord with which benefits are made available to employed workers under certain circumstances have been known to American industry for many years; but it was not until World War II that they became a marked feature of collectively-bargained agreements. Trade unions generally were opposed to the earlier employer-

---

fended these compacts. "I have always believed," he wrote, "that area conferences have rights in entering into pacts or agreements with groups of other organized working people with whom the Teamster conferences must work and get along. More is involved in the right to enter into pacts than simply the question of whether some individuals may like or dislike the organization with which conferences may be entering into agreements. . . .

"I most emphatically deplore the undue attention and publicity which have been given this matter of mutual-aid pacts, particularly when, in my opinion, much of what has been written and said about this matter is purposely slanted and distorted. This creates dissension and confusion and reacts to the great advantage of our enemies."

[12] This decision of the Board was upheld in a two to one decision by the Circuit Court of Appeals of the District of Columbia. An appeal is pending, as this is written, before the Supreme Court. See Supplementary Notes.

financed plans and attempted to provide benefits for their members from their own funds. These were limited and seldom provided anything like adequate protection against industrial hazards. A number of employer-established funds in the 1890s and early 1900s provided retirement pensions usually on a discretionary, noncontractual basis. The development of "welfare capitalism" in the 1920s led to a sounder approach in the form of group life insurance—a device later tending to include other hazards. The premiums were at first paid by the employers but later became "contributory," with employees paying a considerable proportion.[13]

In the 1940s, after court decisions holding that pension and welfare funds fell within the area of collective bargaining as guaranteed by the Taft-Hartley Act, the number and size of such funds increased rapidly. A subcommittee of the United States Senate reported in April 1956 that over 75 million persons, "employees and dependents," were then covered to some extent by welfare and pension plans, and that "this tremendous development has come about principally in the last ten years." The report states that over $6.8 billion are contributed to such programs annually of which approximately $4.5 billion comes from employers and $2.3 billion from employees.[14]

Reports published by Congressional and state agencies [15] emphasize the existence of grave abuses in many of the funds. Nothing like an exhaustive study has yet been made, however, and it is impossible to judge the proportion of the whole number that are justly subject to criticism.

The New York Findings

An investigation made by the Superintendent of Insurance of New York in 1954 covered 162 welfare funds in that state. Of these, 91

[13] Millis and Montgomery, Labor's Risks and Social Insurance (New York: Harper & Brothers, 1938), p. 254.

[14] Final Report of Subcommittee on Welfare and Pension Funds of Senate Committee on Labor and Public Welfare, April 6, 1956, pp. 5–6. A preliminary report was made by this Subcommittee on January 10, 1954, and an interim report on July 20, 1955.

[15] A subcommittee of the House Committee on Education and Labor held hearings on welfare funds in 1953 and reported in 1954.

In 1954 also the Superintendent of Insurance of the State of New York published the results of a study of welfare funds in that state entitled "Whose Welfare?" The same office published a second report early in 1956.

were found, in the main, to be "ably administered in the best interests of the membership." Thirty-seven plans were "subject to some criticism," and "serious abuses were found in 34." These included misuse of funds, loans or gifts to unions and union officers "to finance projects having no connection with the purposes of the welfare fund," lack of proper administrative procedures, discrimination in benefit payments, "kickbacks" to union and fund officials, and nepotism. Public hearings held in the fall of 1954 revealed the practices engaged in by the administrators of some of the funds.

Two managers of a fund maintained for the benefit of the members of a small local union bought annuities for themselves using for that purpose a larger amount of welfare-fund cash than was invested in the same year for the benefit of the four hundred members of the local. The manager of another fund, who was also president of the local, received a salary of $41,000, $28,000 of which was from the welfare fund. This fund, which also paid $100 a week, salary and expenses, to an "arbitrator" who did nothing, absorbed for "overhead" over 34 per cent of the contributions.[16]

The most fantastic story brought out by the New York hearings was about a fund administrator who bought, presumably as an investment on behalf of the fund, a four hundred-acre tract of land to be used as a vacation resort. The land, which belonged to his cousin, was assessed at $10,500, but the administrator paid $85,000 for it. This administrator was appointed for life, with power to fix his own salary—which he did, at $30,000 a year. This fund was nearly bankrupt at the time of the study.

Other drains on the funds were for trips to Florida and other vacation spots, entertainment of friends, and heavy hotel bills.

The Senate Committee Report [17]

The Senate report distinguishes between pension plans and welfare plans. The funds available for pensions are in the main based on

---

[16] The investigation of twenty "selected union welfare funds" revealed an average of 18½ per cent for operating expenses, with a low of 5 per cent and a high of 47 per cent.

[17] Final Report submitted to the Senate Committee on Labor and Public Welfare, by the Subcommittee on Welfare and Pension Funds, April 1956. The statements appearing in this section are either quoted from or based upon this report.

contributions by the employer. Welfare plans, the report states, provide "life insurance or death benefits, disability insurance . . . and hospital, surgical, and medical insurance or direct provision of health services as required," and they "are a joint enterprise of the worker and his employer." The latter statement seems to require some modification. Some large companies pay the total cost of maintaining welfare funds, and the trend in collective bargaining seems to be, to some extent, in that direction. One of the most important of the noncontributory plans resulted from collective bargaining in the bituminous coal industry and is known as the United Mine Workers Welfare and Retirement Fund. The report of the Senate Subcommittee, which contains a full account of the operation of the fund, refers to it as "a far-flung, pioneering, well-run program of immense value to its beneficiaries."

Other important welfare and retirement plans that are largely noncontributory are those of the Amalgamated Clothing Workers and the Ladies' Garment Workers Union. These funds also are described in the Senate Subcommittee report. Both funds maintain medical centers in the larger cities where their members work, available for diagnostic service and such treatment as can be given in a doctor's office. These centers are maintained at the joint expense of unions and employers.

The Subcommittee reported on three types of funds, from the standpoint of administration. Unilateral employer-administered plans, a considerable proportion of which are union-negotiated, account for 90 per cent of all employees covered by welfare plans. In many of these the unions have a voice in the selection of the insurance carrier, and frequently union representatives serve on joint committees dealing with some problems of administration. The employer makes all arrangements with the insurance company, and pays all the costs of administration. The only criticism of employer-administered plans in the report is of the failure of the companies to make their costs known. The Subcommittee believes that since the employees generally contribute a considerable proportion of the fund they are entitled to know what the costs are.

Union-administered plans constitute a "very small minority of all plans and no detailed investigation was made." Among the plans reviewed, however, improper practice appeared to be rife. Cases were found where there were "commingling of union and welfare funds, use of funds for other than welfare purposes, favoritism in the payment of claims, extravagance, mismanagement, and one-man domination."

Plans of the third type were the jointly administered and multi-employer plans. These, which cover "less than 10 per cent of employees receiving benefits under all types of plans," received the major share of Subcommittee attention. However limited in number or scope, it was to these plans that the Subcommittee gave most critical attention. And it was here also that the Subcommittee often found the employers at fault equally with the unions wherever there were abuses.

The Taft-Hartley Act provides that a welfare fund, set up by the joint action of employer and union, must be held in trust for the sole purpose of paying agreed-upon benefits to the covered employees, and must be administered jointly by representatives of employer and employees, with a neutral outsider.[18] It is disregard of this section of the law that opens the way to abuse and corruption.

"Many of the abuses in welfare funds," the report states, "have at their source the failure of trustees to be true to their trust. Union trustees have often used their trusteeships to serve personal gains. Employer trustees have sometimes connived with union trustees in such instances and at other times have closed their eyes. It was frequently found that employer trustees of joint funds completely abdicated their responsibilities." [19] In some cases the trustees had held no meetings "for several years." Sometimes "employer representatives designedly gave full control to the union in the hope that the union would eventually be discredited. On the other hand, employer representatives in some cases were subject to coercion."

The Subcommittee reported on a number of funds, some of which were maintained by the internationals, others by local unions. One of the latter type was an affiliate of the former UAW-AFL (now designated as Allied Industrial Workers of America). The funds, of

[18] Section 302.
[19] In describing a series of events culminating in 1953 in the murder of the president of a union local who was also administrator and plunderer of its welfare fund, the report of the New York Superintendent of Insurance stated: "The employer trustee testified that he 'paid no interest' in seeing that the money contributed by the employers to the fund was not diverted or wasted." *Whose Welfare? op. cit.* pp. 19–20.

which the local officers were in full charge, were merged with other union funds, from which the president of the local withdrew sums apparently as he saw fit. Items of expensive jewelry were purchased as gifts for friends. The president went on pleasure trips to Puerto Rico and to various points in the United States at union (and presumably welfare-fund) expense. Chided by the chairman of the committee, Senator Paul H. Douglas, for this spending of money belonging to the "hard pressed" members of the union, the financial secretary of the local said: "It is expenditures such as these that expand the horizon of labor leaders," so that they can deal more adequately "with what is sitting across the table from them." [20]

A local of the Bricklayers' Union in Chicago handled its welfare funds in an extraordinary way. In spite of the requirements of joint control in the Taft-Hartley Law, the president of the local had exclusive control over the fund and the payment of claims. There was no set schedule of benefits, the committee reported. The president told the committee: "There was no reason for anybody to have any disposition as to who was getting the funds or otherwise, because they were given to those that were deserving of it. . . ." The committee found that the welfare funds of this local were commingled with other union funds, and that checks made out to "cash" were unaccounted for. Other locals maintaining questionable practices were affiliates of the Bakery Workers and of the Plumbers Union.

The Subcommittee reviewed the practices and experience of two international unions maintaining welfare funds jointly with employers. The more extensive study was of the fund of the Laundry Workers International Union, formerly AFL.

The Laundry Workers

This case, the report states, "presents a good example of nonfeasance on the part of trustees." At the outset,[21] the fund had only two trustees: the president of the international union and an attorney for the San Francisco Laundry Owners' Association. Later two addi-

[20] Since the report of the Senate Committee was issued this local has withdrawn from the parent union.

[21] The fund was established on a nationwide basis in 1950. The LWIU had, in 1954, 73,000 members in 125 local unions. *Bulletin 1185, U. S. Department of Labor,* Directory of National & International Unions in the U.S. 1955. As of early 1955 approximately 55 locals were included in the plan.

tional employers and two union representatives were named as trustees. Apparently no outsider was added to the board. Control of the fund and of relations with the insurance company was placed in the hands of an insurance broker who was responsible for transmitting to the insurance company approximately $3¼ million in group insurance premiums between 1950 and 1953. Of this sum, the report states, the broker "diverted or, perhaps more accurately, embezzled approximately $900,000." Over the same period he received in commissions an amount which aggregated $262,500.

The broker did not keep all of this money for himself. His bookkeeper testified that she "forwarded a substantial part" of the $900,000 to Eugene C. James, secretary-treasurer of the Laundry Workers Union, by checks drawn to the order of the Union. An examination of the Union records by agents of the Senate Subcommittee "failed to reflect any accounting of this money . . ." but further investigation revealed an account in a Chicago bank in the name of the Union "into which was traced $573,000 in checks from [the broker's] insurance agencies" on which account "James had sole authority to draw."

James and Byers (president of the union) were trustees of the welfare fund of Local 46 in Chicago—a fund set up independently of the national fund. The sum of $26,500, the report states, "diverted from this fund was located in the previously mentioned LWIU account" in the Chicago bank.

As secretary-treasurer of the international union James also received $2,500 a month from the insurance carrier—a total of $85,000 from 1951 through September 30, 1953, "for alleged expenses incurred by the international union in promoting this welfare plan." These checks also "appear to have been deposited in the account in the same Chicago bank and the money disbursed . . . without any accounting." [22]

The Distillery Workers

The welfare fund of the Distillery, Rectifying, Wine and Allied Workers International Union was established in 1948, and is financed by employer contributions. The insurance broker who handled the account with the insurance carrier was the one who had performed a like service for the Laundry Workers. From the large commissions

[22] For further details, see Supplementary Notes.

paid him by the insurance company, the broker was "alleged" to have "kicked back" more than half a million dollars over a seven-year period to an officer of the union who was also a trustee of the fund, and to two well-known racketeers whose relation to the union is not clear. These three were indicted by a New York grand jury in 1955 for "bribery and conspiracy," but the indictments were dismissed.[23]

In 1955 the contract that the Distillery Workers' welfare fund had with the insurance company was discontinued and the fund became self-insured. Shortly thereafter the salaries of the manager and counsel of the fund were raised from $13,000 and $10,000 respectively to $25,000. The manager, who is a nephew of one of the union trustees, received a Christmas bonus of two months' salary in addition. Two of the union officers who were trustees of the fund received over $700 a month, in addition to their salaries as officers, for acting as "welfare representatives." Two sons of the president of the union, acting as welfare representatives, received respectively $800 and $320 a month.

The Senate Subcommittee disclaimed any intention of suggesting that the administration of this fund is "bad throughout." In some respects it is competently and efficiently managed. But the Subcommittee had "reservations" about certain "definite phases of the administration and operation of the fund." Among these are the payment of salaries for welfare-fund activities to persons holding other full-time paid positions in the union. It found it difficult to understand how these individuals could "competently fulfill the obligations and duties attendant to the 3 and 4 positions they held."

They were disturbed over evidences of nepotism, and about the increases in salaries of manager and counsel at the time that the fund became self-insured. These are "practices," the Subcommittee said, "that can lead to abuse" and can "result to the detriment of the beneficiaries of the fund."

OTHER EVIDENCES OF MISCONDUCT

Through the several investigations of welfare-fund abuses, and other disclosures, it has become evident that a significant number of

[23] The indictments were "reluctantly dismissed" according to the Senate Subcommittee, which quoted the trial judge as saying "Unfortunately, a trustee of a union welfare fund, except when he commits larceny, is not chargeable with a crime for violating his trust even though he simultaneously be an officer of the union." (People v. Cilento 143 N.Y.S., 2nd 705.)

international unions are harboring one or more local affiliates whose leaders are engaged in corrupt practices. In others, individuals with corrupt associations are carrying on illegal operations under the aegis of otherwise respectable trade unionism.

The union known heretofore as United Automobile Workers-AFL, recently renamed "Allied Industrial Workers of America" by the AFL-CIO Executive Council, originally consisted of automobile workers who remained with the AFL when the larger body withdrew and joined the CIO in 1937. It reported to the AFL a paid-up membership of 73,000 in 1955. This union achieved some prominence a few years ago by authorizing one John Dioguardi (commonly called Johnny Dio) to organize workers in New York City regardless of trade or occupation. Dioguardi had served time at Sing Sing for extortion and was said to have underworld connections.[24] After the AFL Executive Council had denounced the issuing of blanket organizing permits to individuals the then president of UAW-AFL revoked the charters of Dioguardi's locals. Soon afterward, the executive board of the union met, deposed the president, and reissued the charters. The locals so organized were later taken over by the Teamsters' Union.

At the meeting of the AFL-CIO Executive Council in August 1956, it condemned the issuance of charters to cover "paper locals," such as Dioguardi had received authority to issue, and notice was served on the Allied Industrial Workers of America that it was under investigation.

The International Union of Operating Engineers attracted attention by holding its 1956 convention behind closed doors. Newspapermen were barred on the grounds of alleged unfair and prejudiced reporting. One of the items on the agenda was an appeal by two former members of the union against their expulsion by a New York local. The convention dismissed the appeal.

The local in question—Local 138—consists of members working on Long Island. Its president, William De Koning, Jr., who received a suspended sentence after pleading guilty to a charge of "coercion," succeeded his father, William De Koning, Sr., in that office, the father

---

[24] Dioguardi was arrested in September 1956 and indicted on charges of complicity in the acid-throwing attack on Victor Riesel which resulted in blinding the labor columnist.

having been sentenced in 1954 to a term at Sing Sing after pleading guilty to indictments charging extortion and grand larceny.

A trial examiner of the National Labor Relations Board issued a report in September 1956 following a hearing at which evidence was presented concerning the administration of the affairs of Local 138. The evidence showed that the local was in violation of the closed-shop provisions of the Taft-Hartley Act; that it had never complied with the requirements of that law with respect to financial reports and affidavits disclaiming Communist affiliations; that the union had three divisions with a total membership of 863, less than a fifth of whom have an "absolute right to vote on all issues." The others may attend meetings but may not vote in the election of officers. On other matters they may vote "only with the permission of the chairman." The voting section had approximately 158 members among whom were "at least 31 master mechanics, assistant master mechanics, foremen, and job superintendents employed by contractors under contractual relationship with the union," together with "an undisclosed number of executives," among whom was the president of one of the largest contracting firms on Long Island.

The trial examiner found that the union was in essential respects "dominated" by members of the employers' association, the "only effective remedy" for which was "to completely disestablish the union as the representative of the employees of the members of the [employer's] Association."

The union members who were expelled had been members of a "reform group" which had been trying to remedy the situation described above. The charge against them was that they had "defamed the union's good name." They were quoted in a press report as saying at the commencement of their fight that they had believed that "the Joe Fay and Bill De Koning type of labor racketeers could be cleaned up by rank-and-file members within our union." [25]

While the 1956 convention, which upheld the expulsion of these members, was in session, William E. Mahoney, president of the international union, was quoted by a reporter as saying that the "international union has nothing to do with the locals." [26] A few

[25] *New York Times*, April 14, 1956.
[26] *New York Times*, April 13, 1956.

years earlier Mr. Mahoney was called to testify before a Congressional committee to explain why he had held a local union "under supervision"—that is, under the control of the international president—for eleven years.[27]

PROPOSED REMEDIES

Before the merger both the AFL and CIO were expressing deep concern about revelations of corruption existing in certain unions with respect to welfare funds. AFL leaders began to give consideration to corrective legislation. Affiliated unions, particularly the Machinists, made public their proposals for curbing welfare-fund racketeers. The Ethical Practices Committee of the CIO, which had been created a year or two earlier, held public hearings to consider the nature of the evil and possible remedies. These hearings were participated in by insurance experts and prominent union officials. From the hearings emerged a report condemning corrupt practices by either union or insurance companies, and the draft of a bill calling for full publicity of the acts both of fund trustees and of companies writing welfare fund insurance.

The AFL-CIO at the merger convention in December 1955 adopted a resolution in three parts dealing with the administration of health and welfare funds. The first part dealt with action open to the unions. It declared that a salaried union official who serves in any capacity in the administration of a welfare fund should not receive any extra compensation for such service; that such a person should be "entirely free of any compromising ties, direct or indirect, with outside agencies . . . doing business with the welfare plan," and that any union official found to be "involved in such ties to his own personal advantage . . . should be removed." Trustees of the funds who accept "unethical payments" should be proceeded against with a view to their removal. Financial operations should be reported "in accordance with the best accounting practice," and reports should be made available to the beneficiaries at least once a year.

"The duty of policing and enforcing these standards," the resolution states, "is shared by every union member. . . . The best safe-

[27] Hearings before Committee on Education and Labor, House of Representatives, 83rd Congress, First Session, Part 10, April 30, 1953, pp. 3257 ff.

guard against abuses lies in the hands of a vigilant, informed, and active membership, jealous of their rights and interests. . . ."

The second and third parts of the resolution contain recommendations concerning federal and state legislation. Congress should enact legislation, the resolution declares, requiring "annual reports and public disclosure" of the financial operation of all welfare plans. These reports should be filed with the Internal Revenue Service, and there should be "criminal penalties for nonfiling or false filing." At the state level, laws should be enacted providing for the regulating of insurance companies doing business with welfare funds, including a code of standards for commissions and charges. State insurance commissions and departments should assume a "greater degree of responsibility for the integrity, competence, and character of agents and brokers who are licensed by the state." Finally, "the fiduciary obligations applicable generally to trustees under state law should be applicable to trustees of health and welfare plans."

Recommendations by the Senate Subcommittee with respect to federal legislation concerning welfare funds correspond closely to those outlined by AFL-CIO. The report called for registration of all plans covering twenty-five or more employees, and annual reports available to beneficiaries on all plans covering a hundred or more employees, with criminal penalties for noncompliance, and for embezzlement of welfare funds.

It should be borne in mind that the overwhelming majority of unions are organized by honest men for legitimate purposes, just as is true of most business enterprises. There are aspects both of unionism and of business, however, that suggest to criminally minded men the existence of opportunities for pursuing criminal objectives. A notorious union extortionist, on entering Sing Sing prison a few years ago, must have come very close to meeting a prominent businessman on his way out, the latter having completed a term for stealing from the pension reserves set up for the employees of the business with which he was connected.

One source of corruption within the unions is the existence of a criminal element in society looking for opportunities to accumulate dishonest dollars. Another source is a certain amount of growth from within. Sometimes men who join unions with no other thought than to advance the legitimate interests of workers, including themselves, discover opportunities for personal gain that they are either too weak, or too limited in moral stature, to thrust aside. It is probable that such misuse of welfare funds as has been discovered in recent years is due in part to the presence of this element.[28]

Leaders of the American labor movement are showing a determination to drive crooks and racketeers out of the unions. This is made manifest by the declarations of policy in the AFL-CIO constitution, in the resolutions adopted by the 1955 convention, and most impressively by the creation and implementation of the Committee on Ethical Practices. At the meeting of the Executive Council of AFL-CIO in June 1956, this Committee was given additional authority and resources for investigating and dealing with instances of corruption in constituent unions. The committee has made full use of its powers. It has reported to the Executive Council from time to time on its investigations and has made recommendations which have led to action by the Council. The latter, at its meeting in January 1957, adopted a policy statement giving support to government agencies investigating racketeering and calling on labor officials to answer "all relevant questions" asked by "legislative committees and other public bodies seeking fairly and objectively to keep the labor movement free from corruption." The statement referred to the Fifth Amendment of the United States Constitution as a "historical right" which "must not be abridged" but declared the policy

[28] James P. Mitchell, Secretary of Labor, has explained the presence of crooks in the labor movement as follows: "There are two types of labor hoodlums—the corrupted apostle of labor's cause and the committed criminal who, after a life of crime, attaches himself to the labor movement. The second invariably depends upon the first to gain access to the movement. Thus, the labor leader who tolerates the existence of racketeering elements in his union is himself suspect." Criminals who enter from the outside "have been drawn to the labor movement for these reasons: First, the ethical nature of the movement provides an excellent and sturdy blind behind which to hide their own desires for personal gain. By acting constantly in behalf of the workers, so they say, while actually lining their own pockets, they have to some extent avoided the detection of public opinion. Secondly, the democratic structure of the labor movement with its many divisions and subdivisions provides cover and opportunity for a man of ill will. Thirdly, the wealth that has accumulated in some union treasuries is considerable and presents a great temptation to unscrupulous men." Excerpts from address by Mr. Mitchell before the Catholic Institute of the Press, February 14, 1957.

of the AFL-CIO to be that a trade union official who invokes it "has no right to continue to hold office in his union."

At the same meeting, following further the recommendation of the Ethical Practices Committee, the council adopted a series of "Codes of Ethical Practices," [29] and gave the Laundry Workers Union, the Distillery Workers, and the Allied Industrial Workers three months in which to clean house "or stand suspended and face expulsion from the AFL-CIO."

[29] See Supplementary Notes.

15

A Closer Look

In the preceding chapters an attempt has been made to present a picture of trade unionism as a functioning organism. Here and there the approach has been critical, in the sense that moral judgments have been implied, or briefly indicated. In the main, however, the facts have been allowed to speak for themselves, as they do with an especially clear voice in Chapter 14.

We now turn from the exceptional conditions treated there to take a closer look at some more nearly typical aspects of trade-union behavior or policy. Here are expressed some personal judgments with respect to these union practices.

ETHICS IN COLLECTIVE BARGAINING

In Chapter 13 it was suggested that a strike or slowdown while negotiations at the bargaining table are in progress raises at once an issue of good faith. This view is sometimes questioned, but I suspect that those who do so would not contradict an assertion that an employer who declares a lockout during contract negotiations is by that act straining the definition of good faith. In either case what we have is an attempt to carry on bargaining in such an atmosphere of conflict that reasoned consideration of factual data becomes difficult or impossible.

A similar situation is created when the bargainers meet in a state of mind that makes resort to epithet seem preferable to a serious exchange of views. Such attitudes are more likely to appear at an early stage, before either union or management has acquired enough experience to approach maturity in the bargaining relationship. Some years ago, when collective bargaining was a novel experience in one of the major industries of the country, the newspapers were full of accounts of grown men facing each other in an allegedly bargaining session and conducting their affairs mainly through the medium of insults and name-calling. Industrial relations in that industry have now reached a higher level; but the earlier practice has not yet been eliminated altogether. Even mature and experienced bargainers sometimes give out press releases during negotiations, each attacking the integrity of the other side.

These are not the usual practices in collective bargaining. The majority of bargaining conferences are carried on without fanfare and therefore presumably in an atmosphere of reason. The exceptional cases where intemperate behavior mars the proceedings are the ones that do harm. That such an atmosphere sometimes prevails, however, cannot be doubted by anyone who has ever had even limited experience as an arbitrator in labor disputes. That this atmosphere of battle—and when it exists both sides are apt to be guilty of it—is harmful both to the immediate issue and to the institution of collective bargaining seems beyond question.

Where bargaining is carried on in an atmosphere of quiet and good temper, the emerging agreement is much more likely to be in the public interest. But there may be another side to the picture, as in a case where the bargaining takes a course that leaves the public in the lurch (See Chapter 13).

A pertinent comment on this point is contained in a memorandum by Dr. F. Ernest Johnson, the consultant for the series of which this book is a part:

"I am wondering if it will ever be possible to complete the confrontation of interests by representation of consumer interest. There is excellent reason for attempting it, I think. For it is this missing economic component at the bargaining table that should supply the 'governor' when bargaining gets into high gear. When the community comes into the picture in its political role, i.e., as the state, the character of the process is entirely altered. The 'people' belong in it—certainly in the first instance—in their economic capacity, as consumers, not in their collective political capacity, as the state. I have come to question whether collective bargaining can sustain itself permanently as a device for setting wage and hour levels with the community (public) an interested but voiceless party." [1]

[1] A similar thought appeared in an editorial in *The New York Times*, commenting on the wage negotiations in progress in the steel industry: "Two parties sit around the bargaining table in steel—the companies and the United Steel-

WAGES AND THE PUBLIC

American labor has been pressing continually for wage increases, especially since the end of the Second World War, and there seems to be no immediate likelihood of a relaxation of effort in this direction.[2] Whether a continuation of such pressure is in the public (and therefore in labor's) interest is a question about which there are differences of opinion. Economists are not in agreement about either the influence of labor organizations on labor's share in the national income, or the inflationary effect of new wage demands.[3] Analysis of contrasting views is beyond the planned scope of this book, but attention may be given to some prevailing attitudes and trends.

A surprising number of individuals and families in the United States receive annual incomes that are below a reasonable minimum. The *Economic Report* submitted to Congress by President Eisenhower in 1955 stated that a "significant number of American families have cash incomes under $1,000 per family," and added the comment, "By current standards, most of them must be considered poverty stricken." The Census Bureau has estimated that in 1955 there were

---

workers Union. But there is a third interested party whose presence should be felt, even if its spokesman is absent from the room: the public. . . .

"The public interest—and, in the long run, that of both parties now bargaining in steel—demands that a rise in prices be avoided like the plague it certainly would be. As the initiating party, labor has the primary responsibility in these negotiations. The union should keep its demands for increased compensation sufficiently within the bounds of possible absorption—through increased productivity and otherwise—so as to avoid an unreasonable sacrifice in profits at the present level of prices. But on the employers rests a countervailing obligation: to hold the line on prices.

"So great is the public's concern with prices that any increase will call for evidence of its absolute necessity. And it would be better that this be given voluntarily rather than be required by some Congressional investigation." (June 1, 1956.)

[2] *Economic Trends*, published by the Economic Policy Committee of AFL-CIO, reported in its issue of November 1956, that average earnings of factory workers were about $2 an hour, and added the following comment: "This figure does not represent the end of the road or even a spot to linger and rest. . . . The next convenient spot on the road ahead is the $3 mark."

[3] See papers by Professors Clark Kerr, Martin Bronfenbrenner, Harold W. Levinson, Sumner H. Slichter, and C. L. Christenson at the 66th annual meeting of the American Economic Association, December 1953. *American Economic Review*, May 1954, pp. 279–366.

in the United States 3 million families with money incomes below $1,000, and altogether 8.3 million whose incomes fell below $2,000.[4]

Many, perhaps most, of those who belong to the lowest income groups are other than regular wage earners—sharecroppers, farmers on infertile land, migratory and casual laborers. These present a social problem significantly different from that confronting the wage earner.

For regular wage earners at the lower income levels a legal minimum wage offers a form of protection. Such laws have been enacted in this country and elsewhere in response to a belief that they are necessary to insure a subsistence income. Combined with this is the conviction that a worker whose efforts are not sufficiently productive to justify such a wage will not, except for short intervals, be offered employment. Congress amended the Fair Labor Standards Act in 1955 by increasing the minimum for certain employees in interstate commerce from 75 cents to one dollar an hour. The new minimum will provide an annual income for the fully employed (assuming 40 hours a week for 52 weeks) of $2,080.

That amount is probably sufficient to meet the absolute necessities for many workers—young people living at home and single men and women without dependents—but it is a scant amount on which to bring up a family. Consequently organized labor and others are seeking a further advance in the minimum as well as wider coverage. However desirable this may be, it does not in itself constitute a final answer. As the 1955 *Economic Report* points out, a minimum wage affords needed protection, but it is not a remedy for low wages. The basic need is for increased efficiency at the level where the lowest wages are paid, on the part of both management and labor.

The pressure for higher wages is not, however, limited to subnormal income areas. The demand finds expression all along the line, and this raises a question that has wide implications. The total wage bill constitutes the largest charge upon business enterprise; consequently the effect on the national economy of a general wage increase—especially in a time of full employment—is something that should be taken into account by those making the demands. It is an area in which organized labor should act with due consideration of possible effects on employment and the purchasing power of the consumer's dollar.

[4] U.S. Department of Commerce, *Survey of Current Business*, June 1956, p. 10.

Complicating the issue is the question of the equitable distribution of the gain resulting from increased productivity. Should unions formulate their wage demands on the theory that all of such gains should go to labor? The use of the term "output per man-hour" to measure productivity tends to create the impression that increased output is due solely to increased labor efficiency. This is surely a factor in specific instances, but the trend toward increased productivity over the years is to be attributed far more to technological improvements than to an increase in skill or in manual effort. In fact, the latter at least has tended to decline in intensity as productivity has increased. What inferences, then, are to be drawn with respect to rival claims to the gains arising from increased productivity?

The "basic principle, to which a competitive system would give effect," writes Professor John M. Clark, "is that such gains belong only temporarily to the persons responsible for making them." [5] Clark adds that while this might take place through reduced prices with money wages remaining unchanged, "unless the improvement made increased demands upon the workers" the actual trend, and presumably the more natural one, has concentrated on increased money wages, leaving problems of adjustment between industries in which productivity has increased faster or slower than the average.[6]

During 1950–55 average hourly earnings in manufacturing rose about 28 per cent. During the same period wholesale prices rose 7.3 per cent, and the Consumers Price Index rose about 11 per cent.[7] Thus it appears that the average hourly earnings of factory labor in recent years have risen faster than the increase in productivity (estimated at 2 to 3 per cent a year) and to have outrun the rising price index as well.

What this means to factory labor as a whole cannot be determined without a breakdown by industries. The average increase in hourly earnings is the resultant of adjustments in many industries. In some cases earnings have risen at a more rapid rate than productivity, and in others they have fallen short. Under such circumstances the wage groups that are far out in front may have set a pattern that initiated

[5] John M. Clark. *Alternative to Serfdom* (New York: Alfred A. Knopf, 1948, 1950), pp. 130–131.

[6] Clark, *op. cit.*, pp. 131–134.

[7] *Monthly Labor Review*, September 1956, pp. 1120, 1121, 1130, 1136.

an inflationary movement—one that will be harmful to the consuming public, which includes other workers, and in the long run harmful to themselves.

Another danger is that "labor union and employer may compose their differences at the expense of the public, including other labor." [8] In the recent period of high demand for goods, and the consequent high industrial activity, management in particular industries has shown a tendency to come to comparatively quick agreement on wage increases and to attempt to compensate for it by increased prices. In especially prosperous industries, when dealing with powerful unions, this seems to have become standard practice.

The explanation usually given for a boost in prices following a wage increase is that it is necessary to compensate for the added labor cost. The observer may wonder whether in some cases the cost could not have been absorbed by the industry without undue injury on the profit side. He cannot have failed to notice that in some industries the price increase has been followed not by a maintenance of the *status quo* as to profits but by an actual increase. This may be *post hoc, propter hoc* reasoning. The rise in profits may be due to other causes—improved management policies or technological advance—but the fear arises that there may have been a mutual willingness at the bargaining table to make a gain regardless of the consequences to the consumer.

The foregoing may suggest that an easy alternative in wage bargaining to bitter struggles between employer and union, each to out-pressure the other, is collusion at the expense of the public. It seems reasonable to believe that a high sense of ethical obligation may find a better way, though this is an alternative that Sumner Slichter believes to be "too utopian to be promptly achieved." He suggests instead that "if rising labor costs force a rise in the price level, the community may properly insist that employers do a better job of bargaining." [9] How the "community" is to do this is not made clear, nor is support offered for the implication that the employer can be counted on to protect the public against the designs of the unions. In specific instances the respective roles may be the opposite of those

[8] Clark, *op. cit.*, p. 140.
[9] *American Economic Review*, May 1954, pp. 345, 346.

suggested. A sense of responsibility in both camps will afford the best protection of the public welfare.

A sense of responsibility or the lack of it is sometimes revealed in public discussion. At a labor convention in an Eastern state a labor official suggested that "sometimes labor can push industry too far, at the expense of loss of jobs and labor's own well-being." He said that while it will always be the legitimate aim of labor to obtain more, "you can't get more than the whole" and added that "management is justly entitled to a fair return on its investment." Another leader replied: "Don't be disturbed about whether you are asking for more than a fair share. The most you can wring out of an employer under the best of circumstances will be a hell of a way short of your fair share. . . . Let the philosophy be: build your union to a degree of strength that you can wring out of the boss every last penny that business will allow to be wrung out." [10]

Comment in an official publication of AFL-CIO reveals both a sense of responsibility and a canny awareness of reality:

It should always be remembered that unions are subjected to a variety of powerful restraints every time they bargain with the employer over wages.

In the first place, the union's wage objective must always be related to economic realities—current demand for the product or services it helps produce, potential substitute products on the market, the wage rates of competing nonunion employers, the condition of business generally and of the employer particularly.

This above all, no union can afford to be indifferent to the reasonable profit requirement of the employer. *Its objective is to improve the jobs of its members, not to destroy them.*

Furthermore, the union is only one of the parties to the bargaining process; ultimately it must always reach a *mutual* agreement with the employer or his association, and in the process it cannot be shown that union responsibility declines with the growth of the size or increase in the scope of the bargaining unit. On the whole, exactly the opposite is true.

Finally, even when union members find that just demands are rejected, they are always aware that all strikes are hazardous. Unionists know too well the hardship a strike may bring, and more, they know that strikes are often lost. Besides, the staying power of unions is relatively limited

[10] *AFL-CIO News*, February 11, 1956.

because neither the members nor their organizations have the great resources of industry.[11]

It is impossible to deal adequately, within the limits of this chapter, with the impact of wages and prices on management, labor and the consumer. Both management and labor, if they are wise, will try to steer carefully between the twin dangers of economic starvation on the one hand and pricing themselves out of the market on the other. Between these extremes there is an area within which the consumer's interests will be protected only if there is an atmosphere of tolerance, good will and restraint at the bargaining table.

COMPULSORY UNION MEMBERSHIP

In Chapter 7 the question was asked whether the unions, by reason of their present strength and the protection of their rights under existing laws, might not now consider giving up the practice of seeking to have written into their contracts with employers a requirement that all employees become union members. The arguments advanced by the unions for a continuance of the policy were there set forth,[12] and the historical reasons for the development of closed-shop and union-shop policies were discussed. The practice grew out of employer hostility and lack of legislative or judicial protection of the right to organize and bargain collectively. The union arguments, however, while they are cogent, do not seem finally to establish the wisdom or the soundness of union-shop policy. If it creates confusion in the shop and mutual ill-will, as the union leaders say, to have members and non-members working side by side, may it not have the same effect to have willing and unwilling members in the same shop—the latter resentful of the compulsion that brought them into membership? Is the coerced member a really useful or helpful member?

One of unionism's great problems is to secure the active cooperation even of the members who have willingly joined. Attendance at union meetings is notoriously small. Walter Reuther has repeated more than once the admonition that he gave the delegates at the last convention of the CIO before joining the merger. "We need to build

[11] *Labor's Economic Review*, published by AFL-CIO, Vol. I, No. 2, February, 1956.

[12] See also the strongly reasoned defense of the union shop in Golden and Ruttenberg, *The Dynamics of Industrial Democracy* (New York: Harper & Brothers, 1942), Chap. VII.

our union stronger," he said, "to organize the unorganized. But more important, we need . . . to concentrate . . . on the task of unionizing the organized, of making the millions . . . who have trade union cards in their pockets understand what trade unionism means in their hearts. That is the great challenge because the power of our movement does not come out of the per capita tax that the workers pay. . . . [It] must flow from the loyalty, the understanding, and the devotion and dedication that the rank and file members . . . invest in our great movements." [13]

The soundness of the argument that essential union discipline is promoted by the union shop and the reasonableness of the criticisms of the "free rider" may be granted. But there is something worth considering in the idea that a union that attracts members by its accomplishments will be a stronger union than one that has a considerable body of membership secured by a measure of duress. [14]

A FAIR DAY'S WORK

Make-work practices exist primarily because of the uncertainties of employment. If there has been more of it than elsewhere in the past at least in the building trades, it is because regular employment is uncertain in that field. If a man has a job in a factory he is not constantly dogged with the fear that when he has finished his immediate task there may not be another waiting for him. But when a building is finished the carpenter or bricklayer or plumber has to find

[13] *Proceedings of the 17th Constitutional Convention, CIO, December 1, 1955,* p. 14. Mr. Reuther's point here is emphasized by a comment in one of the case studies in the series, "Causes of Industrial Peace": "As is true of most democratic organizations which younger generations inherit without having to make sacrifices, the locals . . . face the problem of attracting rank-and-file members to union meetings. They have discovered a new kind of 'free rider.' The old fashioned kind accepted union benefits without belonging to the union, but the new free rider merely holds a union card and refuses to accept responsibility for the conduct of union affairs." (Case Study 9, Colorado Fuel & Iron Co. and United Steel Workers, pp. 17 and 18 of pamphlet report; p. 233 of Summary volume *op. cit.*)

[14] The questionings presented above are in no sense to be interpreted as approval of the misnamed "right-to-work" laws. These laws simply prohibit employers and unions from negotiating union-shop contracts. Such governmental limitation upon the free exercise of judgment on the part of the contracting parties is contrary to the democratic spirit of our country. The fact that such laws are sought by associations of employers who are traditionally opposed to unions as such does not add to the attractiveness of the movement.

another place of employment. To be sure, the factory worker is faced at times by the same problem though usually at longer intervals. Because of this and for other reasons inherent in the employer-employee relationship and in the economy itself, most wage earners are aware of the danger of unemployment. What could be more suited to the nature of the predicament than to make the job last as long as possible, or to create a situation calling for the employment of as many workers as possible? That this attitude tends to manifest itself among wage earners generally is indicated by the evidence of its existence among nonunion as well as union employees.[15]

Frederick W. Taylor, the "father of scientific management," was so impressed with this problem in the nonunion shop where he began his managerial career that it led him—so he said later—in the direction of the studies from which his system of scientific management emerged.[16]

Organized labor, in general, is on record as approving technological advance. In the unions of the building trades, Professor William Haber found in 1930 considerable opposition to labor-saving machinery and many varieties of make-work practices. In a further study of the same industry in 1956, Haber and Levinson reported that while restrictive practices still existed the charge of organized restriction of output "has not been supported by the preponderance of the evidence obtained in this study. Nor have many other widely cited rules appeared upon investigation to be as widespread or restrictive as has often been alleged." [17]

[15] See Stanley B. Matthewson, *Restriction of Output Among Unorganized Workers* (New York: Viking Press, 1931).

[16] See his Principles of Scientific Management (New York: Harper & Brothers, 1911). This book contains as sympathetic an explanation of restriction of output by labor as could be found anywhere. In it he wrote that one of his chief objectives in his study of management principles was to discover those under which a worker could afford to do his best.

[17] Much has been written on this subject: see William Haber, *Industrial Relations in the Building Industry* (Cambridge, Mass.: Harvard University Press, 1930), Chap. VIII; Sumner H. Slichter, *Union Policies and Industrial Management* (Washington, D.C.: Brookings Institution, 1941), Chaps. VI, VII; Joel Seidman, *Union Rights and Union Duties* (New York: Harcourt Brace and Co., 1943) Chap. 3; Millis and Montgomery, Organized Labor. (New York, McGraw-Hill Book Company, 1945), Chaps. IX, X; Stanley B. Matthewson, *Restriction of Output Among Unorganized Workers* (New York: Viking Press, 1931); Haber and Levinson, *Labor Relations and Productivity in the Building Trades* (Ann Arbor, Mich.: University of Michigan Press, 1956), Chaps. VII, VIII, IX.

There is still evidence, nevertheless, of the existence of rules involving the unnecessary employment of individuals, as where an electrician is employed in a theater to turn a light switch, or where a carpenter is required to cut a hole to enable a plumber to extend a pipe through a floor—which the plumber could do with equal competence—and of occasions, particularly in the building trades, where a skilled craftsman is employed to do work that could be done by an unskilled laborer.

On the railroads an obsolete method of calculating pay for operating employees has led to some peculiar results. A day's work in train service is either 100 miles or 8 hours in freight operation, and 150 miles or 8 hours in passenger service. This rule was fixed when trains moved more slowly than at present. Under present conditions with passenger trains often covering as much as 500 miles in 8 hours, and through freights doing 40 miles an hour or more, a train crew, theoretically, might be entitled to better than three days' pay for one day's work. This is prevented, however, by an agreed limit on the number of hours that the train crew can work in a month. Thus individual earnings are kept within reasonable limits but the number of men required to operate the trains is increased. It is not "featherbedding" in the usual sense, but it is a "make-work" device. As Sumner Slichter remarks. "The obsolete definition of a day's work of fifty years ago keeps in railroad service many thousands of men who are not needed there." [18]

Two instances of true feather-bedding that have received considerable notoriety through court decisions involve practices of the Musicians' Union and the Typographical Union.

The Musicians' Union has in its by-laws a rule that a traveling orchestra "cannot, without the consent of a local, play any presentation performances in its jurisdiction unless a local house orchestra is also employed." Under this rule a local of the Musicians' Union in Akron, Ohio, refused to give its consent to the appearance of a traveling band at a local theater unless the local orchestra was engaged to play on the same program. The management of the theater would not agree to this proposal and a traveling band which had been engaged for a performance canceled its engagement. The local union

[18] *Union Policies and Industrial Management, op. cit.* p. 191.

then proposed that the management agree to engage the local orchestra to play, as the Supreme Court put it, "on some number of occasions having a relation to the number of traveling band appearances." The management declined this offer and filed charges with the National Labor Relations Board.

The Typographical Union has long maintained a practice frankly termed "bogus" which was described in a Supreme Court opinion as follows:

". . . a newspaper advertisement was set up in type [and] was impressed upon a cardboard matrix or 'mat.' These mats were used by their makers and also reproduced and distributed, at little or no cost, to other publishers who used them as molds for metal castings from which to print the same advertisement. This procedure by-passed all compositors except those who made up the original form." Facing this loss of work, the court explained, the union made agreements with the publishers under which compositors set up in type, at "regular pay," the matter contained in the advertisement "precisely . . . as though the mat had not been used," after which the type was "consigned to the 'hell box' and melted down."

This practice as well as that of the Musicians was the subject of a charge of "unfair labor practice" before the National Labor Relations Board under the "feather-bedding" clause of the Taft-Hartley Act, which forbids a union to require an employer to pay for "services which are not performed or not to be performed."

Both cases were carried to the Supreme Court after the Board had held that the acts complained of were not in violation of the law. The Court agreed with the Board. It held that even though the services in question were not needed or wanted, the unions were not asking pay for work "not to be performed," but for work that was actually to be done.[19]

Taking into account the basic factors that lead to make-work policies it becomes evident that the problem must be considered in economic as well as in ethical terms. The short-run effect of such practices may be beneficial to the workers. The long-run effect is bound to have an adverse bearing on all factors in the economy, by increas-

[19] National Labor Relations Board v. Gamble Enterprises, 345 U. S. 117; and American Newspaper Publishers Association v. National Labor Relations Board, 345 U. S. 100. Both cases were decided on March 9, 1953.

ing costs and limiting production. What is unsound economics is also usually bad morals.

PICKETING AND VIOLENCE

Certain aspects of picketing were discussed in Chapters 6 and 13. Reference was made to the assumption that strikers are somehow endowed with legitimate authority to prevent others from going to work. This question is complicated by several factors. One of them is the possibility that the strikers may be suffering from acts of injustice on the part of management that can only be characterized as morally wrong. Another factor, usually present, is the existence during a strike of several categories of persons desirous of entering the plant who represent different degrees of threat to the winning of the strikers' objectives. Professional strike breakers may be brought in from the outside, though this is not as common as it was formerly. There may be employees who prefer to remain at work and are opposed to the strike. There are almost certain to be employees who are not involved in a strike of production workers, such as technical men and office workers, and there are management officials who want to get to their offices.

That there should be anything less than a feeling of deep hostility toward professional strike breakers is inconceivable. Their introduction is an invitation to violence.

Employees in the same industrial category as the strikers but who choose not to join the strike and attempt to continue at work present a different problem. One can understand the indignation of the strikers at this lack of support, and their bitterness over what they consider the acts of traitors. That these fellow employees are within their legal rights, however, seems clear. The absence of any legal right on the part of the strikers to make use of force or violence to prevent their access to the plant seems equally clear.[20] To picket in such numbers as to give information about the strike and the reasons for it, to attempt persuasion, and to make clear the strikers' abhorrence of the action of those who prefer to work during the strike would

[20] In a case pending before the Supreme Court as this is written, a union is appealing from a decision granting $10,000 damages to a worker who was prevented by mass picketing from going to work during a strike. New York Times, November 20, 1956.

seem to constitute proper and legitimate behavior. But more than this can be justified, it seems to me, only if the very existence of the strike may be said to confer sudden extra-legal immunities on the strikers, not claimed by them as their right before the strike or after it is over.

As to persons whose work is unrelated to the jobs that the strikers have left, which is ordinarily true of clerical workers or certain technical employees, interference is very difficult to defend; and even more so is the attempt to keep executives from their offices. Yet in recent strikes all categories referred to, except the professional strike breakers who apparently were not involved, have been the object of determined, and at times violent, opposition. Beyond the question of illegality these tactics seem to be morally wrong.

Equally to be condemned is violence for which employers are responsible, and there is much evidence of employer-supported violence during strikes. The more extreme examples, such as the occurence at Ludlow, Colorado, forty odd years ago, or the "Memorial Day Massacre" [21] in Chicago twenty years ago, are not likely to be repeated where the struggle to establish trade unionism has been won, but such incidents could occur again in areas, particularly in the South, where the struggle is still going on, and where modified versions of them have already occurred. Violent attacks on union organizers in such areas are frequently reported in the labor press.

In the midst of a strike early in 1956, in which there were press reports of violence, and responsibility was attributed to representatives of both parties to the controversy, the American Civil Liberties Union issued a statement defining its position with respect to picket-line behavior:

"Intimidation or violence," the statement ran, "should never be allowed to interfere with free entrance to or exit from a place of work by anyone. Such intimidation or violence is an infringement of civil liberties and has no place in a democratic society which respects the idea of individual decision. The frustration of labor organizations and pickets in a strike situation concerning workers who seek entrance to or exit from the plant is understandable. But it is the responsibility

[21] The Chicago Memorial Day Incident, Report of La Follette Committee, 75th Congress, 1st Session, Report No. 46, Part 2, July 22, 1937.

of labor organizations and picket lines not to violate the civil liberties of persons with whom they may be in dispute.

"Intimidation or violence should never be allowed to interfere with peaceful picketing. Again, the distress of management concerning its economic loss is understandable, but such intimidation or violence is an infringement of civil liberties. It is the responsibility of management not to violate the civil liberties of persons with whom they may be in dispute." [22]

SALARIES AND EXPENSE ACCOUNTS

Whether or not the increasingly evident middle-class tastes and ambitions to be noted in labor officialdom are another roadblock to reform is a matter of opinion. We cannot, however, leave this catalog of impediments without at least a reference to a tendency that causes misgivings among some friends of the labor movement.

A few years ago an annual salary of $25,000 for a union president was unusual. While many unions pay their chief executives less than that amount, the figure is no longer unusual, and the trend is upward. Several unions are known to pay a presidential salary of $50,000. There are unconfirmed rumors of salaries higher than this. Lavish expense accounts send traveling union representatives to the most expensive hotels.

There is a belief that this sort of thing is necessary to enable union spokesmen to meet corporation executives at something approaching their own level, and thus to secure better terms for the workers they represent. There is, however, the danger that what is happening is a widening of the gulf between officialdom and the rank-and-file without corresponding benefit.

Perhaps this is a nostalgic appeal to an irretrievable past. Certain it is that the tendencies referred to are characteristic not of labor leaders alone, but of the business world [23] and, though less commonly, in

[22] News release, American Civil Liberties Union, January 18, 1956.

[23] *Business Week* (June 2, 1956) published a statement concerning the pay of the top executives of 132 companies. Three companies paid more than $700,000 (salary and bonus) in 1955. Seven others paid more than $200,000. "This $200,000 figure," the writer said, "is now becoming a sort of benchmark representing the level at which a man becomes a part of the really high paid executive group." But "only eighteen of the 132 companies pay the highest paid officer less than $100,000." (Footnote continued on page 201.)

some professional fields. If labor is criticized for sharing some of the less desirable qualities of the society in which it functions, it is because the high purposes of unionism justify the expectation of adherence to higher standards than prevail among those whose main objective is financial gain. If a union executive is to serve the membership effectively, he should be relieved from at least the grosser forms of financial worries. But the achievement of that objective does not seem to require making working-class leaders into men of comparative wealth.[24]

The dangers suggested here have not gone unnoted in the labor movement itself. Louis Hollander, an officer of the Amalgamated Clothing Workers and president of the New York CIO, spoke recently before a trade union audience concerning the distance sometimes existing between leaders and rank and file. "Too many leaders," he is reported as saying, "live in a world apart—a world in which the badges of achievement are high salaries, expensive automobiles, membership in country clubs and the other appurtenances of wealth." Hollander did not suggest that these are bad in themselves, nor did he contend that "the only true union leader is one who takes a monastic vow of poverty. What requires vigilance is that we in positions of leadership not succumb to the notion that power, public acclaim or good living are the important things. Each one of us derives his strength from the men and women in the shop; we have value only to the extent that we serve them faithfully and well."[25]

A FRIENDLY JUDGMENT

Another authoritative statement may well serve as a final com-

---

However, things are not always what they seem. *Business Week* points out that the top figure of $776,000 paid to the president of General Motors, after the "tax bite," left him with only $121,328, "according to a G.M. estimate."

[24] A relevant comment appears in Barbash, *op. cit.*, p. 409: "I find it . . . difficult to defend what may well be an inevitable outcome of 'bigness'—a bigness, perhaps, made necessary to cope with the bigness of the problems, I miss most of all the kind of personal humility—a consciousness of doing God's work, as it were—on the part of many union leaders that, for me, is a necessary quality of a humane movement, whether it is a labor movement or any other kind. . . . It is possible . . . that I am not alone in these sentiments; that there are union members . . . and the sympathetic public (and even sympathetic employers) to whom a little less posturing, a little less conspicuous consumption . . . might make them feel better about unions and the labor movement."

[25] *New York Times*, February 25, 1957.

mentary on the subject of this chapter. Midway between the passage of the Wagner Act in 1935 and of the Taft-Hartley Act in 1947, Frances Perkins, as Secretary of Labor, included the following in her annual report: "American trade unionism in becoming an established American institution has implicitly accepted certain definite social responsibilities, and its policies in the future must be predicated not only on the welfare of its own members, but also on the welfare of all the people of the United States. . . . The new status is based on . . . statutory protection [which] gives to trade unionism an enormous prestige and a great responsibility." Organized labor, Miss Perkins said, now has responsibilities not for its members alone but "for all working people, for the development and prosperity of modern industry, to the whole people of the United States for sound, intelligent economic, social, political, and moral practices."

". . . the trade unions," she continued, "with their stability protected by law, do not need to use excessive practices. . . . The practice of closed memberships and high dues combined with closed shop have been effective in securing very high wages for particular groups, but the public asks today that some of these practices be restudied by [the] trade-union movement with a view to the public welfare. . . . Excessive methods of picketing and demonstration . . . , raiding (of one union by another), stoppage of work due to jurisdictional disputes, boycotting of goods produced by the labor of other unions and the secondary boycott are all practices deemed by the public to be excessive and not in the public interest. . . . Whether such practices were ever necessary is not now under consideration, but the public believes that trade unions which have legal protection under the National Labor Relations Board should be quick to abandon methods and practices which lack restraint and due regard for public opinion." [26]

[26] *29th Annual Report of the Secretary of Labor, 1941,* pp. 8–10.

16

Concluding Observations

The facts presented in this book are believed to establish beyond doubt the importance, and even the necessity, of trade unions in modern industrial society. As an economic force they constitute the machinery by which thousands of individuals, powerless as such, are enabled to participate in the making of decisions that affect them in the primary business of earning a living. Collective bargaining is basic to the orderly determination of relations with the employer and to the fixing of the terms under which the individual worker will offer to sell, and the employer will offer to purchase, his services. Trade unionism with its method of collective bargaining is a common-sense way of dealing with the problems that arise out of the business of earning wages—as sensible and as necessary as the joining together of other interests in corporations or chambers of commerce.

In view of the significance of trade unionism to the society in which we live, the fact that obstacles to its healthy development exist may well engage our attention. Such obstacles are to be found both within and without the labor movement. An outside force to be noted is the continuance of varying degrees of hostility.

THE EFFECT OF HOSTILITY

Every labor leader, even where management has accepted the unions as permanent elements in industry, feels that he must keep his guard up. This attitude, as pointed out earlier, is contributed to by memories of the past. It persists, however, because there are elements in industry which, though apparently accepting the permanence of unionism, seem constantly poised for attack, as is made manifest by speeches, interviews, and widely distributed pamphlets.

More important in its effect on union tactics is the existence of uncompromising and ruthless opposition to unionism in regions where organization has made little headway. In many Southern communities union organizers have been driven out of town, have been victims of mob violence, and have even been subject to manhandling by local police. In company-dominated towns the clergy have often been enlisted in the anti-union crusade. On the other hand, in a Georgia town where the pastor of a church was favorable to the union, employing companies issued to their workers an "application form" on which the question was asked, "What is your church affiliation?" Those who named the "pro-union" church were at once discharged.[1]

Municipalities in Southern states in recent years have adopted special ordinances to hamper union organizers or to make their work impossible—such as requiring organizers to obtain licenses at extravagant fees, or requiring that they be citizens of the state or residents of the community, or requiring them to meet other conditions that would be inconsistent with their status as representatives of the union.

An example of this practice is the action taken by the City Council of Dublin, Georgia, in April 1956. According to a Dublin paper, the Council, "at a special called meeting," adopted an ordinance "requiring any agent or organizer of any type of organization to pay an annual license fee of $2,500 to solicit membership in any type of organization within the city limits of Dublin. . . . The granting of the license to be wholly at the discretion of the Mayor and Council."[2] To obtain a license, the applicant would have to be a resident of Dublin of more than five years standing, and would be required to subscribe to an oath that he is not a Communist, and that he does not "believe in the overthrow of the municipal or state laws in regard to segregation." Shortly after the passage of this ordinance, a representative of the International Woodworkers of America, attempting to organize in Dublin, was arrested and jailed.

In another Georgia town an ordinance was enacted requiring a union organizer to pay a license fee of $1000 and in addition to pay $100 for each day of activity, or be liable to a fine or imprisonment. A union seeking to have the ordinance declared unconstitutional and its enforcement enjoined was rebuffed in a U.S. District Court. The U.S. Court of Appeals in New Orleans reversed the lower court and

[1] *Economic Justice*, October 1955.
[2] *Courier-Herald*, Dublin, Georgia, April 21, 1956.

remanded the case for trial, declaring that the tax was "exorbitant and punitive." [3]

THE EFFECT OF BAD EXAMPLES

An influence that hampers the efforts of labor leaders to eliminate the evil practices that have appeared in some unions is the existence of bad examples in business, politics, and government. There are businessmen who condone or engage in corrupt practices along with some labor men. This became evident in 1945 at the trial and conviction of Joe Fay, an officer of the International Union of Operating Engineers, for "extortion" or accepting bribes from contractors in return for "keeping labor in line." The president of the Building Trades Employers Association of New York City appeared as a character witness for Fay. He had known him for twenty years and said that his reputation for "honesty and fair dealing" was good. On cross-examination the witness said he had read a good deal in the papers about Fay's activities, but he couldn't remember "specifically" about charges that he had taken $112,000 in kickbacks from nonunion workers, or about beatings he had inflicted on other union members, including an assault on David Dubinsky, president of the Ladies' Garment Workers' Union, just after Dubinsky had introduced an anti-racketeering resolution at an AFL convention—all of which had been reported prominently in the papers.

One of the contractors who testified at the trial that he had paid bribe money to Fay later filed an affidavit in support of Fay's appeal against his conviction, in which he said that Fay "did not extort money by threat or extortion" but was paid for what the witness considered "valuable service on behalf of me and my company." [4]

A striking aspect of extortion or bribery cases is the fact that the employer giving the bribe is seldom prosecuted, although the Taft-Hartley Act makes the offer of a bribe and the acceptance of one equally illegal. As a matter of fact, prosecution of labor racketeers has, in the past, been infrequent enough to suggest indifference or worse in political circles. Friendly relations between crooked labor

[3] *Monthly Labor Review*, September 1956, p. 1069.
[4] Data in files of New York Anti-Crime Committee.

men and government officials have frequently gone on serenely until something happened to create a public scandal.[5]

Three years before the corrupt Longshoremen's Union was thrown out of the AFL, and its president, Joe Ryan, had been indicted for stealing union funds and accepting gifts from employers, the "Joseph P. Ryan Association" was a flourishing organization. Among other activities the Association held an annual dinner at a leading New York hotel. This, says a well-informed writer, "served to dramatize, once a year, the great power and influence which Ryan and his closest associates wielded in New York City's government; their affiliations with businessmen of undoubted means and some respectability; and their influence over thugs and murderers." [6] Guests at the dinners were said, as a rule, to include the mayor, the police commissioner, and the district attorneys of the several counties of the New York City area.

Labor's Defensive Attitude

A further deterrent to forthright action against corruption has been labor's own defensive attitude under criticism. Samuel Gompers repeatedly declared his unwillingness to discuss or admit before the public any errors on the part of the unions. This was the policy followed by the labor leaders at the Congressional hearings preceding the enactment of the Taft-Hartley Act. In the face of hostile questions they would neither admit the existence of evils nor make constructive recommendations.

In the 1930s and 1940s, individual delegates at AFL conventions frequently offered resolutions alleging that racketeering was taking place in the unions, and urging corrective action by the Federation. These resolutions usually called forth heated denials that such evils existed. At the 1940 convention, President William Green said: "I challenge those who condemn the American Federation of Labor to point out where there is any racketeering" in the Federation.[7] The 1941 convention conceded that there might be "a few dishonest indi-

[5] On the other hand, as this is written, the district attorney of New York County and United States Attorneys in the same area, are actively engaged in seeking indictments against labor racketeers.

[6] Allen Raymond, *Waterfront Priest* (New York: Henry Holt & Co., 1955), pp. 42–43.

[7] AFL Convention Proceedings, 1940, p. 505.

viduals" among the five million members of affiliated unions, but it called attention to the principle of union "autonomy," under which "there is no power in the officers and executive council of the American Federation of Labor to exercise disciplinary authority for any offense committed by an officer or member of a national or international union." [8]

An outstanding example of the defensive attitude has appeared in repeated denunciations of the Hobbs Law at AFL conventions. This is the law referred to earlier that makes it a felony to conspire to use violence for purposes of extortion. Such a law would seem to have no relation to any activities of the great majority of unions. One might expect labor men as good citizens to approve and support it. But the law was enacted to curb the activities of a powerful union, and it has been denounced without a dissenting vote in convention after convention of the AFL, together with expressions of approval of efforts for its repeal.[9]

Behind this defensive attitude is undoubtedly the feeling that the unions are facing a hostile world, and that any admission of error will be used against them by enemies of the labor movement. Samuel Gompers said he would condemn wrongdoers within the unions to their faces but not before the outside world. Under the circumstances it was an understandable attitude, and one not without its value. It made for a spirit within the labor movement of fraternal solidarity

[8] AFL Convention Proceedings, 1941, p. 541.

[9] The Hobbs Law prescribes severe penalties against anyone who obstructs interstate commerce "by robbery or extortion . . . or commits or threatens physical violence to any person or property in furtherance of a plan or purpose" to violate the statute. The term "robbery" is defined in the statute as "the unlawful taking of personal property from the person . . . against his will by means of actual or threatened force, or violence, or fear of injury. . . ." The term "extortion" is defined as "the obtaining of property from another with his consent, induced by wrongful use of actual or threatened force, violence or fear. . . ."

This law was directed specifically against a practice of some of the locals of the Teamsters Union. Emissaries of the union would meet incoming trucks at the outskirts of a city and by threats of physical assault, or damage to property, compel the driver either to turn control of his truck over to the emissary for the drive to the intended destination, and pay him for a day's work; or to pay the same amount and so to continue without molestation. Labor critics of the law hold that it is vague and of uncertain meaning, objecting particularly to the use of the word "fear." Some express the opinion that a strike for legitimate objectives, if accompanied by injuries or damage to property, might be held a violation of the Hobbs Law with its penalties of $10,000 fine, or twenty years imprisonment, or both.

and good will. But it had its ill effects. It led to a strong reaction against outsiders who called attention to abuses within the unions, which not infrequently took the form of defiantly reelecting to their positions union officers who had been found guilty of misdemeanors or even criminal behavior.

This defensive attitude, however understandable, creates misunderstandings and fosters misinterpretations of trade-union purposes. Moreover, it weakens the mood for action against recognized evils and tolerates within the labor movement personalities who do it no good.

TRADE UNIONS AND THE COMMON GOOD

Sensitivity to the needs of others is revealed again and again in the utterances of labor leaders and in the resolutions adopted in union conventions. Walter Reuther manifested it in his speech to the CIO convention in 1952, accepting the position of president to succeed Philip Murray. As free labor, he said, "we have a job . . . of doing much more than just bargaining for our membership. We have to assume ever-increasing social responsibilities. . . . We must find a way to realize the tremendous spiritual reservoir that resides within a free people, and translate that power into constructive approaches to the world's problems—if we do that, we can win the battle for peace and freedom."

George Meany gave evidence of the same spirit when he spoke of the fraternal concern of American workers for other workers throughout the world; when he told the merged federation that labor must give "sober thought to the kind of world that we live in"; and when he said to the delegates at the last AFL convention just prior to the merger that under the new regime as under the old a matter of prime importance is "the mental attitude, the question of good faith," which involves a determination "to live up to our responsibilities as citizens."

The Executive Council's report to the final AFL convention called for action in the spirit of an earlier convention's declaration that "We call all men our brothers." In the new era approaching, said the report, "Our first responsibility must be to our country. We must so conduct ourselves, both in the formulation and implementation of basic policies, as to promote at all times the peace of the world, the security of the free American way of life, and its economic and social progress."

Countless resolutions adopted at union conventions have put the labor movement on record on the side of good government and social advance. These resolutions and the speeches of the leaders are not self-implementing; they do not automatically initiate action. But that is true of all good resolutions, including those adopted by church bodies. Nevertheless, whatever the setting, they reflect the existence of an underlying purpose, the very expression of which encourages action. A half-century ago, Professor William James emphasized among other devices the importance of making a "public pledge" as an impetus toward the formation of a desirable habit.[10]

Organized labor in general has in recent years given support to what is commonly referred to as "social legislation." Among specific proposals in this field, which the labor movement has generally viewed with favor, are laws to protect children against employment inimical to their growth or education, and to protect children and youth against the hazards involved in the use of dangerous machinery; the promotion and advancement of education, including federal aid; public health measures; slum clearance and subsidized housing; minimum wage legislation; and social security in all its aspects.[11]

In Chapter 13, "Unions and the Public," labor's concern about world affairs was considered. Both AFL and CIO gave consistent support to the Marshall Plan and the Point Four Program. An extended resolution on foreign policy was adopted at the 1955 convention of AFL-CIO. The merged bodies reiterated their condemnation of all forms of totalitarianism and emphasized the vital need of American aid, both directly and through United Nations agencies, to distressed peoples abroad. The resolution declared its "categoric rejection of any

---

[10] William James, *Psychology* (New York: Henry Holt & Co., 1900), p. 145.

[11] In the Gompers era the AFL was officially opposed to much of the above legislation on the theory that the contemplated advantages might better be secured through collective bargaining without the risk of adverse court decisions. It is sometimes suggested that in its present advocacy of social legislation, labor is merely serving its own interest as before by a different method. However, most of the measures listed above seem likely in some degree to serve all classes.

In other legislative fields labor, like other economic groups, attempts to further what it considers its own interests, though there are at times conflicting interests within the labor movement itself. Tariff legislation is a case in point. Agitation over the St. Lawrence Seaway is another example.

idea of imposing our form of government or economic system on any other nation," and "rejection of all colonialism—the old declining Western as well as the new rising Soviet colonialism. . . ."

Millions in underdeveloped countries, nursing "their grievances and their hopes," the resolution said, "constitute a fertile field for Communist operations." By ministering to their fundamental physical needs and their "burning desire for independence and equality . . . we shall be on firmer ground as we seek to win new adherents to the free world."

AFL and CIO were among the founders of the International Confederation of Free Trade Unions. Through its activities they are continuing to promote and support free trade unions throughout the world. Both have stood resolutely against Communist infiltration of trade unions at home. In 1949 and 1950 the CIO expelled ten affiliates which had come to be dominated by Communist or fellow-travelling leaders. These unions at that time were said to have a combined membership of between 850,000 and 900,000. By 1955 only four of the expelled unions were in existence, with a membership estimated at "approximately a third" of the number in the expelled unions.

By its consistent blocking of Communist infiltration and its firm espousal of democratic, as opposed to totalitarian, doctrines, organized labor has undoubtedly become one of the most effective opponents of Communist propaganda in the United States and a powerful influence in the world.

There are other areas within which organized labor is contributing to the common good. As indicated in other chapters, organized labor is playing an increasingly important role in civic development— through cooperation with social agencies, through financial assistance to the Red Cross and to other organizations on both local and national levels, and through assistance in the planning of community enterprises.

A FINAL WORD

To sum up, what shall we say about organized labor's discharge of its responsibilities? The record is neither wholly positive nor wholly negative. Some of the practices here noted are to be condemned, and are increasingly condemned in labor circles as well as elsewhere. Other courses of action are deserving of praise. The fraternal spirit engendered by men working together for their common good is one of the finest fruits of trade unionism. I have seen organized working-men so joined in righteous purpose as to put me in mind of what I have read of the spirit of the early Christians.

Sometimes in strikes one sees this spirit. I recall a scene back in the days when many of the industrial workers were recent immigrants. Workers of a half-dozen nationalities were on strike, without formal organization, without outside help. They had to figure things out for themselves. I attended a committee meeting and have never forgotten two impressions. First they were drawn together by the crisis as they never had been before. Each had his own native tongue, but it was an alien tongue to the others. So they were forced to try to speak English, and they were doing it brokenly, painfully, but they were taking steps toward a means of mutual understanding. Second, the subject of discussion was not how to circumvent the boss but how to pool their resources so that the babies would not be deprived of milk.

Such evidences of good will do not always transcend class barriers, but there was the story told by the editor of a small-town news-paper. A strike occurred in the local mill. The editor told his re-porters to report all the news. They did, and the local bank called for repayment of a loan to the paper. The editor was in deep trouble. When the printers heard of it they dug into their savings and helped him to tide over the crisis.

In Chapter 1 it was said that the unions, like other human or-ganizations, have obligations in more than one direction. The unions' obligations, it was suggested, are to its members, to other workers, to employers, and to society. One of the values of this study for the author has been the rediscovery of the fact that the discharge of obligations in one of these areas tends to have favorable repercussions in others; likewise that disregard of responsibilities at one point has harmful consequences elsewhere.

By the same token, the ability of organized labor to make further progress toward more socially responsible behavior depends in large part on the extent to which society, in all its inclusive manifestations, is conscious of its responsibility toward labor. One of society's obliga-tions, and especially that of the church, is to understand the labor movement and the necessities out of which it has grown. It has an obligation to search out the good in organized labor and not to permit itself to become blinded to the latter by the occasional examples of evil behavior. For the better men and women in the labor movement, although in the majority, are frequently struggling against heavy odds.

As the manuscript for this book goes to the printer there are stirring developments afoot. The Ethical Practices Committee, whose activities have been briefly sketched (Chapter 14), is probing further into charges of misbehavior on the part of union officials. The effect of its earlier investigations, and the policy statement of the Executive Council on racketeering to which they led, are being made manifest in action. Larger unions than the three now on temporary probation are being subjected to scrutiny; locals of some of these unions have been placed under trusteeship by their international presidents; and local officials suspected of wrongdoing have been suspended and placed on trial. George Meany, as president of AFL-CIO, has suspended certain officers of directly affiliated locals, whose malefactions were revealed by the Senate Subcommittee on Welfare Funds.

The new housecleaning spirit is to be observed in union journals, many of which continue, as in the past, to play down or ignore revelations of misbehavior on the part of union officials. Now, however, some of these journals are treating such revelations as front-page news. "FBI Arrests Hoffa on Bribery Charge" was the headline on page 1 of the *AFL-CIO News* of March 16, 1957.

In January 1957 the U. S. Senate created a "Select Committee on Improper Activities in the Labor or Management Field." Its effectiveness cannot be judged until the Committee has had time to prove itself. As this is written it is in the early stages of what will be, apparently, an extended study of the Teamsters Union. The names of a few other unions have been announced as prospective objects of inquiry, one of which is Local 138 of the Union of Operating Engineers. If the inquiry is conducted objectively and with a determination to obtain all relevant facts—as appears likely to be the case—and if care is exercised to avoid the placing of blame anywhere except where it clearly belongs, the results will be unmistakably salutary. The AFL-CIO is officially supporting the inquiry.

Another test of the intent and spirit of the Committee will be the extent to which it takes seriously the full implications of its title, which refers to activities "in the Labor or Management Field." The study should, without a shadow of doubt, include the role played by management trustees of welfare funds that have been corruptly mismanaged by union representatives; the identity of bribe-givers as well as of bribe-takers; and the assaults upon union organizers in the newer industrial areas of the South.

If the inquiry is conducted on these lines, the effect should be to strengthen honest trade unionism in its relations both with unorganized workers who have been standing aloof and with the discriminating public. The inquiry should buttress the position of the majority in the labor movement who approach their tasks with honesty and fidelity, and facilitate the purging of trade unionism of its crooks and racketeers.

Supplementary Notes

Matter appearing in the following pages is offered for the purpose of clarifying discussion or supplementing treatment of topics in various chapters, as indicated.

SUPPLEMENTARY UNEMPLOYMENT BENEFITS
(See Chapter 4)

The movement launched in 1955 in the automobile industry has spread into other fields. The coverage in early 1956 was said to include over a million workers under United Automobile Workers' contracts in aircraft and farm equipment industries as well as in automobiles—232 companies in all—together with about 50,000 workers in glass and electrical industries, 35,000 in can manufacturing, and a "scattering" of plants in other industries.[1] In July 1956 the principal companies in the rubber industry entered into a contract with the United Rubber Workers which included supplementary unemployment benefits. And in August 1956 all the leading steel companies agreed with the United Steel Workers to establish such benefits.

The steel agreement provides for supplementation up to 52 weeks. Employees are eligible after two years of continuous service and, subject to limitations as to size of the trust fund and number of credit units, are entitled to 65 per cent of weekly net earnings (after tax deductions). The maximum obligation of the companies is $25 a week as long as state unemployment compensation is being paid, and $47.50 "for each week thereafter up to 52." In both periods an additional benefit of $2 is to be paid "for each of not more than four dependents." The agreement further provides that in states where supplementation of statutory unemployment benefits is illegal the contracting parties shall confer on a plan to provide lump sum payments at the end of the period of unemployment.

Earlier Guaranteed Plans

A study made by the United States Bureau of Labor Statistics [2] a decade ago revealed the fact that some form of guaranteed plans had been at least tentatively in effect for a considerable period. Three such plans were in-

[1] *Business Week*, June 2, 1956, p. 54.
[2] *Guaranteed Wage or Employment Plans*, U. S. Bureau of Labor Statistics, Bulletin 906, 1947.

augurated before 1900. Several hundred were under way at one time or another prior to 1946, though the mortality rate among them was fairly high. The report stated that, as of January 1946, 196 plans were in operation. These included all plans that offered any sort of guarantee for at least three months in the year. They covered, altogether, only 61,000 employees. Among these were the three well-known plans of Procter and Gamble, initiated in 1923, of the Hormel Company, in operation since 1931, and of Nunn-Bush, launched in 1935. These accounted for a majority of the 61,000 employees covered in 1946.

STRIKE DATA
(See Chapter 6)

The basic and most reliable source of data on strikes is the United States Bureau of Labor Statistics. The annual reports on strikes cover all those "known to the Bureau" in which six or more workers are involved and which last as long as a full day or shift. No one is required to report a strike. The Bureau must therefore depend on daily newspapers, the labor press, management releases, etc. for information about the occurrence of strikes. Once having learned of a strike, it obtains detailed facts about it through an extended correspondence with the parties involved. It is probable that any strikes that escape the scrutiny of the Bureau are too few in number and too limited in significance to have much effect on the final Bureau figures.

Strike activity is indicated in terms of the number of strikes, number of strikers, and amount of time lost by the workers involved. Of these three criteria the last is far the most revealing, though the number of strikes seems to be the figure most frequently depended on, popularly, as a measure of strike activity. That the number of strikes is a poor measure of strike activity may be discovered by taking a ten-year period such as 1945 to 1954 for examination. There were more strikes in 1952 and in 1953 than in any of the other years in that decade. Specifically, there were 132 more strikes in 1952 and 106 more in 1953 than there were in 1946. Yet, by the measure of time lost as a result of strikes, 1946 not only far exceeded both 1952 and 1953 but was the heaviest strike year in the whole period during which that type of data has been recorded. Moreover, 1952, which had the largest number of *strikes* in the decade, had over a million fewer *strikers* than 1946, and 1953, which was second in number of strikes, was surpassed in number of strikers in five of the other years in the ten-year period.

The principal reason why the number of strikes is a poor criterion of strike activity is that all strikes are counted, regardless of size—a strike of 1,000 workers is equal in making up the count to a strike of 10,000. Another feature of strike recording that needs to be considered is the possibility that strikes may be concentrated in a few industries. In 1954 nearly half of all strike idleness was due to strikes in three industries— lumber, rubber, and construction. The concentration of strikes in specific areas is a factor that should be taken into account in any attempt to reach a judgment with respect to the extent to which workers in general, in any particular year, are resorting to strikes.

UNION BENEFITS
(See Chapter 8)

As stated in Chapter 8 the largest amount paid out by the unions in the form of cash benefits has been to the beneficiaries of deceased members. Old-age benefits, as pensions, stand second. Until 1949 such payments were far below those made as death benefits, but in that year they began to catch up and in 1954 were higher, reaching $29.75 million while death benefits were $27.85 million. The increase in old-age benefits corresponds, chronologically, to the development of retirement funds under collectively bargained agreements. It seems likely, therefore, that the sums included, in part at least, employer contributions.

Sickness benefits also registered a marked increase, beginning in 1948. Prior to that year the payments for this purpose ranged from just over $1 million at the low point in 1934 and 1935 to between $2 and $3 million in the pre-depression years and up to $4 million in 1945 and 1946. They rose to over $6 million in 1948, to over $7 million in 1949, and continued to rise each year until they reached nearly $26 million in 1954.

Disability benefits have generally been considerably lower than death and sickness benefits, ranging between $1 and $1.5 million, or less, and $5 million. Unemployment benefits were as a rule the lowest in the list. The total paid out for this purpose in 1927 was $690,000. Payments rose to over $9 million in 1931 and to $19.97 million in 1932. Of the latter sum the Brotherhood of Locomotive Engineers alone paid $9 million. With the advent of legislation providing for unemployment insurance—which by 1937 had been enacted in all the states—trade-union benefits for this purpose dropped decidedly. The unions had paid nearly $11 million in unemployment benefits in 1936. In 1937 the figure was $1.67 million. Since then it has topped $2 million only twice—in 1938 and 1940. In 1945 it was as low as $132,000. Since 1948 the annual average has been about $1.3 millions.[3]

THE TAFT-HARTLEY ACT
(See Chapter 13)

The Taft-Hartley Act, although often referred to as an amendment to the Wagner Act of 1935, is really a thorough revision of that Act, with many important new features. Whereas the Wagner Act guaranteed the right of employees to organize and bargain collectively through unions of their own choosing, the Taft-Hartley Act guarantees the right of employees to join or not to join labor unions. The Wagner Act regulated the activities of employers in their relations with unions and individual employees. The Taft-Hartley Act is a long and complicated piece of legislation regulating the activities of unions as well as employers and the relations of both unions and employers to employees in cases where the NLRB asserts jurisdiction. Taft-Hartley spells out in great detail the procedure for collective bargaining and requires unions as well as employers to bargain collectively where a bargaining agent has been duly designated. It requires unions and employers to notify each other of a desire to change an existing contract sixty days before its expiration and to give similar notice to state and federal mediation agencies. It requires trade unions that wish to use the facilities of the NLRB to keep financial records and make them available to their members. It makes secondary boycotts illegal and intervenes to help prevent jurisdictional disputes.

It should be noted that under the Eisenhower administration the jurisdiction of the NLRB has been contracted substantially. The result of this action has been to free unions dealing with smaller employers from the restrictions of the Act and at the same time to deny its protection to the employees involved. By the same token it fails to extend to many small employers the protections afforded to other employers under the Act.

Although unions have in their public statements indicated that Taft-Hartley is unacceptable in nearly every respect, they have continued, since 1947, to avail themselves of the protection of the right to organize and bargain collectively which the Act extends to employees and to unions.

In the NLRB report for fiscal 1955 (July 1, 1954 to June 30, 1955)

[3] The figures given here are taken from annual reports of the American Federation of Labor, which include the railway brotherhoods as well as AFL affiliates. The reports emphasize the fact that the figures are for the most part based on reports from the international unions. Very substantial sums, it is said, are paid out by local bodies and not included in the reports.

the union cases filed charging unfair labor practices against employers number 2,626. This, although nearly 14 per cent less than the 3,098 such cases filed in fiscal 1954, indicates that unions are as a practical matter taking advantage of the protection afforded them by Taft-Hartley.

Unions have also continued to make extended use of the election machinery of NLRB. In fiscal 1955 unions filed 6,153 petitions for representation elections out of a total of 7,165 filed by unions, employers, and individuals.

It is interesting to note that in spite of their bitter opposition to the revived labor injunction, in a number of instances unions (including those affiliated with AFL-CIO) have petitioned the NLRB for injunctive action against other unions.

One phase of Taft-Hartley that operates to the disadvantage of unions is that requiring that secondary boycott and jurisdictional dispute cases filed against unions be given priority in handling over all other cases in the regional offices. The administration officials of NLRB are required under the law to direct attorneys and field examiners to stop work they are doing on cases filed by unions and begin work on cases filed by employers. Thus action on the cases filed by unions must await the completion of work on the secondary boycott and jurisdictional dispute cases. In practice this means that employers get a much superior service in these cases than unions ordinarily do in cases which they file.[4]

THE LONGSHOREMEN
(See Chapter 14)

1. Report of the New York Crime Commission

In May 1953 the New York Crime Commission made a report on conditions on the New York waterfront. Its findings were summarized by Governor Thomas E. Dewey as follows:

"For 20 months the Crime Commission of the State of New York made a thorough study of the Port of New York waterfront. It reported that the longshoremen were dominated by a ruthless combine of corrupt union officers and hiring agents. In some cases acting in collusion with employers. The final report of the Commission disclosed appalling conditions of violence, pilferage, extortion and the use of notorious criminals to enforce the combine. These conclusions were fully sustained in public hearings before me and adopted by the legislatures of the States of New York and New Jersey, which were convened in extraordinary session last June to enact remedial legislation."

[4] The foregoing embodies a commentary by a government official.

2. The Bi-State Compact

Extraordinary sessions of the legislatures of the States of New York and New Jersey resulted in the enactment of a bi-state compact on June 25, 1953. The compact, known as the Waterfront Commission Act, is described by the New York State Board of Mediation in its annual report for 1953 as "unique in the annals of labor relations history; it is the first bi-state compact to deal with employment and related problems. In brief, it requires the registration and licensing of long-shoremen, pier superintendents, pier watchmen and stevedores; outlaws the shape-up system of hiring; establishes employment centers run by the State; and outlaws 'public loaders.' "

Article I of the compact reads in part as follows: "The states of New York and New Jersey hereby find and declare that the conditions under which waterfront labor is employed within the port of New York district are depressing and degrading to such labor, resulting from the lack of any systematic method of hiring, the lack of adequate information as to the availability of employment, corrupt hiring practices and the fact that persons conducting such hiring are frequently criminals and persons notoriously lacking in moral character and integrity and neither responsive or responsible to the employers nor to the uncoerced will of the majority of the members of the labor organizations of the employees; that as a result waterfront laborers suffer from irregularity of employment, fear and insecurity, inadequate earnings, an unduly high accident rate, subjection to borrowing at usurious rates of interest, exploitation and extortion as the price of securing employment and a loss of respect for the law; that not only does there result a destruction of the dignity of an important segment of American labor, but a direct encouragement of crime which imposes a levy of greatly increased costs on food, fuel and other necessaries handled in and through the port of New York district."

THE TEAMSTERS
(See Chapter 14)

1. Jurisdiction

The constitution of the Teamsters Union asserts jurisdiction "over all teamsters, chauffeurs, warehousemen, and helpers; all who are employed on or around horses, harness, carriages, automobiles, trucks, trailers, and all other vehicles hauling . . . freight, merchandise or materials; automotive sales, service and maintenance employees, garage workers and service station employees . . . stockmen, shipping room employees, and

. . . persons engaged in loading or unloading freight, merchandise or other materials onto or from any type of vehicle; all classes of dairy employees . . ., brewery and soft drink workers, workers in ice cream plants; all other workers employed in the manufacture, processing, sale and distribution of food, milk, dairy and other products; all truck terminal employees; cannery workers; and other workers where the security of the bargaining positions of the above classifications requires the organization of such other workers."

A recent treatise on trade unionism quotes Dave Beck, president of the Teamsters Union, as saying: "We will not stand idly by and permit infringement of our jurisdiction. If Carpenters take in log haulers, we can do carpentry work. If Electrical Workers are going to drive trucks our men are going to do wiring. If Plumbers are going to do hauling we are going to do plumbing." [5] A. H. Raskin, *New York Times* labor reporter, has written of the Teamsters' "free wheeling tendency to snatch members from other unions and to make alliances with groups cast out of the bona fide labor movement for corruption and communism." [6]

2. Tactics and Personalities

President Dave Beck

In an address at a meeting of the Central States Conference of Teamsters, in Chicago on April 26, 1954, President Beck said, with an extraordinary suggestion of personal authority, "I intend to spend three million dollars in the next three years, organizing in every section where our international union functions. I will match dollar for dollar wherever [sic] you contribute for organizing work where it is determined necessary in the progress of our great organization. I will make available all the money necessary to develop organizing by contributing equally to match money that you contribute."

In 1955, according to press reports, the executive board of the Teamsters' Union voted to buy from President Beck his Seattle home and then give it back to him. The *New York Times* (July 25, 1955) reported that the price was $160,000 and that Mr. Beck was to occupy it rent-free with the union paying maintenance charges and taxes. The *Times* reported that Mr. Beck said he was out of the room when the proposition was put before the Board.

At the January 1957 meeting of the AFL-CIO Executive Council at

[5] Jack Barbash, *The Practice of Unionism* (New York: Harper & Brothers, 1956), p. 24.
[6] *The New York Times*, December 11, 1955.

which the policy statement on racketeering was adopted, Mr. Beck cast the only vote against its adoption.

Vice President James R. Hoffa

In the *New York Times* story mentioned in the preceding section Mr. Raskin stated that "the truck union itself is honeycombed with men denounced by Congressional and state investigators for racket associations." One of the personalities frequently mentioned in press accounts of Teamster activity is James R. Hoffa, a vice-president of the Teamsters' Union. The idea of loaning $400,000 to the expelled Longshoremen's Union was said to have originated with Mr. Hoffa.

A Congressional committee which called Mr. Hoffa "the Teamster boss in Detroit"—though his power in the union extends over a much wider area—reported that he had been involved in a "shakedown and power grab," and that he had been found guilty of violating state and Federal laws.[7] One of his convictions was for attempting to compel independent merchants to join the union and pay dues to it. For this he was fined $500 and costs and compelled to return over $7,000 that these merchants had been obliged to pay to the union. He was also put under probation for two years during which he was forbidden to leave the State of Michigan without the consent of the court.[8]

Since achieving freedom to travel at will, Hoffa has associated himself with Teamster officials in New York City who have never ceased to cooperate with the expelled Longshoremen. He is said to have supported participation in a New York Teamster Union election by elements allied with known racketeers.

Hoffa has many personal interests outside his union. These include investments in various commercial and industrial enterprises including some profitable ventures that are carried in his wife's name. Asked the reason for using the name of his wife instead of his own, Hoffa replied, "Because I am subject almost every day to some kind of lawsuit or some kind of publicity and I didn't care to have her interest . . . impaired by my activities." [9]

It was after the report and testimony before the Congressional com-

[7] Report of Joint Subcommittees of Committee on Education and Labor and Committee on Government Operations, 83rd Congress, 2nd Session, p. 9.

[8] Hearings Before Subcommittee of Committee on Education and Labor (Investigation of Welfare Funds and Racketeering), 83rd Congress, November 1953, pp. 484–486.

[9] Hearings, *op. cit.*, November 27, 1953, p. 463.
See also Paul Jacobs, "The World of Jimmy Hoffa," *The Reporter*, January 24 and February 7, 1957.

mittees above referred to that President Beck, in a speech before a conference of Teamster Union officials, referred to the "marvellous support" he was receiving from "fellows like President Hoffa" of the Central States Conference of Teamsters.

3. The Portland Case

The following provides some details of the "unfair labor practices" of the Teamsters' Union referred to in Chapter 14.

Several locals and other agencies of the Teamsters Union, occupying joint quarters in Portland, Oregon, together employed some twenty-three office workers in 1953 and 1954. A majority of these had held membership in Local 11 of the Office Employees' Union and had bargained through it with their Teamster employers. In 1954 the employer locals refused to bargain with Local 11 over a renewal of the contract, and brought pressure on the employees to drop membership in that organization and to join Teamsters Local No. 223, Grocery, Meat, Motorcycle and Miscellaneous Drivers (sic.) In view of this interference, Local 11 complained to the regional office of the National Labor Relations Board that the Teamsters were guilty of unfair labor practices forbidden by the Taft-Hartley Act. Hearings on this charge were held in July 1954 and were recessed for a few weeks to enable the general counsel of the Board to obtain further data. During this recess four employees were discharged.[10] All four had been subpoenaed by the Board to testify as witnesses for the general counsel at the hearings held in July.

The complaint before the Board was then amended to include the charge that these employees were discharged because of union activity and because they had honored subpoenas to appear as witnesses at the hearings. Both of these are unfair labor practices under the Taft-Hartley Act. Additional hearings on these charges were held in August 1954.

In his report the trial examiner who presided at the hearings stated that prior to the hearings an officer of the International Teamsters' Union conferred with these prospective witnesses and attempted to dissuade them from testifying or, failing that, to persuade them to testify falsely. After failing in these efforts, he asked one of them "to cooperate by going on a long trip." This maneuver also failed.

On the basis of the evidence adduced at the hearings, the trial examiner decided that the several Teamster affiliates, and the International Team-

[10] Five were discharged altogether. One was discharged in June 1954 on the alleged ground of inefficiency; the trial examiner found that the true reason was her loyalty to Local 11 of the Officer Workers, and her discharge was therefore a violation of provisions of the Taft-Hartley Act.

sters' Union itself, had violated the Taft-Hartley Act in that as employers they had refused to bargain and that they had discriminatorily discharged five employees.

In August 1955 the National Labor Relations Board, acting on an appeal by the Teamsters, held 3 to 2 that the union and its affiliates as nonprofit organizations were not subject to the jurisdiction of the Board, and so dismissed the cases "in their entirety." [11]

The dissenting members said that the violations charged to the union had "run the entire gamut of employer unfair practices," and expressed the belief that the decision of the majority of the Board "achieves a paradoxical and unwarranted result in permitting labor unions to deny to their own employees the very right and privileges which unions have so vigorously advocated and won for the employees of others." In fact, the minority opinion added, "one of the most militant unions" in bringing charges against employers "has been the respondent International (the Teamsters) and its affiliates.

Monsignor George G. Higgins, Director of the Social Action Department, National Catholic Welfare Conference, commented on the Board's decision in this case, in The Yardstick (a NCWC organ) on September 12, 1955. After pointing out that the majority did not pass on the merits of the case, but based their decision on a technicality, the Monsignor continued: "The labor movement ought to use every available means to force the Teamsters into line regardless of legal technicalities. This," he said, "will be a good test of the integrity of the labor movement and, more specifically, of the labor press. The fact that uninformed or unscrupulous critics of labor have exaggerated its faults for their own antiunion purposes can no longer be cited as an excuse for labor's failure to wash its dirty linen, and to wash it in public if necessary."

THE LAUNDRY WORKERS
(See Chapter 14)

The Welfare Fund of the Laundry Workers' International Union had at the outset only two trustees, Sam J. Byers, president of the union, and an attorney for the San Francisco Laundry Owners Association. By vote of these two trustees Byers was authorized to appoint "welfare representatives" in each section of the country in which the welfare program was in effect. Eugene C. James, secretary-treasurer of the international union, was appointed to serve as welfare representative for Local 46 in

[11] This ruling was upheld by the U. S. Court of Appeals for the District of Columbia in June 1956. An appeal is now pending before the Supreme Court.

Chicago (of whose fund he was also trustee). For his services in this capacity he "received $77,970 during the period October 1, 1950 through September 30, 1954." Another welfare representative for three laundry union locals in Minneapolis, St. Paul, and Duluth was "one Sidney Brennan . . . seemingly an unusual person for the position, as he is and has been an international representative of the Brotherhood of Teamsters." Brennan received $11,831.47 for three years' services.[12]

This appearance of an officer of the Teamsters' Union in connection with affairs of the Laundry Workers justifies reference to a previous acquaintance that the secretary-treasurer of the Laundry Workers had with the Teamsters. In his testimony before a subcommittee of the House Committee on Education and Labor in November 1953, James Hoffa of the Teamsters told of his relations with Eugene James. James, he said, was "given contempt of court" at a grand jury hearing in Detroit. After "coming out of retirement for 60 days" James came to Hoffa and asked him whether he would "get him a charter." Hoffa arranged with the international union to "grant a charter" to James. But James had no money with which "to start his local union up," and so Hoffa and his friend Bert Brennan of Detroit lent him a sum of money (apparently $2500). When his local "became a going concern," Hoffa and Brennan inquired about payment of the loan. James was willing to pay, and at his request the executive board of his local (Local 985, Juke Box Local of the Teamsters Union) put Mrs. Hoffa on the union payroll at $100 a week to continue until the loan was paid. (Presumably Mrs. Brennan received similar consideration, since the arrangement was that the payment should be made to "our wives.") Asked why the payments were not made directly to Hoffa and Brennan, Hoffa said it was "what he [James] wanted to do." Pressed further, he said it was because of the fact that he and Brennan were receiving salaries from their own locals and "we did not want to appear on another local's payroll," with which they had no connection.

From this time on James made progress. Having established a Teamsters Local in Detroit, he went to Chicago and became attached to a Laundry Workers local there. He remained on the payroll of his Detroit local for a time, however, because, Hoffa said, he did not know whether he would be "permanently employed by the local union in Chicago."[13] But he advanced in the union, became a vice-president and later secretary-treasurer. His financial success in that position has already been noted.

[12] Interim report of Senate Committee, pp. 32–33.
[13] Investigation of Welfare Funds and Racketeering. Hearings before a special subcommittee of the Committee on Education and Labor, House of Representatives, Detroit, November 1953, pp. 435–438.

The Senate subcommittee on welfare and pension funds said in its report in April 1956: "The embezzlement of over $900,000 was traced to Saperstein [the insurance broker] who was obviously in collusion with at least one of the [Laundry Workers] union officials, E. C. James, secretary-treasurer of the international. . . . This case was fully documented by the subcommittee nearly a year ago and was referred for attention not only to the United States Department of Justice and the United States Internal Revenue Service but to the appropriate legal authorities in the five states [in which trustees reside].

"No action has been taken.

"Mr. James is still secretary-treasurer of the international union."

That was the situation when the Senate subcommittee made its report in April 1956. Seven months later, after the committee on ethics of AFL-CIO had begun an investigation of the charges against the Laundry Workers and specifically of the charges involving Secretary-Treasurer James, and on the eve of a meeting of the committee to determine whether to recommend that disciplinary action should be taken against the union, the executive board of the union suspended James from office. A report of this action published in the AFL-CIO News in December 1956 concluded, speculatively, "Whether James' suspension will be made permanent will be decided by the LWIU convention next May."

CODES OF ETHICAL PRACTICES
(See Chapter 14)

At its June 1956 meeting the Executive Council directed the Committee on Ethical Practices "to develop a set of principles and guides for adoption by the AFL-CIO in order to implement the constitutional determination that the AFL-CIO shall be and remain free from all corrupt influences" and directed that such recommended guides and principles be submitted to the Council. In accordance with this direction, and its constitutional responsibilities, the Committee on Ethical Practices submitted to the Executive Council at its August 1956 meeting the first of a proposed series of recommended codes. This code covering the issuance of local union charters was unanimously adopted by the Council.

Code I—*Issuance of Local Charters* (*In summary*)

The AFL-CIO constitution makes it clear that no affiliate has an autonomous right to permit corrupt or unethical practices which endanger the good name of the trade union movement.

The Code stated that each union should require, for the issuance of a local union charter, an application by a group of bona fide employees eligible for membership in the union; that a charter should never be issued to any persons seeking to use it as a hunting license for the improper invasion of other unions; that a charter should never be issued or continued for a "paper local, not existing or functioning as a genuine local of employees"; that a charter should never be issued to persons known to traffic in local union charters for illicit or improper purposes; that the constitution prohibits the issuance of a local union charter to any group suspended or expelled from the AFL-CIO or any affiliated union for corruption or unethical practices.

Following are the essential parts of codes adopted by the Executive Council January 31, 1957.

Code II—*Health and Welfare Funds*

". . . The task of administering and operating health and welfare programs which have been developed through collective bargaining has placed heavy new responsibilities upon the shoulders of trade union officials. The funds involved are paid for through the labor of the workers covered by the plans. They must be administered, therefore, as a high trust for the benefit only of those workers. . . . The malfeasances of a few [trade union officials] have served to bring into disrepute not only the officials of the particular unions involved, but also the good name of the entire American labor movement. For this reason it is imperative that the AFL-CIO and each of the national and international unions affiliated with it rigorously adhere to the highest ethical standards in dealing with the subject of health and welfare funds. . . .

"1. No union official who already receives full-time pay from his union should receive fees or salaries of any kind from a fund established for the provision of a health, welfare or retirement program. . . .

"2. No union official, employee or other person acting as agent or representative of a union, who exercises responsibilities or influence in the administration of welfare programs or the placement of insurance contracts, should have any compromising personal ties, direct or indirect, with outside agencies . . . doing business with the welfare plan. . . . Any union official found to have such ties to his own personal advantage or to have accepted fees, inducements, benefits or favors of any kind from any such outside agency, should be removed. . . .

"3. Complete records of the financial operations of all welfare funds and programs should be maintained in accordance with the best accounting practice. Each such fund should be audited regularly by internal auditors. In addition, each such fund should be audited at least once a year, and preferably semi-annually, by certified public or other independent accountants of unquestioned professional integrity. . . .

"4. All audit reports should be available to the membership of the union and the affected employees.

"5. The trustees or administrators of welfare funds should make a full disclosure and report to the beneficiaries at least once each year. . . .

"6. Where health and welfare benefits are provided through the use of a commercial insurance carrier, the carrier should be selected through competitive bids solicited from a substantial number of reliable companies, on the basis of the lowest net cost for the given benefits submitted by a responsible carrier. . . .

"7. Where a union or union trustees participate in the administration of the investment of welfare fund reserves, the union or its trustees should make every effort to prohibit the investment of welfare fund reserves in the business of any contributing employer, insurance carrier or agency doing business with the fund, or in any enterprise in which any trustee, officer or employer of the fund has a personal financial interest of such a nature as to be affected by the fund's investment or disinvestment. . . .

"8. Where any trustee, agent, fiduciary or employee of a health or welfare program is found to have received an unethical payment, the union should insist upon his removal and should take appropriate legal steps against both the party receiving and the party making the payment. . . .

"9. Every welfare program should provide redress against the arbitrary or unjust denial of claims so as to afford the individual member prompt and effective relief where his claim for benefits has been improperly rejected. . . .

"10. The duty of policing and enforcing these standards is shared by every union member, as well as by local, national and international officers. The best safeguard against abuses lies in the hands of a vigilant, informed and active membership, jealous of their rights and interests in the operation of health and welfare programs, as well as any other trade union program. . . .

"11. Where constitutional amendments or changes in internal administrative procedure are necessary to comply with the standards herein set forth, such amendment and changes should be undertaken at the earliest practicable time."

Code III—*Racketeers, Crooks, Communists and Fascists*

". . . there is no room within the Federation or any of its affiliated unions for any person in a position of leadership or responsibility who is a crook, a racketeer, a communist or a fascist. And it is the obligation of every union affiliated with the AFL-CIO to take appropriate steps to ensure that this principle is complied with. . . .

". . . A trade union need not wait upon a criminal conviction to bar from office corrupt, communist or fascist influences. The responsibility of each union to see to it that it is free of such influences is not a responsibility placed upon our unions by law. It is a responsibility which rests upon our unions by the AFL-CIO Constitution and by the moral principles that govern the trade union movement. . . .

"Obviously, if a person has been convicted of a crime involving moral turpitude offensive to trade union morality, he should be barred from office or responsible position in the labor movement. Obviously also, a person commonly known to be a crook or racketeer should not enjoy immunity to prey upon the trade union movement because he has somehow managed to escape conviction. . . .

"1. The AFL-CIO and each of its affiliated unions should undertake the obligation, through appropriate constitutional or administrative measures and orderly procedures, to insure that no persons who constitute corrupt influences or practices or who represent or support communist, fascist or totalitarian agencies should hold office of any kind in such trade unions or organizations.

"2. No person should hold or retain office or appointed position in the AFL-CIO or any of its affiliated national or international unions or subordinate bodies thereof who has been convicted of any crime involving moral turpitude offensive to trade union morality . . . [or]

"3. . . . who is commonly known to be a crook or racketeer preying on the labor movement and its good name for corrupt purposes, whether or not previously connected with such nefarious activities . . . [or]

"4. . . . who is a member, consistent supporter or who actively participates in the activities of the Communist Party or of any fascist or other totalitarian organization which opposes the democratic principles to which our country and the American trade union movement are dedicated."

Code IV—*Conflicts of Interest*

"It is too plain for extended discussion that a basic ethical principle in the conduct of trade union affairs is that no responsible trade union official should have a personal financial interest which conflicts with the full performance of his fiduciary duties as a workers' representative.

"Obviously an irreconcilable conflict of interest would be present if a trade union official, clothed with responsibility and discretion in conducting the representation of workers, simultaneously maintains a substantial interest in the profits of the employer of the workers whom he is charged with representing. . . .

". . . the trade union leader does have . . . responsibilities which he must assume and respect because he serves as a leader in the trade union movement. And those responsibilities, the Committee believes, necessarily imply certain restraints upon his right to engage in personal investment, even with his own funds and on his own time. In a sense, a trade union official holds a position comparable to that of a public servant. Like a public servant, he has a high fiduciary duty not only to serve the members of his union honestly and faithfully, but also to avoid personal economic interest which may conflict or appear to conflict with the full performance of his responsibility to those whom he serves.

"Like public servants, trade union leaders ought to be paid compensation commensurate with their services. But, like public servants, trade union leaders must accept certain limitations upon their private activities which result from the nature of their services. Indeed, the nature of the trade union movement and the responsibilities which necessarily must be accepted by its leaders, make the strictest standards with respect to any possible conflict of interest properly applicable. . . .

"1. No responsible trade union official should have a personal financial interest which conflicts with the full performance of his fiduciary duties as a workers' representative.

"2. No responsible trade union official should own or have a substantial business interest in any business enterprise with which his union bargains collectively, or in any business enterprise which is in competition with any other business enterprise with which his union bargains collectively.

"3. No responsible trade union official should own or have a substantial business interest in a business enterprise a substantial part of which consists of buying from, selling to, or otherwise dealing with the business enterprise with which his union bargains collectively.

"4. The provisions of paragraphs 2 and 3 above do not apply in the case of an investment in the publicly traded securities of widely-held corporations, which investment does not constitute a substantial enough holding to affect or influence the course of corporate decision.

"5. No responsible trade union official should accept 'kickbacks' under-the-table payments, gifts of other than nominal value, or any personal payment of any kind other than regular pay and benefits for work performed as an employee from an employer or business enterprise with which his union bargains collectively.

"6. The policies herein set forth apply to: (a) all officers of the AFL-CIO and all officers of national and international unions affiliated with the AFL-CIO, (b) to all elected or appointed staff representatives and business agents of such organizations, and (c) to all officers of subordinate bodies of such organizations who have any degree of discretion or responsibility in the negotiation of collective bargaining agreements or their administration.

"7. The principles herein set forth apply not only where investments are made by union officials, but also where third persons are used as blinds or covers to conceal the financial interests of union officials."

POLICY STATEMENT ON INVESTIGATIONS OF RACKETEERING ADOPTED BY EXECUTIVE COUNCIL OF AFL-CIO JANUARY 1957
(Partial Text)

"We believe that Congress, in the interest of enacting corrective legislation, if the same be deemed and found necessary, has the right, through proper committees, to investigate corruption wherever it exists, whether in labor, industry or anywhere else.

"It is the firm policy of the AFL-CIO to cooperate fully with all proper legislative committees, law-enforcement agencies and other public bodies seeking fairly and objectively to keep the labor movement or any other segment of our society free from any and all corrupt influences.

"This means that all officials of the AFL-CIO and its affiliates should freely and without reservation answer all relevant questions asked by proper law-enforcement agencies, legislative committees and other public bodies, seeking fairly and objectively to keep the labor movement free from corruption.

"We recognize that any person is entitled, in the exercise of his individual conscience, to the protection afforded by the Fifth Amendment and we reaffirm our conviction that this historical right must not be abridged.

"It is the policy of the AFL-CIO, however, that if a trade union official decides to invoke the Fifth Amendment for his personal protection and to avoid scrutiny by proper legislative committees, law-enforcement agencies or other public bodies into alleged corruption on his part, he has no right to continue to hold office in his union.

"Otherwise, it becomes possible for a union official who may be guilty of corruption to create the impression that the trade union movement sanctions the use of the Fifth Amendment, not as a matter of individual conscience, but as a shield against proper scrutiny into corrupt influences in the labor movement."

THE SECONDARY BOYCOTT
(See Chapter 15, p. 202)

The boycott is a device that is called into use, ordinarily, to supplement a strike or as an alternative form of pressure when a strike has failed. A primary boycott is directed at the employer who is involved in a controversy with the union administering the boycott. In such an instance the union attempts to induce consumers to refuse to purchase the goods or services of the employer. A secondary boycott is one that extends its arresting hand beyond the area of the original controversy. It may attempt to induce consumers to refuse to patronize retailers who handle the goods of the employer concerned. Its more drastic form appears in jurisdictional conflicts where strikes are called against employers who use the services of members of the union considered to be invaders of the jurisdiction in question. Or it may involve refusal to handle goods produced by non-unionists. The secondary boycott has been resorted to at times as a means of reprisal against a union which is being opposed on other grounds—as when it was used as a weapon between AFL and CIO unions before the merger. It has been used in some instances merely to obtain more work for union members within a specific area—as when members of a union have refused to install electrical devices manufactured outside the protected area, even though union-made.

The secondary boycott is often criticized as being directed against employers who may have no relation to or responsibility for the practices against which the boycott is directed. The unions question the innocence of this third party, particularly when he is accepting goods for further processing from an employer whose workers are on strike. In such case the union view is that he is an ally of the first employer and that his employees are being asked to "scab" on fellow workmen.[14]

The Taft-Hartley Act makes it an "unfair labor practice" to call a strike having as its purpose, among other things, the forcing of an employer to cease handling the products of, or to cease doing business with, another employer; or to require him to discriminate in employment in order to satisfy jurisdictional claims.

[14] See Barbash, op. cit., pp. 221 ff.

Index of Topics

Index of Names

For Federal agencies, see United States Government

UNITED STATES GOVERNMENT